STREISAND

STREISAND
The Mirror of Difference

Garrett Stewart

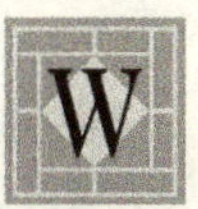

Wayne State University Press
Detroit

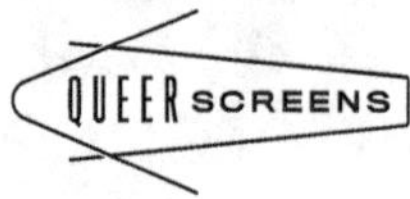

ISBN 978-0-8143-4908-3 (paperback)
ISBN 978-0-8143-4909-0 (hardback)
ISBN 978-0-8143-4910-6 (e-book)

Library of Congress Control Number: 2022942186

Wayne State University Press rests on Waawiyaataanong, also referred to as Detroit, the ancestral and contemporary homeland of the Three Fires Confederacy. These sovereign lands were granted by the Ojibwe, Odawa, Potawatomi, and Wyandot Nations, in 1807, through the Treaty of Detroit. Wayne State University Press affirms Indigenous sovereignty and honors all tribes with a connection to Detroit. With our Native neighbors, the press works to advance educational equity and promote a better future for the earth and all people.

Wayne State University Press
Leonard N. Simons Building
4809 Woodward Avenue
Detroit, Michigan 48201-1309

Visit us online at wsupress.wayne.edu.

For Jim Chandler,
keen interlocutor and provocateur,
who first helped lure me into
taking a Barbra lecture on the road

SET LIST

OVERTURE

Reflection, Refraction, Diffraction

Do you think beautiful girls are gonna stay in style forever? Any minute now they'll be out—*finished*! Then it'll be my turn!
—Intro to "I'm the Greatest Star," Funny Girl (1964/1968)

"Mom, how did it feel . . . being beautiful . . . looking at yourself in the mirror, with such appreciation?"
—The Mirror Has Two Faces (1996)

Like the title of her last self-directed film, Barbra Streisand's mirror has always had two faces: the one looking into it with a confidence ready to power beyond insecurities, and the other angled past her, framed as if for the audience alone. Where, to put it mildly, the image reflected from the start an entirely new slant to screen stardom. Where, to vary *Hamlet* with her own inimitable variance: in breaking the mold of form, that image became the new glass of fashion. A two-part and unabashedly fictionalized biopic of Jewish comedienne Fanny Brice, a debut and its sequel, can be understood to bracket a first major phase of Streisand's Hollywood career (1968–75). This twofold storyline begins and ends with a mirror, as well as bearing down on one in the debut film's penultimate dressing-room scene—and then pivoting on (and around) another two, again in the star's dressing room, in the sequel's most explosive number. In the momentum of her impersonated transformation from 1968's *Funny Girl* to *Funny Lady* in 1975, then on to Funny Boy (for her male disguise as a Yeshiva student in 1983's *Yentl*), there are numerous other turning-point mirrors angled our way—and narratively reframed for inspection—in scenes that pace the ongoing differentials of gender energy and ethnic heritage. Continuing into the later films she directed in the 1990s, such mirrors appear both by the inevitability of decor and by a deep visual, and ultimately cinematic, instinct. And return again in 2000's *Timeless* concert.

Discussion ahead will be looking into these mirrored surfaces, as the camera does, for their own—often audiovisual—subplots, all deriving from the figure (embodied image and metaphor alike) of self-reflection under duress. This is the duress, the tension, that comes from recognizing in those framed inner planes, on the character's part along with her audience's, a difference within—especially its veer from the strictly visual when the portrayed heroine is at odds with herself, cast loose from all moorings. Such emotional precariousness is brought to the point of ethnic as well as psychic crisis for the gender deception of her earliest self-directed film. In the new-century setting (1904) of *Yentl*, the first openly Jewish screen star, long-time feminist activist and philanthropist, is seen defying, in the starring role itself, the strictures of her own historical culture—only to release in the end a new mode of disclosed femininity no longer masking its needs and ambitions: neither Girl nor Lady, just Woman on the move. That career turn in the "helming" of *Yentl* (through to its closing transatlantic voyage) seems to rehearse a logic that was there from the Hollywood career's first on-screen line, addressed to her stylish mirror image: "Hello, gorgeous!"—a greeting of the self as remade other. The mirror of difference for the proverbial one of a kind: a swerve from the merely "generic" even within a full battery of ethnic signifiers—for a persona at once markedly begotten and entirely self-made. From genus (or kind) to the singularity of genius, as derived (etymologically) from inborn.

Beyond testimony to her fabled work ethic, "genius" is indeed the word one hears repeatedly about Streisand's aesthetic instincts, always eyes-on, hands-on, as well as tuned to her preternatural ear: praise not just from lyricists and co-stars but from music arrangers, recording technicians, lighting engineers, and cinematographers. Yet, for all the industry admiration and her international popular renown, entrenched resistance has always been evident, in and out of print. Complaint has never been quite drowned out by adulation—and never easy to separate from a misogyny camouflaged as diva allergy or an ethnocentrism that survives the early thesaurus for "funny looks" ascribed, sometimes euphemistically, to the unabashedly Jewish newcomer. In a book like this, however, reflections on Streisand's "mirror of difference" can reasonably imagine an audience only among the predisposed. For such interested parties, this is the first full-length analytic appreciation of the cumulative interplay of Streisand's album and screen work, or more to the point her ultimately inseparable singing and acting—quite apart from numerous career guides and web archives, glossy photographic volumes, and unauthorized biographies. Still, such a study can do little more than put some further words, more exacting than usual, to established popular reactions. And elicit unnoticed lines of connection in the process. Connection, rather than sheer celebration. It would be pointless to preach to the choir in the jammed arena balconies of her sold-out late concerts, in the sloped, then raked darkness of her film openings, or behind the wheel listening to car radios or tape decks over the decades. Nor are converts likely to be made either, certainly at this late date. But by now there's a long view to be had. In pursuing it, my title is after more than "difference personified." The optical figure of speech is meant to evoke a living figure not fixedly self-centered but in itself differential in its own variable probing. The difference in view, therefore, isn't just the difference the mirror reflects but the difference it helps make. Beyond any narcissistic model, self-scrutiny becomes instead the framed field of disclosure, discovery—and ultimately of performance.

The evidence is all there, right from the start in her first film: an irony propelled forward (if back in time) when Fanny looks apologetically into a second (chronologically earlier) mirror—this time within *Funny Girl*'s two-hour-long flashback—during the opening number ("If a Girl Isn't Pretty") on the way to a hoped-for audition in Ziegfeld-era New York. The first epigraph records what happens next: the burst of self-manifesto as cultural sea change in this openly reflexive biopic, Streisand's story as much as Brice's. Fanny's is a rhetorical question growled out in an accusatory fashion by Streisand—regarding the toppled hegemony of "beautiful girls," whose days are numbered—at two flabbergasted boys, interrupting their hopscotch game next to the theater's backstage entrance. The polemic yelp of our funny wannabe girl vaudevillian is here prepping a young male generation for her own coming-thing as the restyled avatar of "gorgeous" rather than merely pretty: the former a word of "unknown origin" (say the dictionaries) for fine, elegant, refined.

So, too, with the untraceable origin story for a vocal talent (an unencumbered "gift") quite unrivaled in the annals of popular music—and for a screen photogenesis that the craft of the renowned cinematographer on her first three musicals, Harry Stradling Jr., and then again, before his death, on much of *The Way We Were*, cannot begin to explain. Streisand's is a relation to the camera whose emphasis on internal reframing this book will be repeatedly charting. As when, just before her assault on the female fantasies of those unsuspecting boys midway through the "I'm the Greatest Star" number, her "What are you *blind?*" line coincides with the slamming of a mottled glass door in her face at the attempted audition (fig. 1). Mottled, translucent—and in fact diagonally wire-meshed, her stippled image screened (out). Thus the suggestive optic echo in *Yentl* when the disguised heroine shuts the distorting glass door on her tailors—who are having trouble fitting her (as the male Anshel) for her transvestite wedding—just before her exasperated "people are *blind!*" in the "Tomorrow Night" number. Along with the three full-length mirrors behind her in the tailor's shop, here is yet another partially occluded reframing in the screen's looking-glass of difference (fig. 2).

Funny girl: not just comedienne but anomaly. Funny, abnormal. And from the expectations for female stardom that she arrived precisely to queer, this odd-one-out—once

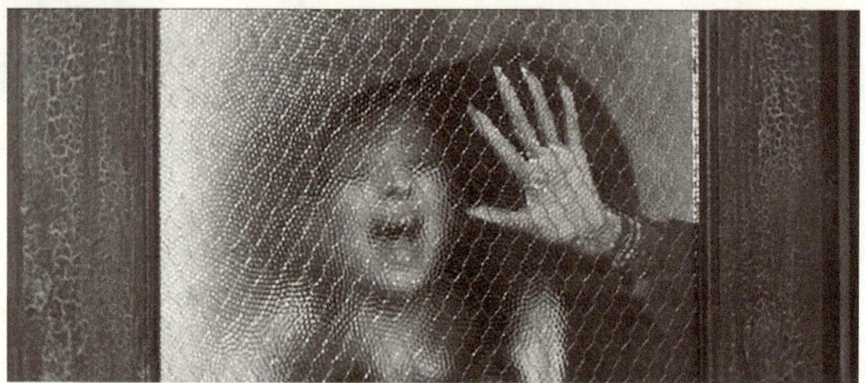

1. Blocked from audition (*Funny Girl*: "I'm the Greatest Star")

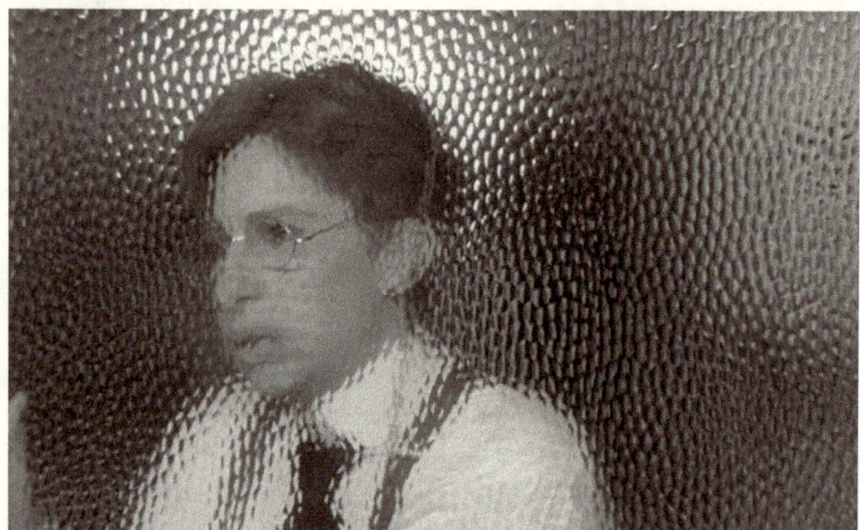

2. Trapped in a role (*Yentl*: "Tomorrow Night")

her talent was released, uncloseted—emerged peerless. Streisand seized the screen like no star before her not just by gorgeous singing but by *acting beautiful*. And the colossal effort of creative will entailed in this is replayed, across the scene from which that first epigraph is lifted, as the true launch of the jubilant big-screen debut that audiences everywhere lined up for. In her frustrated denigration of the cosmetic norm, Fanny has just been rebuffed by the back-door theater guard openly baffled by her claim to be one of those "8 Beautiful Girls 8" boasted by faded cliché on a weathered poster ("Well," goes her riposte, "the makeup helps a lot!"). Quantified and regularized beauty as couched in that emblematic symmetry (8 beauties 8: signage as message in its cramping chiasm) is just the fixed standard that Streisand's own looks—or say the *looks of her talent*—are destined to upend and confound, queering forever an abiding Wasp stereotype from the coming song forward.

Just before this run-up to "I'm the Greatest Star," we have heard from Fanny's mother in the previous song: supportive in a way that Streisand's own wasn't, nor the mother played by Lauren Bacall three decades later in *The Mirror Has Two Faces* (addressee of the second, self-doubting epigraph). Mrs. Brice asks defensively of her female cohort, vocal as they are in throwing cold water on Fanny's stage chances, whether a "nose with deviation" constitutes "such a crime" against "the nation." The tacit ethnicity behind that combined legal and demographic phrasing is hard to miss. Building directly off this, in the first of Fanny's own numbers, it is in fact her strange mobile face that is celebrated when, in "I'm the Greatest Star," she brags about having—via the sound play of internal rhyme—"six expressions more" than can be found in "all them Barrymores put together." Point taken, as currently exemplified in the mugging comic gauntlet of this up-tempo performance. That previous number, therefore, featuring her mother's defense of difference, has set exactly the terms of these chapters. By enrolling Barbra Streisand on the roster of this up-and-running academic series, what the term "queer" is testing for is just this: a difference mirrored back to gender and ethnic norms from within the entirely pardonable aesthetic crime—the transgressive energy—of her disruptive exception, where "deviation" becomes a case of convention both defied and revitalized. When asked in interviews over the years what she thinks explains her devoted gay following, her best answer has been "I guess because I'm different too."

When taking the Broadway stage as the lead in *Funny Girl*, the twenty-two-year-old prodigy was already a recording sensation. But who could have known that her time-based artistry would not just extend beyond Broadway belting to film but find its perfect fit there in the rhythms of visual as well as vocal delivery? Who but Streisand herself?—who always sensed her career destiny in insisting on herself as an actress singing for her supper until the acting roles came. As a public image apart from the routine lighting of early TV guest spots, she was at first—with her picture solely on newsprint or glossy paper in her early days as a recording star (or on cardboard album covers)—nothing if not photogenic in her eye-catching angularity of visage and intensity of gaze: the classic camera object. On-screen as her image soon was, first in the videotape close-ups of her fabled TV specials, then in widescreen color, the motion-picture camera could barely keep up with the exuberant motions of its object, that expressive face and body, in the gestural cadences of its own emotional quick cuts, double takes, flash inserts of recognition, slow dissolves of reactive emotion. At first, on paper, the question of beauty could plausibly remain in the eye of the beholder. On-screen, with the additional evidence of a many-faceted personality to inflect that memorable face, and a voice to beat the band, the question was moot. Pretty or not, yet gorgeous with or without quotes, here was, with her supernatural dose of charisma, an altogether ravishing phenomenon. Under cultural redefinition, she was all 8 beauties together—in a whole new performative mix. Invincibly herself, with a talent myriad but adamantly her own: always the same (identifying) difference.

A 1965 Emmy for Outstanding Performance, then a 1968 Oscar for Best Actress: these were only the beginning of the industry laurels. Yet it was always a danger that the epicure of difference would be cursed with repetition—even if never the swindles of versatility that have been the calling card of many pop performers since. The stamina of Streisand's numerous bounce-backs is the heroic side of this book's narrative. Reporting on them has involved rediscovered astonishments hardly few and far between, on record and screen, as well as a confirming sense of intensities never slackened, even when misdirected. A dramatic narrative Streisand's career certainly is on the face of it—a tale full of incomparable sound, sometimes dramatic fury, otherwise humorous velocity, and a story, at that, many times told. I should say up front that my "credentials" for this coming version of the tale amount to little more than the fact I have been there from early on, the "primary research" ready at hand—and still vividly in mind.

As a college junior in Los Angeles, three of her LPs by then on my shelf, I caught at the Hollywood Bowl (an actually affordable date night in that phase of Streisand's ascendancy) the tail end of her first—and for over a quarter century her last—tour, "An Evening with Barbra Streisand," just before she had to call off further engagements because of her pregnancy. A rapturous rather than laid-back "My Funny Valentine," the stentorian World War I rallying cry "Stout-Hearted Men" intoned with newly amorous inference—these stood out among other transfixing moments, including the already mandatory showstoppers "People" and "Happy Days Are Here Again." And happy such nights, however short-lived her touring would turn out to be. Pregnancy aside, a different pitch of expectancy cascaded through the banked seats from song to song—with everyone, by concert's end, very much aware of the birth of something else: a stardom that would soon make anything less than such a healthy seating capacity, or anything resembling its then modest pricing for that matter, a thing of the past for any "evening" with the star.

Along with being there as her scintillating high notes sliced the night air, it bears mentioning that I was also writing about her from these early days. Sort of. As it happened, I was working that summer with my favorite English teacher, helping her find telling examples of grammatical finesse in contemporary prose for a composition textbook she was developing, and I soon raided the concert program for an example of strategically "broken parallelism." This from an anonymous review of one of her early club dates: "She is alternately gamin-like, sexy, mischievous, innocent, confident, insouciant, girlish, and radiating warmth." I wanted to highlight the way the "sprung rhythm" of that last participial phrase is snapped loose from a chain of adjectives begun only with near similitude ("gamin-like") for a one-of-kind stage presence—and not unlike, come to think of it, one of her own songs' rhythmic twists. Prose like this was what my note cards were sorting under effects variously understood as "mimetic syntax," in this case skewed to the quirkily disparate aspects of the star's oscillating persona. Before taking up this feature of her talent in its irresistible detail, then, we can put it like this: Streisand's multifarious advent had a way of queering even the grammar of accolade into nonconformity and extra impact.

The astral "flare up" boasted by Streisand's first electric film number, "I'm the Greatest Star," locking into rhyme the world's responsive "stare up," builds into its trope, latently, the one problem Streisand's ambition—and ignited dedication—was never to face: burnout. But as the lyric's echo suggests, star wattage must keep in rhyme with its audience—and so in step with the times. "Everything you do, you still audition," she would sing years later in additional Sondheim lyrics for "Putting It Together" (from *Sunday in the Park with George*)—long after she had failed or been flatly refused auditions in her own teenage Off-Broadway scramble. This is the kind of struggle enacted in effect, though backdated to vaudeville in the character of Fanny Brice, for the opening song from *Funny Girl*. Says Keeney the club owner when she's later been slipped into the lineup of chorus girls: "You've got skinny legs. You stick out—and you are out." Crucial, that turn of phrase in turning her away: difference as exclusion. But, of course, stick-out is redeemed as stand-out in every wrinkle and twist of the film from there on. And in the screen career it jump-started. The much later, if related, problem for Hollywood's greatest star: familiarity rather than anomaly. The difference she delivered to stage and screen, to mic and camera, was inevitably in peril of becoming an "effect" to be mirrored each time out. The story here is indeed the resistance to this predictability at the heart of her persistence as artist. It is not easy to think of any screen star before or after Barbra Streisand who has fought off this downside of renown with more long-term, if intermittently flagging, vigilance.

Splitting the Difference

Streisand entered the recording studio as the least "generic" postwar talent since Elvis, Dylan, and Aretha—her first album following Dylan's and Franklin's by only a year (with Aretha actually covering "People" in 1964 when they were both at Columbia) and coinciding with the Beatles' debut in 1963. Streisand's challenge, her trial, once skyrocketing to Hollywood fame a fast half decade later, soon became, and remained, one of *genre* in both song and screen material. With the new star arriving as difference personified in ethnic and cultural terms alike—and in the magnitude of her "stylistic" gifts, both as singer and actor—the challenge was how to vary and ramify both talents together: differentiate each from within over time but not by wholly segregating them. Her advent was clearly too late for canonical musical comedy—since even the star power of her untouchable voice, meeting commercial defeat in her second two films (*Hello, Dolly!* and *On a Clear Day You Can See Forever*), proved that the classic Hollywood vein was largely played out. One inevitable instinct was to split her ambition's commitment between an ongoing recording career—still in the phase of its robust and luscious resuscitation of the Great American Songbook—and her current screen contracts: in short, between music and comedy. And even there genre was a challenge: with folk and rock beckoning (at first gingerly) on the recording front, along with the call of updated Hollywood screwball (all too obviously) for this vaunted screen "funny girl." Quickly the specter dawned: the danger that the sui generis would become a genre unto herself. Rather than as a force for difference and transformation, one came to recognize the too formulaic "Streisand picture." On offer: the increasingly under-invested mood swings between the romantic and the raucous, charm and feistiness, sex appeal and the dreaded "zany." The last was a trait so far from what the world was coming to know about Streisand the committed and exploratory studio artist, the driven "perfectionist," and the concerned liberal citizen that it became an increasingly false note when sounded, let alone glaringly exploited.

Clearly unstable on its own terms, given radically changing popular tastes, still the recording career was less troubled, less commercial trouble. With that voice of voices, there was only so far wrong she could go, and with many cuts per album, the rein was freer—the variance and evolution, even its setbacks, more fascinating to follow, to tolerate, to take and leave at once: always, song by song, at least on first listen, entirely engrossing—and often downright astonishing. But new directions came hard. As the ironic counterpoint dialogue has it in that rewrite of Sondheim's "Putting It Together" for 1983's *The Broadway Album*—an album taking listeners both by surprise and by retro storm after the pop triumph of *Guilty* (1980)—we hear corporatized male voices in a commercial chorus as oppressive background to the artist at work. Though "it's not what's selling nowadays," pipes up one dubious voice, another comes to the defense of the project on the basis of reputation alone ("But she's an original")—corrected at once by a deflating "was!" So goes the chorus of resistance at every turn of her career. In particular, the threat of repetition, of formula, had set in early. It was only to be temporarily alleviated by Streisand's gratifying tack from now lackluster, now frenetic and slapdash, comedies like *Up the Sandbox* and *What's Up, Doc?* (your author being the rare Streisand follower left cold by the latter hit farce) to the Oscar-nominated seriousness of her winning performance (and near-miss second Academy Award) in *The Way We Were*. This turn, in that 1973 film, was further invigorated by a sense of the heroine's Jewish leftist drive playing truer to type—but in no straitjacketing way. The one-off, however, did not a genre make. What next?

Symptomatically, in *The Way We Were* the famous title song wasn't sung on camera. It thus worked to *underscore*, so to speak, the continuing risk of divided loyalties in Streisand's developing ambition: Hollywood phenomenon doubled by what would become the best-selling recording career of any female artist in American music history; and redoubled in the process by the kinetic, quasi-cinematic splendors of her vocal delivery from album to album. Analysis gravitates here to the dramatic space thus laid open, probed and surveyed, delved and traversed, by that voice's negotiation of an inner topography—however much elicited or enhanced by a given camerawork under pressure of narrative context in full-length musical features. Short of that Hollywood manifestation, in every successful song performance, filmed or not, the "actress-who-sings" (as she always wanted to be known, even from her early club appearances) deploys, above and beyond her mobility of facial affect, a voice that directs its own condensed monodramas. It is heard setting their scene, adjusting the mood lighting by mere shades of intonation, pacing their approached pivot points, building toward climaxes taxing but unforced, easing into denouements with a never discharged battery. And exceeding the theatrical, all the while, and certainly the standards of Broadway belting, with a more panoramic vocal sweep. Hers is, in short, not just a dramatic but a cinematic singing, full of a mobile thrill in its dynamic surprises. And with a visceral effect as much like that of exhilarating camerawork as like microphone stagecraft. When one listens closely, the nearness of the ear opens to a placeless inner space cross-mapped between the anatomy of the voice and the body of audition. An almost palpable *feel* for the Streisand sound is a somatic, a haptic, phenomenon that Roland Barthes's sense of the singing voice as "carnal" event will help us to appreciate more fully in the opening chapter. Not easy to annotate in any but the plasticity of the songs' own heard wordings, this is what the coming pages will nonetheless try listening for in prose.

Where the claim is in part that sound has its own specular as well as tangible dimension, with voice making the hearer see things, not illusions but rather further materializations: variants of the waves and valleys that modulate the air in transmission. That's the "screening" we are to find always at stake, at vocal issue, in assessing the Streisand sound in performance. In a mode of embodied synesthesia, that's the *ear mirror* to which a Streisand song plays—and plays across, in every ripple of syllabic voicing. The fact that Streisand is unable to "read music," but learns a sheet of lyrics "by ear"—in all its open cues to variable phrasing—may be part of the airtight pipeline that makes her stresses so actorly, so emotively attuned as well as on key. Music to one side, lyrics are first of all, for her, not note patterns—but meant words. So it is, then, that one is tempted to prolong the optic model for the mind's eye of her sighs and dives and lifts. In this sense, the fabled mirror of difference shown forth to initial movie audiences—both in its reflected original image (and originality) and in its glinting ironic refractions—is matched in song reception by a keen sense of vocal *diffraction*, equivalent to the filtering, then splaying out, of light through a narrow aperture. When Streisand opens her throat in song, there has never been anything like it, in its still colloquial spread and resonance. But after *Funny Girl*, there will never be any way not to wish it leashed as tightly as possible to character in screen performance. And no way not to wonder (at times in the disappointed sense) about some of the non-singing parts to which the established star gravitated instead.

The cliché of a persona "larger than life" may apply with special aptness to this actress-who-sings when she shuts off that latter vent of expression. In minor comic roles, the Streisand persona may either leak out to render the performance, however vivacious, unconvincing—or may seem unnecessarily bottled up. And the singer faces the same double bind as the actress. What—asked the sated or impatient at the time—not just more translucent ballads and incandescent torch songs? Alternately, what now: why is she betraying her true strength in taking up the torch of folk rock? Not another stage musical in adaptation! But, then again, why isn't she singing in this feature? Yet beyond that "larger than life" measure, and its pitfalls, another cliché, understood differently, is closer to the spirit of this book. For in Streisand's case there is a star chemistry at work beyond the usual figurative sense. The most sustained emphasis, or argument, of this study, is that one "gets" Streisand best when apprehending those moments, in a stricter chemical sense, of *supersaturation*: those transformative flashpoints when too much is just enough, resulting in a certain *crystallized* brilliance. This is where vocal genius and performative intelligence do more than gel in their spellbinding way—but achieve a shimmering condensation of the talent in its full prismatic array. Such are the moments this study hopes, with the help of YouTube, to keep in frame and in earshot.[1] The scale of Streisand's achievement is beyond debate; only the interaction of its many facets bears new scrutiny. As with her mounting high notes, bent to their own destined peak, so with the never-final, yet always definitive, omega points of her recording and screen career, where everything that rises, at least in moments of unique control, can—if not must—converge. A book like this has, therefore, no need of hyperbole—but no excuse for restraint, either, when the typifying triumphs reveal themselves.

My approach, in sum, has a bias and a brief at once. Or lump them together as a working assumption. Its partisan view: that the most vivid and arresting presence on the postwar American screen since her idol Marlon Brando—simply as an expressive image and voice, a cinematographic object—is nonetheless only fully Herself, as star, when singing. This bias leads immediately to the brief: that one can only come to grips with the expansive ventures of her career by tracing the interplay of lyric impact and narrative impersonation in and across both the recorded dramatic singing and the screen performances, comic and dramatic alike. And whether in traditional musical comedy or in the rejuvenation of the genre that Streisand gradually achieved. This assumption explains in advance why *Funny Lady* and *A Star Is Born* share the same third chapter as a pivotal diptych; why the further innovations of *Yentl* claim a chapter of their own; even why her tentative return to live singing in a televised fundraiser, *One Voice*, cohabits in chapter 5 with her most serious dramatic role in *Nuts*; and then certainly why such a career trajectory points toward the audiovisual ingenuities of her two luminous and epitomizing concert tours at century's end. For these are stagings every bit as performative, and almost as narrative in form, as a traditional screen musical. Moreover, that there are strategic mirror scenes, not just shots, in some cases many such scenes, in each of the films singled out at length in these chapters, and even in the second concert, 2000's *Timeless*, is by no means a merely incidental tendency toward self-consciousness in the mise-en-scène of her craft. Given the cultural optic of gender or ethnicity reframed on-screen by these emblematic reflecting planes, this book's title mandate is to entertain exactly those screen differences, both on camera and eventually behind it, that Streisand's artistry tends to maximize and refract. About which, despite mountainous press over the years, there is (perhaps surprisingly) much left unsaid, singing out for recognition. This book answers what it can of that call. For besides the scant attention paid to the actual inner *drama* of Streisand's vocal delivery in recorded song—apart, of course, from its much-discussed technical virtuosity—the scholarly silence regarding her screen acting can only be called blinding as well as deafening.[2]

Looking back as one does, it may seem inevitable that only a literal self-direction on Streisand's part—from behind the lens and the editing room door alike, first with the song numbers ("musical concepts") in *A Star Is Born*, then with *Yentl* start to finish—could get a sufficient internal distance on the singing actress. Only this could fully navigate between musical intention and embodiment: could, in other words, triangulate the mirror once held up to sheer difference not just with a recovered sheen but at gratifying new angles. Inevitable too, then, though long merely a fan's pipe dream (given her decades of stage fright), that only her return to self-directed, video-enhanced live concerts—after two more movies directed, we might say, by the actor only, or maybe the intuitive musician, but not the singer—could retrieve again the impact of the original Streisand amalgam. That, at least, is this book's sense of things. Which must begin with a material sense of that thing called voice.

Program Notes

With that emphasis uppermost, I have chosen to pace investigation, not with Contents tabulated but instead via the program format of a career performance carefully staged and phased. The resulting Set List is keyed to the evolving self-differentiated career of a "multi-hyphenate superstar" (as Streisand was often called after her directing debut): actor-singer-songwriter-producer-director. From this ex post facto Overture on, one question guiding the book's own analytic "program" is the extent to which, and in what varying combinations, those hyphens mark segmented but tightly interlinked facets of her talent or operate more like rungs of a turnstile between them. And part of an answer waits in the considered interstices between her clear successes. These are examined in two "Intermissions" on the unsettled question of genre: assessing, from setbacks not least, where some true fusion of her talents might, if not comfortably reside, then thrive in continual transition across developing commercial and aesthetic possibilities.

The Streisand difference—in that levitated play of contrasts her persona can so brilliantly equilibrate, at least when not in danger of becoming just a juggling act within a given plot—did seem too often separately farmed out across half-hearted projects in the wake of the first big musicals. Potential disappointment lurked at every diversionary turn. In the non-singing roles that preoccupied her filmography in the early 1970s, it would have been hard for viewers not to feel the comedown of the dour *Up the Sandbox* after the rousing fun of *The Owl and the Pussycat*. Who could tolerate, let alone warm to, *For Pete's Sake* after *The Way We Were*? Who thrill to *The Main Event* or *All Night Long* following on the visceral excitements of *A Star Is Born*? Or even see in the brave ferocity of *Nuts*, for all its dedication and histrionic force, a promising new direction after the monumental accomplishment of *Yentl* in its sinuous dramaturgy of song, a film queering the straitjacketings not just of gender but of genre? Certainly the typical alternation of drama and comedy, Streisand's rare strength within a given film, often seems the motor of these shifts between projects—as even, though with a swerve less violent, in her later directorial ventures from the 1990s, after a quickly ditched flirtation with MTV: the combined romance and melodrama of *The Prince of Tides* over against the rom-com of *The Mirror Has Two Faces*. Without song to orchestrate some genuine new merger, viewers may simply take their choice.

No such need with the two self-directed concerts mounted in tandem (it might seem) with these early and late 1990s films. Each is melodramatic in the root sense of melodic stagecraft, and filmic in inflection: multiple screen narratives in themselves at times, with punctuating video backdrops, but brought to the boards (and stadium screens), and then to HBO and DVD, in a new mode of the autobiographic stage musical. This is what Act III imagines as a "homecoming," a return to those first big-budget efforts at "Screening the Streisand Sound" in Act I that propelled the star through one musical comedy per year at the turn of the 1960s, from *Funny Girl* through *Hello, Dolly!* to *On a Clear Day You Can See Forever*. And in the global control she exerts over the later carefully "plotted" concerts, she builds on her decision—or call it her hard-won contractual authority, chronicled in Act II—to work from behind the lens as well as in front of it. At the level of conception as well as performance, at last she is in every sense calling the shots as well as being framed by them in role—with results that, especially in *Yentl*, have entered the annals of musical film's most inspired innovations, not likely to be topped or soon forgotten.

This, then, is an *auteur* study with a difference, extending back before the star-turned-director moment to include the artistic reputation and commercial clout that made that transition possible. And the difference is Streisand. There are two phenomena (in every sense) rendered inseparable in this largely self-authored career: star body and its immediate expressive gifts, on the one hand, vocal and dramatic alike; on the other, a restless curious virtuosity—in front of both mic and camera and then eventually behind the lens and megaphone.[3] To begin with, of course, the sine qua non of those twin anomalies and their impact: the Streisand sight as well as sound. As her camera-ready features seemed distilled by concentration on-screen, one thing grew clear: Streisand had always been, if just barely, pretty enough to become unreasonably beautiful. And the voice not too grand to be steadily sensational. Curator of her own look from the start, inventor of the mercurial kook persona of her early TV spots ("I was a personality before I was a person," she has often said), executive composer of her music style in each phase of its pop and show-tune transformation, protective editor of her public exposure, and always coauthor of her scripted screen timing, she became, as the fame gained traction, the consummate "author" (uneven film direction included) of her own career and its dramatic instincts—straight through to her self-directed autobiographical concerts. No popular artist ever worked harder to make sure her talents weren't shortchanged or downright wasted. Not to mention left unrecorded. There were certainly miscalculations, even when she was in charge, but they were gambles, perhaps often too cautious, not squanderings or exploitations.

A watershed moment for this survey of her work comes in January 1992, when she had just released what Stephen Sondheim, in introducing her for the Grammy Legend Award, called an "extraordinary audio history of a unique career and an exceptional artist," alluding to her *Just for the Record* box set. That four-disc anthology was certainly a lavish and replete look back, an invitation to listen again—and again. Sondheim summed it up perfectly: "She not only possesses one of the most exceptional voices in the world but her musical instincts are unsurpassed . . . and that's a formidable combination." When graciously thanking her fans in her acceptance speech, Streisand also "released," in an unexpected spurt of lyric, what one now sees in retrospect as an extraordinary look forward. *Just for the Record* begins and ends with "You'll Never Know," the closing version a transitional duet between instances of the famous voice half a century apart. Concluding her remarks at the Grammy ceremony, she recalls "standing at a microphone" for her thirteen-year-old first recording of the song, and then suddenly sings out, unaccompanied, in front of the present mic, the eight words of its refrain—this time to her fans: "You'll never know how much I love you." As if to prove it in advance by a comic tease only to be slowly realized over the next couple of years, she quips immediately, with a wry laugh: "Who says I'd never sing live again?"

Just a year later, with suitable orchestration, she does sing live—and for more than a line, three songs for a large if handpicked audience—at President Clinton's first inaugural. She then follows that arena return, a year later yet, with the beginning of her career's last great concert phase, its definitive early itinerary the subject of Act III. In thus rounding out the professional circle begun with the early musicals and the club dates that led up to them, she returns to stage lights for the display of her deliriously rich vocal gifts as well as actorly monologues. And what Streisand delivers with the brimming excitement of these prolonged performance pieces, saturated with retrospect, does indeed crystallize—as never so intensively before—a talent of utter originality, rare theatrical command, tested versatility, unrivaled staying power, and undimmed creative drive, to say nothing of an aesthetic and cultural influence still being felt, steadily re-estimated, and more and more widely proclaimed.

Well before the latest decades of overnight notoriety culture in the U.S. media, Streisand wanted shamelessly to be famous, but famous at something, renowned for what she could *do*, not for who she was. Acting, singing, something. Not just as someone. The success of the effort could count as unprecedented. Yet, predictably, she never took to the "star" exposure that came with it. In the uneven development of celebrity and self, in her case unhedged performance energy versus a guarded personal life, the admission of being "a personality before I was a person" has a revealing extra dimension in theatrical terms. Powerful acting, on camera or on record, requires both. Or say needs that third thing: the conduit of persona. This book is about what the artist as star, finding herself quickly at risk of being frozen into icon, cemented by legend, therefore worked to do—on both screen and album, against the odds and with intermittent but striking success—to keep incubating the persona anew in performance. The late concerts see that effort sprout new wings in an electrified air of intimacy and scope. Portending them, in her Grammy Legend acceptance speech, she insists that she thought of herself not as a legend but as a "work in progress." That figure of speech, subsuming the subject of fame to the gauge of its performances, says it all. What follows is just some small segment of the evidence.

Act I

THE SINGING ACT

CLOSE LISTENING

Terrains of the Voice

Anticipating the title of the second chapter even in this first, it is fair to say that well before Streisand, as "song stylist," goes before TV, and later Hollywood, cameras, there is a way in which her vocal terrain is "screened" in its preternaturally smooth—but also deeply valleyed and steeply ridged—contours. This subliminal optic, this filtering of voice as all but visible as well as tactile soundscape, is what one listens for—whether on vinyl or disc, from the speakers of small screen or large, but in any event always *streaming* through to the visualizing ear, where affect is carved out. Such is the eerie grip, the queer breathed immediacy of feeling, sustained by her voice's instantly recognized precisions and their variable "scenic" and emotional shifts. There is, in this respect, a curious symmetry across the span of her talents. In commentary accompanying the anniversary DVD edition of *Yentl*, Streisand emphasizes the way directing a movie has much in common with the rhythms of a musical composition, its "legatos" and "staccatos" in her examples. This may remind us, in turn, how much mental camerawork there is in the tracking, panning, and cosmic zooms of her own vocal blocking and its perspectival dynamism.

For those who didn't happen to catch her early nationally broadcast appearances, 1961–63, on the TV shows of Jack Paar or Garry Moore or Dinah Shore or Judy Garland, including her several returns to *The Ed Sullivan Show* and more to *The Tonight Show*, the initial impact of the Streisand sound came with the first cut on her eponymous first album. This was the pounding flood of comeuppance on the "Cry Me a River" track, as well as, first on the flip side, the anomalous downbeat rhythm of "Happy Days Are Here Again." In pitched contrast, in the very pitch and tempo of delivery, these throbbing ironic ballads were strategically varied, one on each side again, by the "comic relief" of the lesser upbeat numbers "Come to the Supermarket in Old Peking" and "Who's Afraid of the Big Bad Wolf?" Simultaneously released in stereo in these early days, there was nothing monaural about this launching album even in the alternate pressing to which I was reduced with my cheapjack freshman-dorm record player. Either way, patented for all to hear, was Streisand's own version of surround sound: immersive by force of performance alone, apart from technology. A later joke from *Hello, Dolly!* applies retroactively to what one might call the *multichanneled* choice of song material rather than audio quality. "If you've gotta live from hand to mouth, you'd better be ambidextrous." Here, the mouth did double duty as well. As confirmed in the TV guest spots, where she was routinely given two songs rather than just one, usually slow versus up-tempo, the Streisand sound, quickly becoming a recognized style of tonal surprise, made its twin mark within this polarized spectrum of expressivity: accentuating not just the difference she constituted but the differences she could command. The elegantly shaped hands aside, and before they were a signature part of her screen image, the voice was itself ambidextrous—and broadcast as such.

For her first appearance on *The Ed Sullivan Show*, in November 1962, less than three months before the release of her first album, Streisand began by showcasing just over three minutes of what amounted, mounted, to a compressed five-act play followed by a downbeat ironic finale. There could be no clearer instance of her acting and singing in dialogue with each other, in virtual duet, than this more than ordinarily operatic delivery of a song whose narrative phases are all part of a single post-romantic denouement. In her rendering of "My Coloring Book" (Kander and Ebb, written before their big Broadway hits), Streisand's nervously mercurial intensity of shifting expressions, in fixed medium close-up, seems to enact the very lament over ephemerality at stake in this lovelorn song. (Readers who would become listeners to the full drama of the singing in question should take to YouTube, here and hereafter, in taking some measure of Streisand's incomparable dramatic as well as vocal "coloration.")[1] According to the full lyrics of the verse lead-in to "My Coloring Book," as she later recorded it, the figurative "crayon" tones (and musical tonalities) by which the listener is enjoined to "color me"—unfolded on their own without preamble in the TV version—range across a full gamut of *picturable* deprivation. They do so by tabulating every probable emotion—except self-pity—in an optic dance of avoidance with the direct eyeline gaze of the camera (a rule violated only briefly, pointedly, at the early line "these are the eyes"). Regret spreads across the rhyming dissonance of emotional desertion from "gr*ay*" (those same eyes having "watched him" as he "went aw*ay*") through a heart "bl*ue*" (discovering him no longer "tr*ue*") to the "some*how*" of loss with arms colored "empty *now*" (Streisand's own arms opened out in vacancy at this grievance, extending past the bottom of the TV frame). The details to be "colored" by audience projection extend next from worn beads turned "gr*een*" with jealousy (now that an unnamed "she" so cruelly "came betw*een*") to the imponderable chromatics of an unrhymed abstract "lonely." All this, amid the fleeting winces and held-back tears of betrayal, works itself through—in what will become a typifying Streisand fashion—with sufficient reserves of banked fire to sear away any trace of female abjection. After this fivefold litany of heartbreak, the song bears down on the last impossible coloring of absence per se when the phrasing of a man once depended "up/*on*"—after the lyric's own dependent syllabic drop—is put into slightly skewed rhyme with the need, in the recursive refrain, to "color him *gahwnnnn*." And right there, beyond the bracing facial dramatics—right there in the ironic continuum and slow attenuation of that poignantly held (as if clung to) last note—is a hallmark moment of Streisand's mimetic instinct. Call it in cinematic terms, in its thematized diminuendo, a phonic reverse zoom. In any case, it offers an early sign of what would soon become a recognized Streisand specialty: the gradually relaxed yet steadily clarified tenacity of her purest exit notes.[2]

Wide celebration of the talent and its variety quickly ensued after her first album—as Act I ("The Singing Act") will continue retracing through its exponential early stages. With the sequel album's tracks including "My Coloring Book" less than a year after its TV debut, the cover of that even more dramatic and remarkable *Second Barbra Streisand Album* underlined "The Second" in red. By now its fans were just calling it "the Second Album," as with the simpler (as well as more presumptive, some must have thought presumptuous) title of *The Third Album* to follow. The curated stardom was well underway. Despite the missed chance of titling the most recent of her studio productions *The Thirty-Sixth Album*—its anti-Trump protest urging *Walls* instead—those nearly three dozen intervening studio productions, with four times as many singles spun off from them, were interspersed with nine compilations. This prolific audio record has been compounded as well by a further measure of dramatic charisma beyond her rare vocal talent: fifteen soundtracks, beginning with assembled musical excerpts from her first of several Emmy-winning TV specials, *My Name Is Barbra* (1965), and then resumed four decades later in concert albums from HBO and PBS specials once the singer rose again to the challenge of the live stage.

In that first special's opening credits—over a lackluster photo of Barbara Joan Streisand at five years old, and in a tinkling run of babyish high notes—the off-screen voice tames the coloratura of Leonard Bernstein's 1943 song cycle *I Hate Music!: A Cycle of Five Kids Songs* in the special's title number. (Bernstein, who would later accompany her on piano in 1968 for his own anti-war composition "So Pretty" at the Broadway for Peace congressional fundraiser, had earlier jumped to his feet to lead a standing ovation for her 1962 solo turn as "Miss Marmelstein" in her Broadway debut, *I Can Get It for You Wholesale*.)[3] At the start of that first TV special three years later, deferring her glide into moving-image embodiment (guest spots aside) for a still mostly just-listening audience—across a dolly-in on the childhood photo to an outsize, frame-straining live close-up—Barb(a)ra sings dismissively of her mother's sexual euphemisms about where babies come from: "baby bottles," "baby bushes." Nothing doing: "*I* don't believe in storks, either [the rhyming *I*-thur] . . . They're all in the zoo." And then, as a lingering segue to her moving image, there is the panache of non sequitur after a dubious aside ("And what's a baby bush anyway?"). It is here, in an abrupt shift of lyric focus, that she sweetens and distends her vocalizing to emit the whole point of this irrelevant preamble: her way cleared for self-origination with the Bernstein line (originally in normal spelling, of course), "My name is Baaarrrbrrrraaaa." In that enunciation, the roll of those flanking middle *r*'s seems extended to insist by overt repression on the syncopated missing second *a* deleted from her compressed "stage name." In phonetic manifestation of the star's own backstory, this TV moment rehearses the auto-gestation of a persona later to be embodied—in one character after another across her musical performances, on- as well as off-screen—by the variable means of self-*engender*ment.

Nearness by Ear

For starters—inauguration in every sense—that lighthearted rejection of origin stories makes way for the sheer fact of presence and self-nomination. It stands as the first of a half dozen signal moments across the mating of body to sound in the star's unprecedented one-woman television specials that can help in sorting through the ramified deviations and dichotomies cultivated by the Streisand sound on ever-widening screens. For a second example, we can speed to the close of this first TV special for an audiovisual effect playing just before the credits in the famously ironic interpretation of her first true signature song. Long before she would restore for political celebration the original upbeat spirit of this FDR-era ballad, there is the superimposed tripling of Streisand's image (fig. 3)—seemingly fragmented by its own intensity—on the three hammering last notes of "[Happy] *Days Are Here*" before the almost tensecond sostenuto of "Agaieeeeehn." As if perhaps to suggest, with those punctuating cuts on the *here and now*, that this particular vocal happiness is emphatically before us for the first time. But then this closural timing develops another valence as well in future iterations of this showstopper. In the early treatment of this lyric, Streisand sustains a brassy and sarcastic false note, in mood rather than melody. In later concert versions of this requisite hit, the effect is further notched up syllabically with a pulsional self-iterative "Agai-ai-eh-eeeeehn." In an irony tonal as well as vocal, once seems not enough in sounding out either this sarcasm or, on happier national occasions, its impulsive optimism.

[An aside on notation—or "transliteration," one might call it—quite apart from any inferred semantic play in a given case. I refer to the challenge this book sets itself of

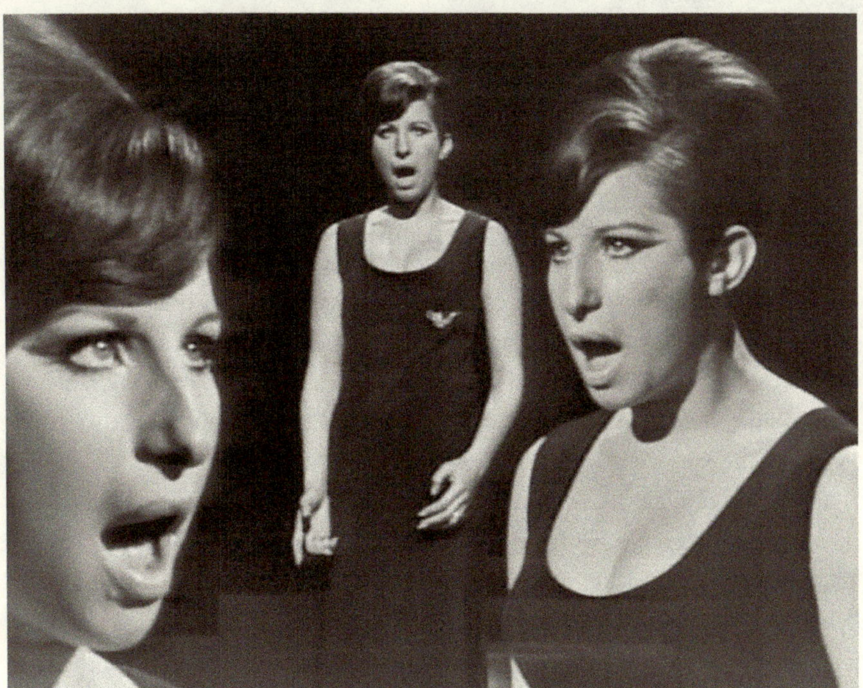

3. Happy . . . DAYS / ARE / HERE (*My Name Is Barbra*)

strictly alphabetic (often phonetic) transcription—wildly more complex in Streisand's case than any sheet music rendering of her material, more sheeted in its very phrasing, layered, sheared away and remade within a single note by internal drifts and skids. My notation of such notes will continue to attest in this ad hoc alphabetic way to the spontaneous mysteries that pervade the scalar eddies, crests, and riptides of her delivery: a matter at times, a materialization, not just of inner sonic differentials but of dramatic emphasis, with a breath control that takes only the listener's breath away. Even where individual screen numbers can be readily linked to on YouTube (to be assumed throughout, even when not specially signposted), my alphabetic transcriptions would be meant as a kind of underscore, lending interpretive stress to even the most unmistakable gusts of enunciation—as if to say "spelling out" what the unaided ear may merely be struck by.]

In the mating of such contoured sound to visual pace, space, and focus, the series of emblematic or reflexive moments I have in mind from these early one-woman TV outings includes, next, the ironically inset archaeology of beauty in her second special, *Color Me Barbra* (1966). Its opening coloring-book logo (and first image) soon mutates into a metropolitan museum setting in which the star's profile is matched against sculpture and painting from Nefertiti to Modigliani. These comic effects have a way of anticipating that non-chorus-girl beauty asserted in *Funny Girl*, almost cubist at times in its exploited angularities, that may indeed (varying our first epigraph) "stay in style forever." Despite the common vicissitudes of mass popularity, such is the suggestion of Streisand's millennial prototypes at the Philadelphia Museum of Art. Here, too, is another TV venture that knows where it's going (in the idiom of one of its closing song numbers), knows its own dramatic vector, capped as it is by another concert finale in which the star is poised on an abstract cantilevered staircase (compared to the more modest set she descended at the close of *My Name Is Barbra*). The vanishing point is now somewhere in midair, stage rear, no real end in sight—as the star sends into voice the equivalent of that terraced ascent's own upward thrust.

This happens, in fact, across a three-song sequence in the move from spatial to temporal horizons (beginning with the open-ended "Any Place I Hang My Hat Is Home," and followed by the rhetorical question of the equally jazzy "Where Am I Going?"). What completes this triple play on destination is a yet more challenging star turn on the part of the Streisand sound—still establishing its signature reach in the pace and space of performance—when she delivers the more opulent legato of "Starting Here, Starting Now." It's as if that huge-throated love song were fulfilled, in sound alone, by the prolonged embrace of the final "Noooouuwww." And by *now*, in performance time, the amorous lyric has been abstracted to a kind of musical odyssey in the offing: inaugurating—in intended company with the applauding audience itself as early fan base, and as the rhyming lyric has it just before—"the greatest journey" that "heaven can allow."[4] A journey figured in transit via lap dissolve to an even more expansive "starting now" refrain and climax (fig. 4): a markedly prolonged double image in which one Barbra is leaving the other behind—as troped in the shift to long shot—in transition to the final blazing reprise. The voice laddering up in this way, the career journey has certainly taken off. In detailing the lilt, the melting lift, of this staircased transition, it is hard not to sound, or to make *it* sound, overly melodramatic. In fact, the cinematographic effect feels as effortless as the vivid singing. And answers to the very space opened by the latter. As with the triple self-reflection at the close of her first special, this more fluid effect locates an early benchmark in Streisand's screen work. Camera technique, breaking with the general transparency of star display, and in this case courting a momentary translucency matching the lustrous opacity of sound, unfolds to complement—and further enact—a chromatic vocal terrain in the very contour of montage. Here, then, is one visualized point of departure from sound into emotive scenography in this entirely *expansive* career. For the audience of that second special, if not before: starting there, starting then.

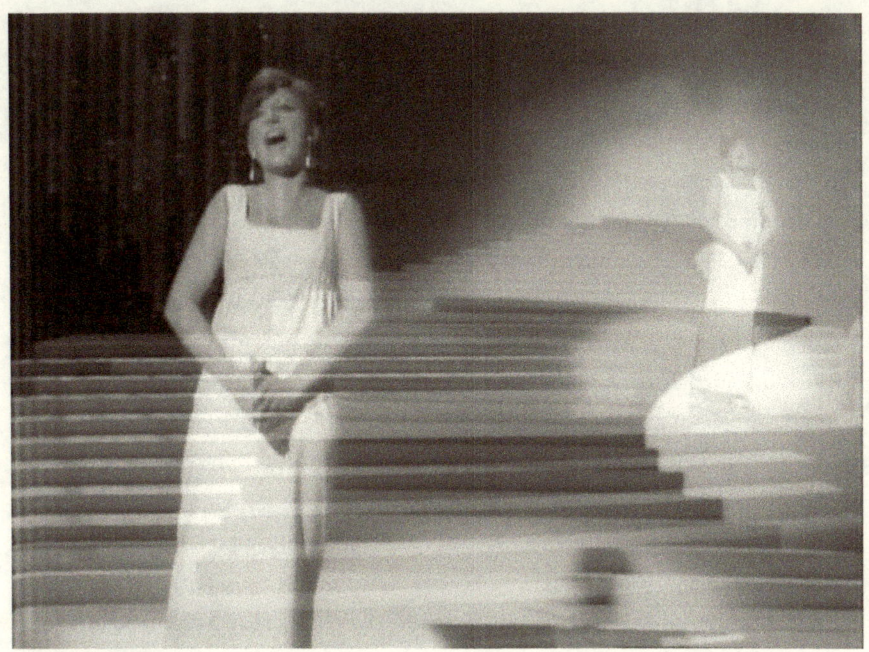

4. Starting here / there / now (*Color Me Barbra*)

The rest, as they say, is history, but a richly sedimented one, rewarding one dig after another into its layered and variably textured buildup. I think back in this respect to the silly Howard Bannister figure (Ryan O'Neal) in *What's Up, Doc?* (1972), mockingly characterized as a "musical archaeologist" who believes that Pleistocene stones were the first musical instruments—and who is thus set up for a throwaway joke about getting his rocks off with his prosthetic tuning fork. Having nothing to do with the Streisand heroine's aggressive pursuit of him in that misbegotten plot, still his job description does name one important motive in any review of Streisand's song career. It is part of the implied prospective longevity of the public's love affair with the Streisand sound, as tacitly invited by that dilated last syllable in "starting noooouuwww" from the second TV special, that is further captured—in the present audiovisual archaeology—by a subsequent plateau moment worthy of being singled out, among many, from the rapid sequence of these pathbreaking TV specials.

In 1967, as a vaudeville darling in *The Belle of 14th Street*, containing in (thinly disguised) propria persona some of the most ravishing vocals—and close-ups—Streisand ever recorded, she also doubles at one point as the guest artist, the lampooned German diva Madame Schmausen-Schmidt, for a send-up of a ponderous "Liebestraum." This impersonation is next interrupted by, and then submits to a duet with, a young boy down front, all in green, who couldn't hold back "their" exquisite voice (Barbra also in this third role) in the German's labored version of "Mother Machree." In this context of high operatic chops versus folk sincerity, let alone the gender dichotomy that anchors it, Streisand confronts those ponderous bellowing big notes with her own choirboy sweetness—for what is in fact her first "trouser role"—in a face-off resolved only with the assured star fusion of the Belle herself when she reaches the stage. This occurs in dazzling renditions ranged across another dichotomy that gets assimilated to a negotiated spectrum, moving from the shimmering clarity of "I'm Always Chasing Rainbows" and "My Melancholy Baby" to an earthy belting in the closing Sophie Tuckeresque medley of "A Good Man Is Hard to Find" / "Some of These Days." That combo is probably the punchiest and most uninhibited—and sexiest—"jazz" performance Streisand ever put on film, or in this case videotape: verging on raunchy as well as raucous—and anticipating the vamped comic fire of the "So Long, Dearie" number in *Hello, Dolly!* As with those *three faces* of emphatic vocalizing (via superimposition) at the "Happy Days" close of her first special, here in these three narrative personae is another synthesizing triangulation of Streisand's whole vocal and dramatic register at once. Ambidextrous—and then some.

Move now (or more like glide) to one more emblematic moment from later that same year, 1967, just as the movie version of *Funny Girl* was about to premiere—and to change the expectations of big-screen female stardom as if overnight. In this live TV special based on Streisand's free Central Park concert, an outing indeed, what is delivered up is a spectacle, an event—in the titular lingo of the time, a "happening"— that still, decades later, even though miked unevenly across a shifting summer wind, remains transfixing from song to song. In its TV edit, the *Happening* begins, behind the credits, with a quiet love-song delivery ("The Nearness of You") accompanying a leisurely helicopter shot over Manhattan, crossing miles—and many skyscrapers' worth of vertical distance—to close in, over a sea of heads, on Barbra floating alone on a plexiglass stage. She is framed there in close-up completing the last camera-filling four words of the Hoagy Carmichael standard, with its swooning sense of being able "to feel in the night" the "nearness" of the private amorous "you." It is, as it happens, a number lifted midstream—and edited forward—from the live song sequence of this *Happening in Central Park*. Happening, event, advent. Here, if never before, the Streisand sound has found a defining image for its fervent aerial reach. Distance is indeed crossed and closed by the gravitational pull of that voice, even from the elevated terrain of an unlikely intimacy—and even in the deliberately counterindicated context of one of the largest crowds ever assembled, at that point in performance history, for a single-artist concert.

Figured or not in the proximity of its affect, the voice had brought the singer to this mass renown. Against mounting rebuffs in early job interviews and auditions, the upward struggle was short-lived but legendary, the breakthrough so meteoric it remains hard to parse. But, in sum, how the "nearness" of the Streisand sound—since early in the 1960s' run of club dates—had saved her career from its premature dead end as an actress makes one of the great thrift-shop-rags-to-riches sagas of show business lore. There's no doubt that the game was stacked against Barbara Joan Streisand at the outset—before she could play her full singing-actress hand. Judged either too "plain" or too "odd" for the dramatic stage in early auditions, an unlikely misfit of ambition, with "homely" and "eccentric" at frequent cross-purposes in such rejection, the still-teenage Streisand turned to the recording studio instead. This was her own version of Fanny's back-door entrance. One of the funniest lines in *Funny Girl* comes when dashing Nick Arnstein introduces himself to her outside her dressing room after her opening night smash at Keeney's modest music hall. With an overdressed blonde glamour-puss on each arm, Nick invites her to join them for dinner, offering graciously to "wait while you change." With a glance of chagrin at the renewed symmetry of 2 beautiful girls 2, Fanny shoots back: "I'd have to change too much. Nobody could wait that long." Even long before landing this part, Streisand herself didn't think to change, but nor did she actually have to wait all that long herself, since the Broadway stage—recognizing the deep "histrionics" of her nightclub act—quickly came calling.

Though an instant national celebrity with her first albums, even then she was so much a force of nature that she seemed to some ears forced, artificial, the sound itself too assertive. Against the growing cascade of awe and adulation, there was always some undertow of complaint—and its contradictions. Supposedly too quirky and undisciplined at first, she was soon dubbed too aggressive a perfectionist. Though boasting, as it were, an uncontested power, the singing was deemed too nasal for some ears, too strident for others. Her persona, vocal and otherwise, was too bohemian for the Midwest clubs, later too aloof for Vegas, not schmoozy enough in either venue for mainstream ingratiation. As her stardom solidified, her unevadable talent was often critically sidelined as too late for the fading genre of Hollywood musical comedy, in vocal style too overmastering for their standard-issue duets anyway, too scene-swallowing for ensemble drama, too anomalous for traditional rom-com leads. After being found too young for Dolly, too old for Yentl, too Jewish for Christmas carols, too cautious with classical, too staid and operatic for rock, too stately for disco, she was then thought, after the *Guilty* album, too lucratively pop-identified for a return to Broadway ballads. And even when her work was hailed, the star was nailed as behind the scenes too demanding, out front too political for her own good, and certainly too brazen later in wanting to break from entrenched custom and take over her own screen direction. On it went, the naysaying, and on so many fronts at once: the star was just *too too*, too much. Too true—but more in the superlative than the comparative sense of that phrase. Less may often be more. But the maximal has its magnetism as well, and Streisand rarely dialed herself back or down, even when the eventual script choices seemed ill-considered.

Once her dramatic talent as pitch-perfect comedienne as well as singer was unleashed, Hollywood was inevitable. But the Streisand soundscape was, I've been suggesting, already a widescreen phenomenon before movies came knocking. For when I speak of "screening" her sound I mean, again, a filtered attention on our part, regarding film or disc, that frames and mediates the heard as a mode of theatrical deep focus. Audition matches itself to the way the voice sieves its effects through a closely meshed grid of dramatic inference: an inner optics of focal as well as vocal adjustment. One rolling terrain after another is traversed by phrasal tracking. Expansive vowels dolly in and out within a single syllable, alternating the intimacies of caressed phonic close-ups with the achieved scale of virtually telephoto long shots, to say nothing of fluid dissolves and sometimes overt jump cuts, all focused by the listener in the mind's eye of the voice's almost material scope, reach, velocity, and diaphanous vanishing points. This synesthetic audition, in a disposition of "close listening," is where musicology overlaps with dramaturgy—and eventually with the star's own control of cinematography—in Streisand's evolving performance of voice.

And not only, it should be stressed, in singing numbers. Her rich speaking voice, later mellowed and honeyed with age, though with its comic patois and Brooklyn ethnic twang very much on call when needed, has always been a strangely unmentioned part of her screen magnetism in non-singing roles. But that is only to stress, in complementary terms, a more important fact about her musical skill. For the Streisand sound is *always* on a felt continuum with the speaking voice. Even when she stopped doing only pre-contracted musicals on-screen, each of her films was punctuated by little arias of appeal or diatribe—all the way through to her last lead role in 2012's *The Guilt Trip*. And if she never stops singing her big lines, she never—as odd as this may sound for a voice so studiously "grand"—stops *talking her songs* even at their most lushly orchestrated and sumptuous in delivery. The seamless ease with which she moves from chest voice to head voice, as well as from contralto through mezzo to soprano, holds even the most flamboyant performance within the realm of a kind of musically scored soliloquy. This, more than anything else, is the rarely mentioned secret of her vocal style: where a determined lucidity of enunciation, never verging on operatic elocution (or its transcendence altogether into pure tone), is always persuasively vernacular in any register, low and high notes alike, never sheer phonic abstraction. [It is this phenomenon that lends justification, I like to think, referring to a similar side note in the previously bracketed paragraph above, to this book's sometimes lumbering mode of alphabetic emphasis on the inner lining of Streisand's syllables. To treat otherwise, in strictly musical ciphering, these wide-angle enunciations and distensions—as entirely a matter of half-notes and holds, for instance—would miss their always still-speaking force as wording as well as musical phrasing.] From her debut album on, one miracle of Streisand's effortless huge notes, schooled in theater, is just this vernacular acuity: their materialization as speech as well as voice. They embody not just singing but the drama of song, its emotions set to music while spoken forth as orchestrated line readings. Such is the impressive benchmark as well as unique trademark—the true *earmark*—of Streisand's given gift and her genius at once.

Granularity in Action

A vocal theater of expression, yes, with the likes of a deep-focus thematic resonance. At the same time, Streisand's lyric "readings"—as ours of them in turn—also register what French theorist Roland Barthes, about classical song delivery, called the almost ineffable "grain" of vocalization beneath the dramatic text: material through and through, yet none the less an appreciable "text" in its own right. Certainly an "indelible" sound like Streisand's is ripe for the textualist approach to voice in Barthes—including his call for audition at magnified range. When his well-known 1972 essay "The Grain of the Voice" is followed the next year (in order of original composition) by his even more famous *The Pleasure of the Text*, Barthes surprises us by closing the latter with a sudden rhapsody about the voice track as its own kind of screen "close-up."[5] The critic famously indifferent to the time-based medium of cinema, in favoring instead the contemplative fix of the photograph, finds in the temporality of the soundtrack a revelation all its own—and a supposedly decisive analogy. It is, we hear, a matter more somatic than semantic.

In the earlier essay, Barthes lifts an influential dichotomy from theorist Julia Kristeva, distinguishing between the generative matrix or core, the funding energy, of a linguistic form, on the one hand, and, on the other, its generated surface discourse, each open to decipherment: in reverse order, the pheno-text over against, over and above, the underlying geno-text.[6] From the ground of production up, call it the voicing beneath the messaging. According to Barthes, and despite the decline of melody in the art song, the aural component—the tangible voice itself—is as much a part of the legible text of vocal art as is any articulated lyric. In song, what's left of it as aesthetic category, lies the obvious "pleasure," whereas in the voice alone rests the enhanced, but also primal, realm of "bliss," where the *generative* body may be said to inhere in, and even transcend, the performance *phenomenon*, narrative or otherwise. The joys of opera or ballad may have to do in part with plot as well as with vestigial melodic motifs; its ecstasies instead, its erotic *jouissance* in Barthes's terms, with the fabric and nap of vocalization itself. This entails the particulate tactile grain of the loosened throat, its friction and liquidity: an immanence of voice quite apart on-screen, for Barthes, from script (as otherwise from lyric in the art song).

Just before a climactic and telltale passage in *The Pleasure of the Text*, Barthes does grant the place of familiar song within the order of textual pleasure: "A certain art of singing can give an idea of this vocal writing; but since melody is dead, we may find it more easily today at the cinema" (67). Not at the cinema of the movie musical, certainly, with its dated melodic center, but at the technical realization of the "projected" voice itself—at once enhanced and artificially isolated: bodily production dissevered from image in the mechanical soundtrack. What counts for Barthes is the way "the cinema captures the sound of speech close up (this is, in fact, the generalized definition of the 'grain' of writing)." Such a foregrounding of speech sounds made audible on the movie track—in unsaid associative connection with the screen's visual close-up—is what, in Barthes's giddy run of hyperbole, can "make us hear in their materiality, their sensuality, the breath, the gutturals, the fleshiness of the lips . . . fresh, supple, lubricated, delicately granular and vibrant" (67). Despite Barthes's disclaimers about melody, what could better describe the Streisand sound than this stress on the *text of voice* beyond or beneath its words? Or, as this book's main syllabic stress, *within* them: "the voluptuousness of vowels, a whole carnal stereophony" (66). For Barthes, as he puts it for once rather tersely, this hearing "shifts the signified a great distance" (68). Implicitly displaced by the tangible phonetic signifier, the effect is ravishingly detached from meaning. It is at this point that somatic production rather than semantic content achieves its erotic penetration for Barthes: succeeds, that is, famously, "in throwing, so to speak, the anonymous body of the actor into my ear: it granulates, it crackles, it caresses, it grates, it cuts, it comes: that is bliss." Or in other words, again, orgastic charge and release. Barthes's "throwing" ("so to speak") evokes, aptly enough, the "thrown voice" of ventriloquism, which makes the smitten auditory body vibrate along, silently, with that of the performer. As I hope will become ringingly clear from the attentions ahead, with their many cited examples, listening to the Streisand voice has its unmatched way of sustaining, over decades of variety and invention, something of this joyously transferred somatic thrill—making listening itself an uncanny act of shared embodiment as well as secondary visualization.

Certainly Streisand's voice weds Barthes's cleft textual pleasures of song versus sound, melody versus vocal texture—welding as her projection so effortlessly does the "text" of vocalism per se and her dramatic voicing of a given musical text or lyric. Listened to "close up" in her screen musicals, and regardless of camera position—whether in a space-catapulting long shot or at intimacy's tighter grip—what we audit is that cusp moment between the story told by a song and the hold of its notes, in themselves and upon us. In other words, though still in her enunciated wording, once the radically non-"anonymous" body of this actor arrives on-screen, the Streisand persona, what gets underway is a genre evolution in the movie musical that climaxes under subtitled revision—and under her own direction finally—in *Yentl: A Film with Music*. In progress toward that screen occasion, that ongoing cause célèbre, such singing has found ways, or tried, time and again, variously, flamboyantly, to textualize voicing twice over—or say to re-narrativize it. The result is that our sense of vocal grain becomes its own kind of terrain, a plotted topography, dramatized from within the furrows, swells, and striations of sound itself—and all with no loss, just a channeling, of its intrinsic phonic bliss. On-screen or off, and always "close up," even when a film shot has backed a good distance away as if to figure oral volume in its own right—including at times an aerial vantage that the voice itself has seemed to reach in its wild climb—this is the dramatized trajectory of voice as text in the Streisand sound: song by song, a variegated inner passage and its punctuating, often piercing, t(h)rills. Grain and articulation at once: a scintillating friction and a dramatic frisson—serving to trope space by timing and intonation alone. At their best, each strain, in the musical sense, becomes a fertile as well as a furrowed terrain all its own.

This is vividly the case in the last triumphant addition to Streisand's roster of signature treatments, debuted live (after a previous video rendition) in her politically troped *One Voice* (raised in defiance) fundraiser broadcast in 1986. It is a song then further canonized in her repertoire for the 1994 *Streisand—In Concert* finale: namely, Leonard Bernstein's and Stephen Sondheim's "Somewhere," from *West Side Story*. In its unspecified asymptote of arrival, the titular utopic "where" is floated as possibility only in the topography of notes sustained in approaching, and then opening wide across, the eight elating sub-syllables in Streisand's evocation (her evocalization) of an idealized "SUH-uh-um-WUH-er-er eR-ERE." Utterance itself is revved up—and spread wide—by being lifted into its own ethereal clime: a space translated from the inward body out of which it issues. In registering the grain of such voice, our sense of its time-released encapsulation leverages a separate conceptual zone altogether, a "place for us" in the midst of listening, highly dimensional: a kind of 3D sphere of identification, "narratively" motivated by the actress from within the song. Streisand's is in every sense a volumetric sound, mobilizing not just the grain but, again, the varying *terrains* of voice. My reading of its "text" will thus continue to be a kind of topographic reading—where, in a concentration on the musical films and videoed concerts, the articulated space of cinematography will be vocalism's most immediate complement. But the point of this establishing chapter goes beyond, and back before, the actual filming of the Streisand sound in production. In the hyphenate spectrum of her talent, on this book's auteurist view, it isn't just the actress who finds her earliest and some of her best parts in song but the eventual screen director who, from the first, has dynamized their lyrics with what amounts to a contoured mise-en-scène and a mobile camerawork alike.

As with the filmography, so with Streisand's discography. It too can be combed anew for effects in the occupied soundscape of voice that clarify her on-screen re-alization of vocal "range" as emotive space, now compressed, now expansive. These include the stage duets she reduces to monologues with herself on record (as with Sondheim's "Move On") or the many medleys she puts together for their lamination of two or three separate dramatic moments or personae (hear Rogers and Hammerstein's "I Have Dreamed" / "We Kiss in a Shadow" / "Something Wonderful"). Through it all runs the frequent imitative potential mined, or better mimed, by her scrupulous ear for the visual choreography—again, the tacit cinematography—of song. To give just a pair of examples from the four-disc archival box set *Just for the Record* (1991), there is her electrifying version of the Buddy Rogers song, and 1963 Lenny Welch hit, originally on her *Barbra Joan Streisand* album. This is hardly a mere "cover" but instead a complete rethinking that scales the heights—and titular figurative plummets—of "Since I Fell for You," all in a remarkable high-wire, high-dive performance, its peak the pumping admission (and repetitive innovation on the original's straightforward adverbial lyric) that "*I'm still, I'm still, I'm still* in love with you." In its clinging itera-tion, this superbly judged effect drifts off—and up—into the higher-yet cross-word rhyme between the phrase "We*ll I*-i-i-I guess" and the reversible phonetic alliteration (and internal chiasmus) of "*I'll* never see the *ligh*-i-i-hi-ightt."[7] The blindness of love finds vent in these swooning lifts of sound.

Equally stunning in delivery, as culled from the unreleased corners of the archive on *Just for the Record,* and again in Streisand's richest mimetic vein, is the Kander and Ebb/ Sondheim medley bridging from "A Quiet Thing" to "There Won't Be Trumpets," where love sneaks up unheralded, on "tiptoe" notes in the first lyric, then phasing over into the tandem melody's searing blare of "who needs trumpEHEHEHHHHTs?" Textualized in the latter metallic thrust—as before in the counterindicated crystalline shimmer of "the bells don't ring"—is a "compensatory" vocal effect that indulges the clarion fanfare it rejects, that harbors and then releases, almost as if to exorcise, the fantasy it disavows. It does this, trumpets this very catharsis, in the process of rendering a sustained vocal image of piercing brassy thrill. Such, and more, always more, are the insignia moments of a singing gift that, in such prolongations not least, embodies—and euphorically emits—the gift that keeps on giving. Without ever yet, at this writing, giving out. With a kind of aural irony in that previously unreleased number, the disclaimed clamor of trumpets is put at the same distance that their peal so vibrantly traverses. This is to stress again that Streisand in song is always latently a moving-picture director, staging the mise-en-scène of the inner ear, making little motion clips out of her vocal micro-dramas, screening the inner topography of her lyric framings. Again, every track the tracking shot of a unique vocal terrain.

Microphonics under the Microscope

Regarding the analytically magnified granularity of voice, Barthes's theory keeps un-expected good company with hands-on practice, if from an unexpected source. In particular, regarding voice embodied and projected from an on-screen image, and then felt from within by the body of the listener, an excellent *aide d'entendre*—in an assisted hearing of one signature song's worded music—is provided from the video blog of British Indie rock guitarist Fil Henry, under the stage name Wings of Pegasus. His is an ear-opening appreciative study, "phrase by phrase," of "just some" aspects of the "plethora of vocal technique" that Streisand commands.[8] His chosen example is in fact her self-composed "Evergreen," though not the screen version from *A Star Is Born* but the one filmed a decade later at the 1986 backyard fundraiser, *One Voice*. Yet the word-by-word (though not exactly word for word, but rather note for note) emphasis offered by Pegasus maps back quite precisely onto the filmed rather than just videoed version as well—whose ecstatic circular pan in *A Star Is Born* captures the "dance" of "spirits" on the "rise" (and melodic return) that the song both describes and enacts.

With his own meticulous attention in video replay being as "bang on" as her high and low notes alike, some of which he approximates in revealing falsetto, Wings of Pegasus helps with unprecedented care to step off the inner architecture of her vocal production in "Evergreen." The emphasis is entirely on production, not on this un-usual case of her own composition. But by the time he's through you marvel all the more at the perfect fit of lyric and technique in that #1 hit, as if the novice composer were indeed writing exclusively for her own throat. When Pegasus says he intends to "put her vocal cords under the microscope"—and, at times, implicitly, her breathing under a stethoscope—he is doing the expert work whose complement in response is the kind of thematic audition my phonetic annotations are hoping to net. That he can demonstrate so much with one of her least showy numbers, if certainly one of her most popular and enthralling, is a source of fascination in itself, especially given the abundance of craft drawn out from this one love song—and readily extrapolated to her other performances, live or studio—not to mention its pivotal (and visually revolved) place in the film from which its uplift is lifted. One result of this rock musician's up-close listening is to remind us how it is exactly sound under the microscope that the song numbers in *A Star Is Born* ("musical concepts" by the supervening star herself, as we'll explore in Act II) are themselves out to enhance dramatic focus in the laboratory of cinematic framing.

And not the least strength of this video analysis of a video rendition, coming from a stage performer like Pegasus, is the emphasis not just on the "skeletal" shape and resonance of the singer's head (and his relief that she didn't tamper with it via the often encouraged nose job) but on her own bodily movements in delivering the song. He stresses how she's never studiously searching (as singers often do) for her "center of resonance," not straining to maximize the play of the diaphragm in aid of breath support, but instead following the logic of the composition with her gestures of head and torso. This analysis helps us appreciate not just the actorly drama of Streisand's performance style but how it is that she can sound always colloquial, if never just talky—singing, we might say, in the key of speech. This musicological precision on the part of Pegasus enters this book's own commentary, that is, for the way his attention stresses not just vocal range and technique but the resulting "authenticity" of the sound as song drama. As usual, the main gain of such listening (as my own ungainly liberty with spelling will continue trying to bring out) is to trace the close coupling of semantics with phonics. Though sketching out what amounts to the narrative superstructure of "Evergreen" as music rather than lyric, Pegasus, to whose video analysis we'll return in a moment, helps at the same time to suggest how the vocal cords can repeatedly be found sounding the focal chords of a song's lyric plotline rather than just its musical "theme."

Streisand's ability to work the diaphragm naturally, without being preoccupied by the physical logistics of sound production, has been not just striking but foregrounded and almost self-consciously enacted in her mobile stage presence from the start of her career. Yet this divergence of bodily "concentration" between the anatomy of sound and the dramatics of its delivery is easily forgotten when listening to the subsequent polishing of her craft in the studio albums—or in the more statuesque claim on the mic in her much later return to live delivery. Before the closing "concert segments" of her first two TV specials, there is surely no better example of this on video record than her hyperkinetic version of "Down with Love" in her 1963 guest appearance on *The Judy Garland Show*.[9] The snarly ironic splendor of this performance is a compendium of the early Streisand sound when "screened" by dramatic context, with its typical swings between tingling purity and grit. In this anti-love-song's frenetic oscillation of tempo and temper, almost feral at times in its "attack," a metallic belting can get funneled on demand to a melting high note, all danced out by an upper body in full subordination of vocal technique to dramatic expression. And the song is preceded on that same Garland special, by contrast, with the tempered mellow wonder of "Bewitched, Bothered, and Bewildered," rendered in a fixed medium close-up in which shoulders, neck, and head are, as Pegasus might have it, productively mobilized within the tight frame of the performance's variably gleaming high notes.[10] So sensational were these separate numbers, to say nothing of the fabled and ubiquitously clipped duet (cum duel) with Garland herself on "Happy Days" / "Get Happy," that Streisand garnered her first Emmy nomination for "Best Performance in a Musical or Variety Program" just for this guest spot.

Two decades later, at the opposite end of the dramatic and melodic spectrum from the brassy "Down with Love," comes the rolling erotic affirmation of "Evergreen" in live performance for *One Voice*—but yet again with the body discounted as mere instrument and thrown instead into emotion. And the subsequent video analysis of Streisand's delivery by Wings of Pegasus is especially telling in its annotation of the notes not just hit but slid into. This is explained elsewhere by Pegasus (in his blogging on Sinatra) as a matter of "pitch bending," where anything celebrated as "perfect pitch" is not a clear hammer blow but often a waver and glide that only comes to rest, rather than landing immediately, where it belongs. And such bending, such vocal torque, is guided not just by the throat but the whole torso. This emphasis emerges from the close attention given by Pegasus, not just to the exactions of the larynx, Streisand's in particular, but to the way they are enhanced by what amounts to the *body language* of the actor (the performer, not her diaphragm alone) in emitting the singer's instinctive emotive precisions of breath, volume, pitch, and skid. One result is that this video commentary, for all its musicological clarity, amounts to a rudimentary narratography of the Streisand sound as well. It is within the orbit of such realization that my further emphasis will continue to fall on the elongated or clipped connotation of such embodied notes, across their inner syllabic (and sub-syllabic) shape, in the mating of voice and lyric: the true galvanizing duet of every Streisand solo.

Although the work of noting the low Bs and high Cs of a given delivery can certainly leave cold the untrained ear, as in numerous other websites celebrating and anatomizing the Streisand range, I'm well aware that my own accompanying (rather than alternate) phonetic sketches can only lend a dreary ear, as well, to the actual recorded effect. The hope is that glossing a rudimentary if seamless division of labor between singing and acting, between notes hit and words theatrically released, can, though far from simulating, at least help remember for you—or send you to with new curiosity—those unmistakable contours of Streisand's intonation that, on first hearing, always take the listener by surprise. Suffice it to stress again, though, that no spoiler alerts are necessary. No emulated spread of letter sounds on the typographic page can take the bloom off the space-making timbre and bend of the Streisand sound itself, the room it opens within single words, the inner difference it effects.

Exemplary in its own right, the Pegasus analysis wings its way, to begin with, across the fine line Streisand is able to maintain between breathing and singing, noting how she can get "closure" with her vocal cords on the very cusp of producing just pure air. In "Evergreen," he points first to the opening line's softly delivered synonymy for love as an "easy ch-air," with (one might add, as my typography is meant to) its all but punning emphasis on relaxed breathing itself, in any case a phrasing comfortably sunk into. Such an effect is certainly pursued further by the song's breathier-yet rhyme, for a second simile, in the terraced downward slide of "mo-oh-o-rni-in-ng aiiiir"—delivered in the *One Voice* performance with a downward jut of her jaw and a slight smile, as if at the vocal feat itself. For all the difficulty of such calculated sighing at the point of unforced vocal delivery, its mimetic effect approaches a low-keyed, kicked-back, breath-easy pleasure in love, enacted, as Pegasus is at pains to stress, a full octave below the famous humming notes she opens with: notes, we might think, that pitch (in the sense of advertise) a further reach coming. Without putting it this way, his stress on this bracketing difference serves to draw out one unmistakable inference of his video commentary: that we've already heard the song's phonic destiny in its prologue.

After two lines headed by "love"—its second iteration made more spacious (I'd add) with the extra breath of "luh-ah-uhve"—"Evergreen" finds its third and more emphatically stretched emphasis edged open on approach with the "Wuh-uh" in the first word alone of "One love"—though still as much relaxed as insistent. As Pegasus hears this, the vocal cords get only just enough "closure" to turn deep-breathing into a sung note—this before her voice traverses the almost one-worded ligature "I ha*ve found*" ("Ivfound")—found (that "one love") with the song's addressee. As second person enters the lyric in its narrowing down from ode to love song—with the slightly roughened (read: earthy) gradient in descent through "I" to "have," as if in a kind of throaty contracted "I've"—it is just here that we find the commentator's chief example of "vocal fry." Achieved by bringing the vibrated vocal cords so close together that their friction skirts a kind of mellifluous rasp, the effect seems complemented a split second later with the zeroing in and down on the second-person object of "hav(e) found with you." At which point, in the lyric's third simile, Pegasus notes the onset of Streisand's renowned high-speed vibrato in the song's most extended note yet, "Like a *rohohose.*" This is essentially where the phrase-by-phrasing commentary on "Evergreen" stops, with a sense of the endless virtuosity in the "skill set" it has only spottily sampled in a few illustrative strokes. But Pegasus has our hearing g/eared up—to listen further on and in. For that first identified lift into vibrato opens the most complex phrasing so far, trailing off into the loosely grammatical inversion completed by the next line's "I was always certain": certain of the fact that love "would grow." Alerted to pitch-bending and breath control, we trace more closely the voice's descent along the downslope of an extra-syllabled "ceruhtain" in slipping free from the constrictive sibilant hiss of "wa*s* alway*s* *c*ertain"—and thus rendering erotic confidence even more relaxed, more the stuff of whispered confirmation than forced insistence.

The professional musician's video exegesis is suspended just before this, yes, but not without scoring probably its most revelatory point, early on, regarding the convergence of vocalism and compositional symmetry. Thanks to his demonstration of note shifts on the frets of his guitar, he helps us hear how the opening hum (more abstract but just as famous as the revving-up phonetic "uhmm" of "uhmMem'ries" at the start of "The Way We Were") does its real oblique work. The abstract "um-um" of "Evergreen"—mutating into "ooh-ooh-ooh" in the same high register—comes just two notes short of the climactic high at the end of the song, where it is "time" itself that "we've learned to sail above." At that late point—in the float of sense upon sound, its sematic updraft—Streisand has set sail above her own momentarily stabilized tone. Timed neatly to this, the lyric switches its keynote noun from inverted object (time having been levitated above) to the new subject ("time won't change"). Denied thereby, in a negative predication, is the usual damage ("change the meaning of" a committed passion) that this particular evergreen bond believes itself capable of staving off. Timing is everything in Streisand's shimmering delivery of this lift-off switch (fig. 5).

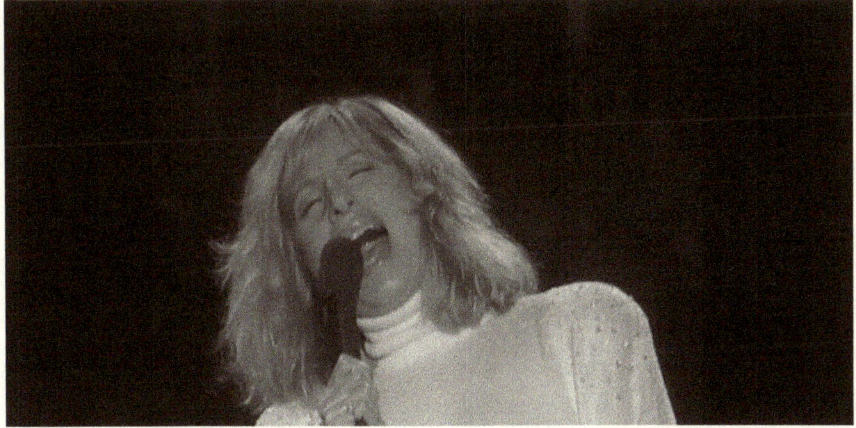

5. "Time . . . to sail above" (*One Voice*: "Evergreen")

One can't listen too hard. As if dissipating the word from within, exploding it with the sound of its own pitch-b(l)ending high note, the noun of mundane duration is edged ahead, and transcended from within, by the temporal spread, in iteration, of a ringing ignited "Ti-i-i-m-e." It is an effect that has a related antecedent in the possibility of the classical repertoire as well.[11] Streisand's unique turn occurs before the voice's trailing off in a tempered end rhyme on what time at least "won't change": namely, the bonded alliterative "meaning *of* one *love*." That passing feathery echo is elicited without the vocal fry, this time, on the muted fricatives of those two last words, softened by now with yet more confident relaxation. Following which, even more lyrically explicit in its stair-stepped descent, is the extra onward force of repetition in the vocally subsiding but thematically persistent closure with "ever, ever, gree-ee-ee-eennn": a little different and variously sustained in every one of its dozen or so recorded live versions over the years since. As so often in the alignment of vocal with thematic continuum in Streisand's repertoire, *now*'s and *evermore*'s are mimed by voice in their own performed duration—as will *forrrrevvvverererrr* be, even more strenuously, in the last song from *A Star Is Born*, a protesting-too-much long after the dream of invulnerable love has done itself in. At the apogee of the film's earlier "Evergreen," however, time's normal erosive course seems defied by voice's own prolongation, the threat of loss forestalled from within the lyric as much by vocal climb as by phrased claim. This is the same defied loss to be answered—and broached through other means, elegiac rather than ecstatic by then—in the film's closing number.

But even on the internal cinematographic evidence of the Oscar-winning "Evergreen" (when returned to its site-specific delivery in the film), there is music in the optic movement itself, adding its own accent to the lyric's rotary notation. For the camera literally circles round to the final high note from the song's opening ("voiced" but not "spoken") bars—that absorbing launch coming in from off-frame as Streisand reaches for the microphone with one hand, an earphone held in place with the other. The point that the Pegasus videolog has stressed "phrase by phrase," though based on her later *One Voice* performance of the song, applies to the film version as well. And in ways narratively strategic as well as compositional. What his trained ear recognizes in her humming out a "C5 and a B#5" at the start—thus preceding the melody only "two notes (one tone)" under the "mountain-climbing" final dyad at "ti/iiime," before dropping back an octave to begin singing on a G#3—is that the Streisand sound has done more than tease the ear with the destiny of this particular song as it scales again to and beyond this at first unsung but sounded high bar. It has actually limbered up her own vocals for that steady ascent. This is a compelling thought: the song as its own exercise in possibility. Enunciated lyric thus comes round to its own promise, as so perfectly captured in the wheeling camera of its recording booth version in the film (figs. 6–7)—a lateral mastery by cinematographer

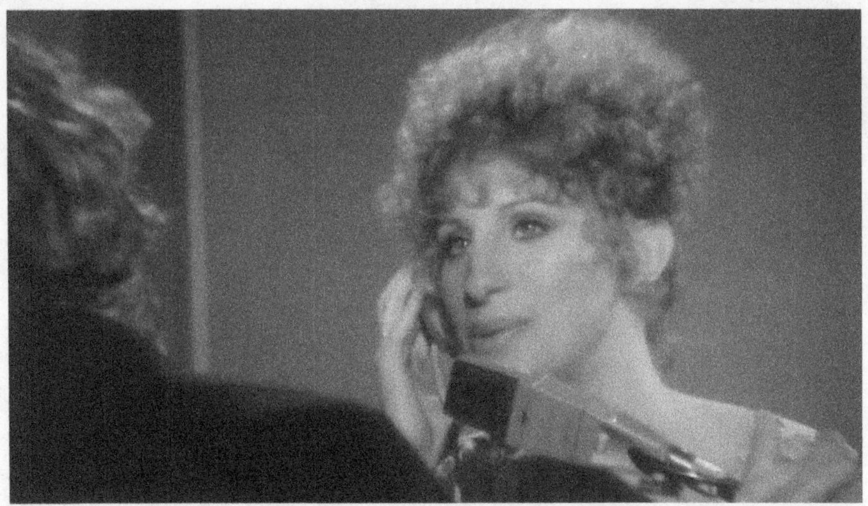

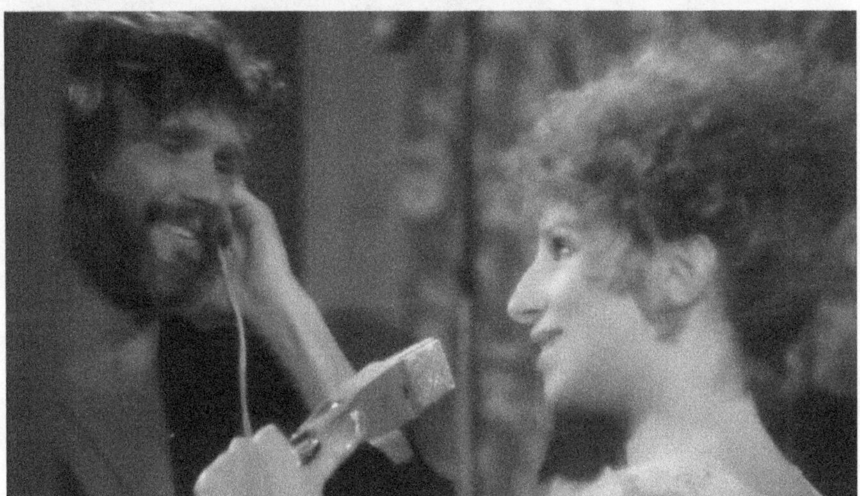

6 and 7. Closing time's circle (*A Star Is Born*: "Evergreen")

Robert Surtees that brings down to the level of parity and rapport the lovers' however one-sided duet (Streisand with Kris Kristofferson). Closing this erotic circle on-screen is the perfect objective correlative to the acoustic arc of Streisand's own most memorable composition: a virtual parable of lyric form, with onset manifesting its own sonic upshot.

And regarding the song's unworded syllables as tune-up, there is a confirming out-take from *A Star Is Born* as well. The phonic (before phonetic) skeleton of the film's studio track is there, in rehearsed version, on the cutting-room floor, in a deleted scene recently retrieved in the ephemeral Netflix issue of the restored *A Star Is Born*—though long available online.[12] Any sense that the famous humming teaser at the start of

"Evergreen"—suspended until its drop into lyric simile (a mimetic descent itself "soft as an easy chair")—has located the tonal core or matrix of the finished number is certainly backed up by the cut scene. For there we watch Streisand's own guitar work, fingernails on one hand pared back, as she picks out, without lyrics, the wordless notes of a composition not yet a song: the same "Evergreen," but all humming lead-in at this stage. On request by the rock star she's just met, the delicate oo-ooming and lu-luing of her character's tentative demonstration of the melody, in a muted ripple stopping far short of ululation, does turn out, lullaby-like, to have sent the mostly mesmerized soon-to-be lover (Kristofferson as John Norman Howard), drunk as always, head back in delight, suddenly to sleep. Our listening will continue to be more attentive.

And it has its grand precedents, not just in the pop expertise of Pegasus but all the way from the unstinted admiration of classical pianist and essayist Glenn Gould, using the occasion of *Classical Barbra* (recorded 1973; released 1976) to wax ecstatic about her more familiar repertoire, through to *New York Times* classical music critic Anthony Tommasini singing the praises, and praising in detail the singing, of her jazz-influenced *Love Is the Answer* album over thirty years later.[13] Gould's enthusiasm, however, can't be improved upon. An unapologetic "Streisand freak" ever since he previewed "an acetate of her first disk" that was making the rounds at Columbia studios in 1963, Gould actually (if obliquely) volunteers in his review to produce her next classical album. He had in mind material that would liberate her from a hampering awe and timidity in front of the Masters, even while noting her coup with Karl Orff's "In Trutina," where "Streisand, using the fastest vibrato in the west and the most impeccable intonation this side of Maria Stader's prime, provides a reading second to none in terms of vocal security while stripping this rather vapid air of its customary theatrical accouterments."[14] Yet one is drawn especially to Gould's generalizations, as they bridge Streisand's widening choice of material: "For me, the Streisand voice is one of the natural wonders of the age, an instrument of infinite diversity and timbral resource"—and, when teamed with the right material, capable of "heartbreakingly beautiful intensity." Or this, the shadow double of "mannered" when a complaint rather than, as meant here, an accomplishment: "Streisand is one of the great italicizers; no phrase is left solely to its own devices." And it's the emphasis itself, richly unpredictable, that is for Gould the measure of her vocal "intimacy," as if we're thinking along with her, off-script. In celebrating her gradual finessing of a natural trouble spot in her vocal equipment—"breaking the C-sharp barrier in low gear"—Gould singles out, among the myriad accommodations that her vocal ingenuity has devised to turn this "impediment to an advantage," what he hears as "a moment of special glory." This is the "'Nothing, nothing, nothing' motif, securely focused on D flat and C natural, from the final seconds of that Puccini-like block-buster, 'He Touched Me.'"

And part of the "special glory" of this terraced, incremental negative in Streisand's pathbreaking technique, dramatic as well as vocal—played out so emphatically for its filmed performance in Central Park, then reprised a quarter of a century later for the 1993 *Concert*[15]—is the pounding threefold insistence ("suddenly nothing, nothing, nothing is the same") on the momentous change made. I alluded earlier to the listener's "almost palpable *feel* of the Streisand sound." Her rendition of "He Touched Me" is certainly one ready (and heady) touchstone of this effect, this bodily affect. Amounting to a break from sameness in popular performance style as well as in the narrated moment of awakened desire, what we hear enacted is precisely the elation of difference mirrored in a delivery avid, vibrant, almost delirious. Streisand's theatrical touch has never been surer. With the climactic doubling of the title phrase, its verb elongated to at least three or four syllables in refrain ("tu-uh-uh-ch'd"), the emphasis does more than shift focus from glancing physical contact to the more deeply "touching" advent of early desire. In the enhanced phonetic texture of the renewed phrase, Streisand's familiar move—as if uniquely thematized here—is to transfer the song's depicted moment of haptic rush and upheaval to the tactile reach, the caressed terrain, of voice itself in its bodily contact with the listener.

When I also imagined, earlier, a certain cinematic dimension to the Streisand sound, one that finds potent scenic extension on-screen, I meant that, even in just hearing her instrument, one listens with the mind's eye, spatializing the vocal dynamics, scaling with her the assured exploitation of her range. But at the same time, when the power of that voice is fully released, we can of course be said to *take it in*. We don't just visualize phonic space; we feel its explored topography—in our own somatic register—somewhere between spine and throat, chest and cranium. To put this audiovisual sense of voice, with its full sensory impact, in the lingeringly channeled words of aroused thrill from "He Touched Me," redirected to our own response, the smart of such listening often delivers "a sudden tingle . . . a sparkle, a glow." Where the sparked vocables feel optically "aglow," as if spotlit, even while taken inward by the scintillated ear. To this end, it is the unique ease in Streisand's verbal delivery across the potential gulf between word and note, the sheer vernacular immediacy of her tone and enunciation, that encourages us to think along with her lyrics in the rhythms of inner voice. And the latest physiology of speech recognition has its own way of confirming such internalization as an actual motor function. Mirror neurons are now thought to have their rough counterpart in echo neurons. In that polished mirror of difference that is the Streisand sound, when one is fully tuned to its wavelengths, every touching moment, every *gripping* song, is a private sing-along in its inward haptic feedback. Barthes again: the tangibly fleshed-out charge of voice's "whole carnal stereophony."

One can certainly be grateful to Glenn Gould for instigating such a pause over the "He Touched Me" number. But again his generalizations ramp up the local appreciation: "With the possible exception of Elisabeth Schwarzkopf, no vocalist has brought me greater pleasure or more insight into the interpreter's art." And interpretation is work: in this case an actor's work, Gould speculates, practiced in the loose improvisation of self-scrutiny—and in a "dressing-room" setting inseparable from her theatrical screen career. Hence this extended "fantasy" in Gould's imagination of Streisand's craft: "that all her greatest cuts result from dressing-room run-throughs in which (presumably to the accompaniment of a prerecorded orchestral mix) Streisand puts on one persona after another, tries out probable throwaway lines." She is so much committed to the bodily force of theatrical performance, as Gould seems to sense even in recorded song, that—very much in the spirit of the present study's own mirror paradigm as well—he pictures to himself how she "mugs accompanying gestures to her own reflection." In her mixing of "registrational couplings" (the "street-urchin" versus "sophisticated-lady" intonation, for instance), Gould conjures her as she "performs for her own amusement in a world of Borgean [*sic*] mirrors (Jorge-Luis [*Borgesian*], not Victor) and word-invention." Moving Streisand's delivery out of the imagined dressing room, and watching her take up her vocal stance in front of the film camera's actual automated mirrors, is of course the main work of this book.

Short of this, as a rhapsode of sonority, the classicist Gould, with no mention of screen presence, joins a fellow (rock) practitioner—and enthusiast—like Pegasus and a theoretician like Barthes in locating the reflected throated body of song production. For Gould, the imagined mirror of differential effort: try-ons and outtakes, where exploratory musical reflection is at one with the resulting mode of inventive lyric wordplay, often a kind of syllabic plasticity, that the coming pages will have many further occasions to specify. Again, varying Barthes: listening a granular matter concerning the very text of the voice, its micromanaged textures (with "phrasing" in this melodic sense, rather than grammatical, being submitted to Gould's notion of "italics"). But through both senses of such *determined* audition in Streisand's case, listening is also fastened by interpretation to the fashioned voicing of a given lyric text, both leagued with and unleashed by wording. Determined, purposive: such are the effects we are *hearing for*.

One symptom of the Streisand sound's originality and affective edge has a negative—or better to say absent—manifestation. Despite the consistent chart-topping singles and gradually established trademark perennials, there is a notable market deficit, in its own way epitomizing. Regarding one common fate of so-called mainstream mate-rial, the rippling, then cresting stream of Streisand's voice is typically too turbulent, or at least urgent, for pre-programmed background music in the familiar venues of bars and restaurants: too inflected, yes "italicized," and thus distracting in its shifts of pitch and volume. With the rare exception of the *Guilty* tracks, troweled smooth by the rolling Bee Gees rhythm, even her most popular numbers don't make for the kind of sonic wallpaper to which Sinatra's sound, by contrast, is so eminently suited. Rather, her voice tends to sculpt its lyric surface into more aggressively contoured dimensions, with orchestration following suit. These shifting contours narrate in relief a dramatic space all their own, too ridged and specific for ambient sound. It has always been wrong, then, to find her vinyl records, later her CDs, filed in the "Easy Listening" bin. Neither relaxed nor relaxing, her vocal drama claims a more focused attention, never just passive recognition. Quite apart from any exaggerated "diva" reputation (that phobic *hauteur* theory that has dogged her career from early on), the voice is, on its own fervent terms, undeniably pushy. The elation she reaches for doesn't come easy—even at the receiving end. In its vocal command, the sound alone is *demanding*.

Discussion ahead exists to keep answering its call. But two very different further examples are all this one chapter has space to close in on. In Gould's exemplary pop citation, "He Touched Me," the escalating tripled "nothings" are, as we've heard, the prelude to a transfiguring implicit *everything new* in the ecstatic negative assertion of the final "nothing is the same." A later and more explicit coming-of-age song, written in 1972 by Tom Baird and Ron Miller for a musical adaptation of William Inge's play *Bus Stop* (titled *Cherry*) that never made it to Broadway, is a number to which Streisand gives the full stage charge it was meant for in its 11 o'clock spot. "I've Never Been a Woman Before"—lifting like "He Touched Me" (and the later cover or "Since I Fell for You") to a comparable run of final high notes under lyric iteration—begins, in direct address this time, with "*You* touched me." The specification "in the sun" comes into rhyme with her sense of herself as the "only one" (she "somehow knew") that her virgin lover had been with. Detached from the stage play's own characterizations, this sexual awakening seems transferred on record to the vocal persona as well. They've both "walked away from time" long since, but in a song aptly included in *The Way We Were* album, the female voice wants back this "wonderful" rite of passage—and gets it rehearsed on her own part by a grammatically elusive return, in pulsing refrain, to a recovered present ("present perfect") tense.

After admitting to having "done everything" that a "girl could do," including the long-held extra insistence on "and more" (rhyming with the "every door" she's already "been through"), this immersive vocal flashback in "I've Never Been a Woman Before" peaks finally (with the alliterative *I've/nev* rather than the logical "I'd") in a kind of double climax. This is achieved under the thrust of a mounting transition that withholds from full-bore release the final stretch of the "ore" rhyme. Building toward it, "But *I've never been a woman before*" is pressured by an emphatic "No" (with its rising overtone of "oh") into the immediate zing of iteration ("No/oh, I've never"). And this smoldering eroticism is fanned with a fiery clipped lift on "*wooo*man" when the phrasing comes round again: a reminiscent bliss made present when unfolded in the pivotal shift from the breathy "beehnn" to "beeee—fo(oh)rrre." Sailing rather than trailing off into pure aerated sound rather than syllable, the last ten-second note embodies a freed-up erotic high from which even the voice wants never, it would seem, to let go. Via a paradoxical time loop in grammar that only music's immanence could excuse, what she had never before been she is now still in the recovered process of becoming. So there again—here again—the inimitable timbre of Streisand's vocal intensity. Listening for such moments—riding the wave of sound, climbing with it in its slowed velocity and hover—we are very much listening *in*: attuned (there is no other word for it) to her voice's inner cinema. Neither easygoing nor low-keyed, but at once huge and nuanced, such is the matchless intimacy of Streisand's aural melodrama, scanning terrains of its own excavation in a roving audial POV. And this with a power, as the next chapter is meant to demonstrate, that singing on camera, actual Hollywood cameras, neither deflects nor counteracts. Just as much as hearing her voice on record, tape, or audiodisc, watching Streisand sing is still—and sometimes all the more, sets and costumes aside—looking through her own sonic optic into the shaped space of a vocalism not just granular but specular: an affective vista sequentially revealed in the shapes and reshapings of sound. The acoustic mimesis of desire's coruscating private terrain becomes, in these terms, the differential mirror of voice's own eros.

And to bring scattered evidence of this up to the (retrospective) moment with Streisand's latest archival mining, a sequel with the punning title *Release Me 2* (too), it is no surprise in this 2021 raiding of her vault that the only frog in the throat of the anthologized rarities is Kermit the Frog in a reworked, interspliced duet of the Muppet ballad "Rainbow Connection" from the late 1970s. In this gimmicky counterpoint, it is, in fact, his gravelly acknowledgment that he too has heard them "calling my name," certain dream voices, that foregrounds Streisand's interpolated onomatopoetic coup in transfiguring just this sonic climax of the lyric. His twang sets off to further perfection, that is, the sibilant undertone of her mimetic float in the alliterative echoic surge from "*have* you been *half* asleep" through "*HAVE* you heard voi*ces?*" to the silky sirenlike question, overarching Kermit's line, about whether "this" may not well be the "swe-e-e-e-eet sou-ou-nnd" that, in epic tradition, "called the young sailors." In one sense, of course, "this" sound is operable right here and now, its spell let loose in the vibrant amplitude of Streisand's self-instancing delivery. Another voice, far more nasal than hers, and antithetical in its croak, only serves to showcase the ethereal and seductive otherness of her own.

SCREENING THE STREISAND SOUND

This chapter moves forward with the momentum of the star's career by hewing to the two senses of its title: screening her sound, sifting it, assaying its granular texture when filtered free, to the extent possible, of lyric content—even while tracking its power in narrative performance on film. For it is there, first in a brief but stunning resuscitation of the classic Hollywood musical, that we may sense voice itself performed in character, not just the other way round. Singing, of course, is its own kind of acting—especially Streisand's. But, in retrospect, the unquestioned destiny of her consolidated talent lies in screen capture, a celluloid rather than just vinyl imprint. And what an imprint it was, beginning with the widescreen mark made by the 1968 release of *Funny Girl*. The natural gleam of the silver screen caught the star's differential reflections perfectly.

And if her inaugural Hollywood performance seemed almost literally glowing, it wasn't just the incandescent range of "expressions" ("six more," as we've noted, than those boasted by the Barrymores), along with her detonated comic timings, that sparked the screen into this surprising radiance. The smooth luminescence now, years later, popularized for Zoom use as the so-called ring light—lending a less stark visual presence to one's self-presentation—has been known in the industry as the "Streilight" ever since Harry Stradling Jr., her first and afterward coveted cinematographer, devised a makeshift version of such diffused light in portable form. A best boy was assigned to follow the star around with it on the *Funny Girl* set, just out of camera range. One imagines it did wonders to smooth out the irregular shadows to which her profile might well have been vulnerable. In this respect and every other, cinematic framing had met the challenge of the Streisand difference head-on. The issue was never an impersonation of Ziegfeld star Fanny Brice in this freely adapted biopic, in the run-up from hard-won fame to failed marriage, but rather a definitive new screen chapter in the ongoing Streisand story.

Reviews of *Funny Girl* tended to notice the camera-ready comedienne with more emphasis than that given even to her singing, often citing the great days of Hollywood heroines in 1930s comedy. And the line readings were indeed "pitch-perfect" in their own right, including a later allusion to the more/Barrymores line when she is asked whether she can look on at Nick's crucial shipboard poker play without, as it were, giving the game away. Her reaction is couched in the same ethnic rhythm of her throaty, high-handed, broad-gestured response before her first roller-skate number—simply repeating the question there, with an italic twist, as if its answer were obvious: "Can *I* roller skate?" This time it's "Can *I* watch with no expression?"—as the camera quick-cuts to a glove-biting frenzy of potential visual giveaways at the gaming table. Even halfway into her first film, a hyperexpressive persona has been so firmly entrenched that the character can allude to the star's own established facial versatility, within the plot, as a sudden comic liability, the antithesis of a poker-faced stare. One might as well ask if Streisand could sing with no affect whatsoever. Certainly it is the interplay of expressive registers that defines the scope of her difference, as Glenn Gould knew in imagining her song rehearsals before the actress's dressing-room mirror, trying out the verbal surprises of her "line" readings before staging them for the microphone itself.

8 Beautiful Girls 9

Invading big-screen space for the first time in *Funny Girl* is the lambent intimacy of the Streisand sound: a singing voice that theatrical amplification delivers at uniquely close range, despite the scale of auditorium projection. She magnetizes the movie crowd at the same time that within the plot she's bringing audiences to their feet for the young Brice. Before Fanny is told that she "sticks out," and is thus bounced from the chorus, Streisand makes her first on-screen and homely ethnic appeal: "I'm a bagel on a plate full of onion rolls!" But the music-hall owner Keeney won't even "try it." Pure difference, under the name of innovation, may go figuratively untasted. But we already know better, of course, savoring the irony, because this is part of the extended flashback structure of the film: her early career struggle remembered from her seat, ahead of the audience, at another of her sold-out Ziegfeld shows. This reminiscent flashback is begun with the hailing of one Mrs. Strakosh from this soon to be unfolded past, one among the Lower East Side chorus of neighborhood doubters regarding young Fanny's hopes for the stage.

Framing all this in the present, the star has deliberately gotten to the theater early, needing time to think, nervously expecting her husband's return from prison for white-collar (and his signature "ruffled shirt") crime. It's a perspective new to her, the stage when not on it. And the camera has followed her to this reverse point of vantage by a perfectly calculated star entrance, one of director William Wyler's most expert touches. After the saturated color images of pre-flapper New York City fading in and out behind the credits, the screen goes to a faint photographic sepia of the Ziegfeld marquee, only gaining full color as the publicity lights go on around the star's name, Fanny not Barbra. But it is very much the latter, in the role of the former, who comes walking—gliding—into frame, pausing, her back to us, for a glance at this token of her fame, her name literally up in lights as the projection of her story begins. The camera then tracks, all but stalks, her across the street and down the alley, her face still unseen. At this point that same camera lets her get ahead of it in entering the privileged back door and moving past a security guard, seated in a booth half off-frame, who barely looks up from his newspaper to note her authorized presence.

This progress has all been aptly underscored (in both senses, not that we need recognize it yet, on first viewing) by the low-key and dissonant strains of her first number in the pending flashback, "I'm the Greatest Star." With Fanny pausing to look left, onto a cluttered stage, rather than going straight to her dressing room, she now moves amid the disarray of jumbled props, followed at a still-discreet distance by the camera—until she stops cold before a full-length, freestanding, gilt-framed mirror. The camera then patiently catches up with her in its measured steady track, sidling now into position to catch her reflected image over her leopard-coated shoulder, as well as her famous greeting, "Hello, gorgeous" (fig. 8). Self-hailing—and then some, as the flashback plot will soon reverse engineer. Just here, with the film's first edit, say its first explicitly narrative rather than pictorial move, it cuts to a full frame view of the mirror image, still marked as such by a swirl of gilding at the upper left. No reverse shot of the heroine herself yet, just the image under scrutiny: sheer stage presence beamed back from a gaudy stage prop (of the sort multiplied a dozenfold in the later "Beautiful Bride" parody). Though only barely recessed as a frame-within-the-frame, this is what we've come for: the image plane of performance. In follow-up to Streisand's famous opening line, just after uttering the words to her reflection in the medium shot, she smiles wryly at her

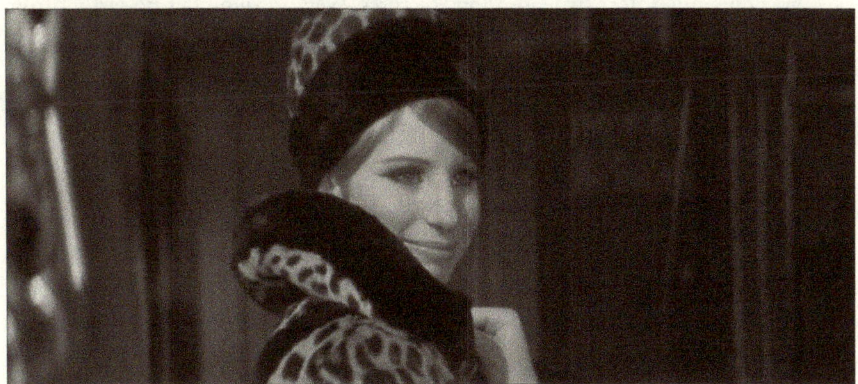

8. "Hello, gorgeous" / Goodbye Nick (*Funny Girl*)

own ironic braggadocio with a tear quite visible in one eye. In this initial glance, hers and ours alike, the film's mode is openly announced in this overlap of comedy and sentimentality, as matched to and anchored throughout by the star's high-wire balancing act in one flourish of deprecatory self-celebration after another. But more will soon unfold in recap, across story rather than discourse time.

Did I say first viewing? Did anyone see *Funny Girl* just once? Given its canonical status in this fabled film career, and in the latter-day roster of successful musical comedies, certainly this book couldn't have been written with such a viewer in mind. There'd be too much plot summary, and especially too much legwork in the evocation of the star's freshness, line by line, lyric by lyric, to leave room for drawing out the genre template and its complex, often vexed, genealogy. Pauline Kael, awed by Streisand's performance, wrote with prescient anxiety in her *New Yorker* review about the genre challenge facing this gifted newcomer, as if foreseeing the box-office fall-off with her next two traditional musicals. She feared that commercial calculations would sever the star from her true uniqueness, "her ability to extend a character in song."[1] That ability was hard to argue with. But it needed enabling by formal constraints and guidelines. Among them was the precise angle of that "extension"—whether laterally, toward another character in the drama, or just forward toward the audience. In musicals like *South Pacific* or even *Oklahoma*, location is the selling point of transport, its distance from the Broadway theater's own stage. Thus exotically marooned, characters make music from what they have or seek in common. Suspended disbelief is at a premium in the shunt between dialogue and song. By contrast, in the "naturalized" backstage musical—a subgenre of the hybrid theatrical form of musical comedy, and always a piece of metatheater in its own right—music is what the characters tend to share professionally in looking for something more. Tend to share—or at least seek to. Streisand's scale of talent militates against many a duet in this backstage mode, however, let alone in her next two "location" pictures, even if exiling her no farther from Broadway than upstate (Yonkers) or uptown (Upper West Side). This is the price she pays, in genre terms, for that absolute fact of her difference. It is a running recognition of this book that on-screen duets were, for the singularity of the Streisand sound, extremely hard to arrange, ultimately rare, held when broached mostly to a brief line or two, and sometimes (as in the sequel to *Funny Girl*) rendered entirely subvocal, like intersecting (or not) internal monologues.

Yet it was the "backstage" subgenre, casting the singing actress in the role of just such a performer, that lent *Funny Girl* so much of its emotional force and unembarrassing appeal. *My Fair Lady* offers another obvious foil to *Funny Girl*—and in more than name only. Gifted singing comes as a surprise from a heroine taking rudimentary voice lessons in non-Cockney phonetics. In contrast, Streisand the singing actress is at her most plausible and compelling in her early screen work when she gets to play one. It seems to me hard to overstate the importance of this in the varying emotional conviction of her first films. But neither is there any way to exaggerate the magnetism of the debut effect itself. One of the most telling anecdotes about Streisand's unholy triumph in the stage version of *Funny Girl*, as only magnified on-screen, came from Isobel Lennart, author of the play's book. Here was a writer scrambling night after night, once the show opened, to moderate its comic apologia for the plainness of its heroine. "Did I have trouble with Barbra?" she asks rhetorically, and spells out the main problem. "How would you like to write a libretto about a homely little girl" and have "what seemed to be a homely little girl engaged for the part," but then "the first time she has an audience—on opening night in Boston—have her turn beautiful in front of your eyes? And get more beautiful at every performance, so that—by opening time in New York—she's obviously one of the great beauties of all time. What do you think that did to all my 'homely little girl' jokes?" The thing is, they still work— that's the new star's comic brilliance in this part—so it was good "trouble" after all.

Although Streisand, through song especially, could emote her way into a weirdly luminous beauty, she could also play the awkward and unprepossessing girl-next-door with equal aplomb. And in so doing, turn her difference to account—almost into an ethical stand. Is "a nose with deviation" inevitably "such a crime"—and "against the nation?" at that—asks her disgruntled mother of her kvetching friends in the film's first song, insisting in her own slightly deviant asymmetrical rhyme that a face "off balance" is nonetheless accompanied by "golden talents." As with the bagel analogy in the next scene, Jewish ethnicity itself is rendered demographic in that former rhyme, even as the plot quickly reworks the "deviation" into a case of talent as its own kind of mass cultural defiance. And one further detail is prototypical in this opening comic song, for this book as well as for the career it is studying. In its lead-up to the star's own exhilarating first number at the end of the opening matronly chorus, this first move of the flashback chronology has offered a prolonged and defining mirror shot answering to the mother's ironic "condolences" for her daughter no longer being "cute." In the foreground we see Fanny disproving the aspersion by primping bemused in a series of comic facial shrugs, cuteness personified, over the shortcomings of her image on her way to a hoped-for audition (fig. 9). No "Hello, gorgeous" yet. So the muted ugly-duckling jokes—an entire "Schvan" Lake parody tacitly built around them later—do click, though now as part of the assimilated arsenal of the star's own protective sarcasm, as in fending off Nick Arnstein's dinner invitation in that epitomizing line: "I'd have to change too much . . . nobody could wait that long." Some differences can't be

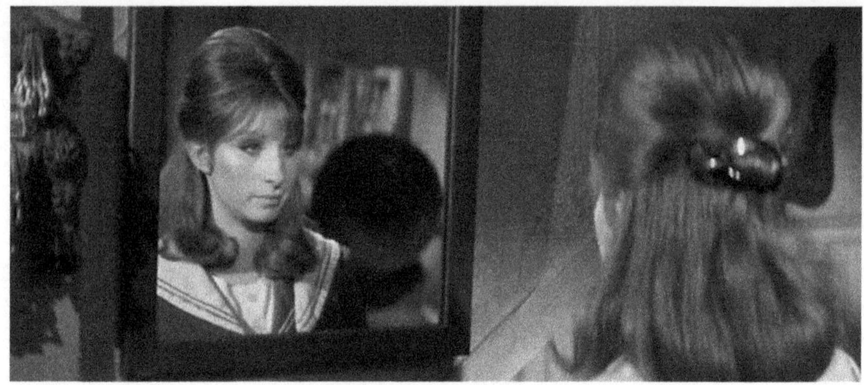

9. "Like a Miss Atlantic City" (*Funny Girl*: "If a Girl Isn't Pretty")

effaced or outlasted. But the internal changes Fanny does put herself through later in the narrative, once accepting a second invitation from Nick—when they make love in a private dining room to the tune of "You Are Woman, I Am Man"—are something to behold in their intoxicating gauntlet of comic pique, erotic heat, and ultimately vaporized sexual diffidence.

Even as amorous consummation, though, that later song remains a duet for one. Backstage or offstage in *Funny Girl*, Nick is never really asked to sing, just to mouth a few mandatory lines in this one number. Before that, more awkwardly, he is cast in the role of solo audience to Fanny musing out loud in the "People" number—or, more to the point, performing for him on a deserted street that makes them the only titular subjects of the lyric: two dawningly infatuated people held within the orbit of a kind of overheard soliloquy. Other vocal liberties—other free-floating song numbers—are more strictly generic. The "Sadie, Sadie, Married Lady" montage samples Fanny's private home-alone monologues as the compulsively happy bride, and the added title song, new since the stage play, is sung, at first, alone in court chambers after Nick is taken away to prison—and then transferred as segue into its open-mouthed but emotionally throttled conclusion in huge profile from Fanny's orchestra seat at the end of the flashback. The key word, the adjective "funny," has been transformed from its original congratulatory epithet in Nick's usage, directed now at herself across the expanded sigh of a long-held note of idiomatic irony: Funny, in effect, how it doesn't feel that way—how it "ain't *so-o-o-oh* funny, funny girl." The rest of the big theater numbers, and the biggest one coming soon in the finale, are all staged before an audience, typically punctuated by laughs and ovations, with the signal exception of the breakout vocals in the lead-up to "Don't Rain on My Parade." This is a song seconding "People" in the need for more than an audience—with Ziegfeld hanging up on Fanny when she insists on leaving the tour to follow her man. Anticipating her soliloquy to the dead husband Ephraim that introduces "Before the Parade Passes By" in Streisand's next musical, *Hello, Dolly!*—hoping for his blessing in her recommitment to life, to people, to acknowledged needs—*Funny Girl*'s "Parade" number licenses her own offstage desire just before (as later in *Dolly* as well) the breather of an intermission.

The earlier film's metaphoric parade is already very much in progress as the song builds, moving across three additional modes of vehicular transit (taxi, train, boat) in addition to the vaulting voice itself. It is a voice coming in and out of interiority until it vies in full-throated defiance with the blare of her rented tugboat's whistle in New York Harbor. As she plows after Nick's ocean liner, her knowing gesture of freedom matches the raised torch of the Statue of Liberty with the rain-drenched bouquet of her own flame's latest gift, his signature bouquet of yellow roses. Only one number, as her marriage bottoms out in the second half, can top this. And part of its closing power is its strategic negotiation, again, with the backstage musical format, the subgenre of performance as such, with the heroine doing her night job as Ziegfeld star—and no longer trumpeting in broad daylight her confidence in taking on the real (offstage) world. Very much backstage is the film's last dialogue. Though Nick has just been released from his jail term for embezzlement, it's soon sadly clear to Fanny, as anticipated, that he has no intention of returning to the confinement and second billing of their marriage. Another mirror sends back, this time, the hollowness of mere image. Turned away from him in his exit, Fanny's tear-streaked face is redoubled in her triptych vanity mirror (profile left, full-face center), the back of her head toward us, the right panel just barren space (fig. 10)—as her man disappears behind the door he is closing on their marriage (visible in the central panel) before she even struggles to utter her own belated "Goodbye, Nick." From the camera's perspective, the looking-glass

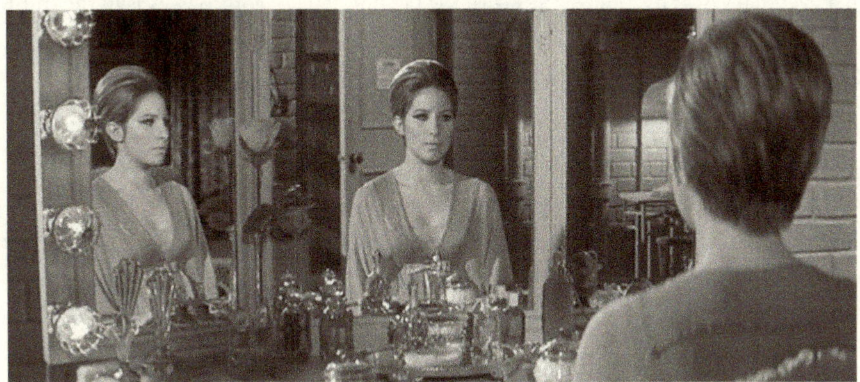

10. Vanity mirror exit (*Funny Girl*)

tells the truth, in its three-paneled emblem, at once about the preparatory space of her public persona—including that face she must nightly put on for the world—and about the emptiness by which it is now flanked.

"Don't Like Goodbyes," Streisand had sung, aptly enough, on her 1964 *People* album, while she was delivering that record's title song nightly on the stage of *Funny Girl*. Especially not a "goodbye" rendered so soon, in lived time if not plot time, after her arresting "Hello." When, in the Overture, I distinguished between a model of narcissism and one of performative self-scrutiny in the figurative mirror of Streisand's star persona, I had in mind her career's first and most famous on-screen mirror—and a similar if elusive split there between self-consciousness and dramatic rehearsal. Elusive, because the easily forgotten flashback structure of the biopic trajectory may well induce in progress a second forgetting. What is likely to get lost in the discrepant contexts of a multiple echo across the romance plot are, in the narrative timeline, two marked chronological anticipations of their dramatic upshot in that mirrored self-address that famously sets the story in motion—arguably postwar screen history's most famous opening line. This is to say that the praise in the greeting "Hello, gorgeous" has a checkered career well before this in the film's unfolded retrospect. In one of those bait-and-switch maneuvers of comically cornered dialogue that will later typify the self-corrective script turns of *Yentl*, Fanny, stunned into a sudden "gorgeous" when first introduced to the dashing Nick in the backstory, is forced to deflect this spontaneous reaction onto his snazzy ruffled shirt instead. Yet her first impression is later confirmed by her mother as well, in exactly that notable epithet. So that when Fanny, on the verge of Nick's return from prison, seems to greet herself ironically as such, in the mirror of a teary mock-vanity, she is, in whatever defensive gesture of an insecure ego, also in effect—a double irony—rehearsing the feared doomed reunion (hello and goodbye at once) with the man she won't have managed to keep. Greeting her eventual Oscar for Best Actress with the tag line "Hello, gorgeous" was in the spirit of this same other-directed address, even while mixed again with the wit of wry self-congratulations. It awaits her later career to elicit yet more pressure on the cross-gender identification entailed in the amorous "gorgeous" of this otherwise unapologetic debut address—through mirror and screen at once. (Hello, reader: for more on the subtext of "gorgeous" in the implications of this frame narrative, look ahead, via *Yentl*, to Y2K and the turn-of-the-millennium *Timeless* concert in the last chapter—where another source of masculine validation, father rather than lover, is explicitly foregrounded in the twist on a single song lyric.)

In true subgenre form in *Funny Girl*, needing to "go on," Fanny is soon back on stage from the backstage dressing-room defeat—and ushered there across a sound bridge bearing the first chords, and anticipatory applause, of her big solo. The singer, as suffering subject, now works her way—fighting back swallowed tears—through a number not in the original Broadway show. It was debuted from Fanny Brice's own repertoire on the closing night of the play's Broadway run, and delivered on camera in the same spirit of homage three years before this film finale, in the closing concert segment of her first TV special, 1965's *My Name Is Barbra*. But all deference to Brice is long gone in this incarnation of Fanny as Streisand, who brilliantly insisted on recording this last song live, against all Hollywood tradition—because, as she's explained in interviews, its emotional immediacy would be spoiled by her inability to time her tears to the playback. What happens instead is a magisterial vocal drama. In a subtle shot sequence splendidly blocked out and lit, first against trios of stage lights (pink, white, and blue), the camera then shifts at the song's open-armed take-off ("When he takes me in his arms"), coasting rightward to frame the filmed singer entirely against the seamless black void out of which, even in her avowal of abject devotion, she is struggling to emerge in performance.

At the song's and the film's final climb, there is a climactic cut from close-up to medium shot, almost framing her whole figure isolated on stage. A sliver of light rims her thrown-back head after the plaintive, sustained, and throbbingly syllabic "ehh/vehehr/mohohre" (closing out the last subsuming and fiercely insistent rhyme of "I am his" with "whatever my man is")—and then a full cut to black before the credits. We've heard at the song's start, in a long shot, the packed audience applauding her in her saddened, tentative entrance, but the lyric confession has come to its conclusion in her space alone, not theirs: a survivor's performance gone gradually inward in its catharsis. No on-screen applause—though no little of it in those early movie-house screenings. No one initially seeing Streisand, in unstinting vocal embodiment, put through this climactic wringer—in the chiaroscuro shimmer of mint-condition celluloid on the huge roadshows screens—was likely soon to forget it. Nor were audiences thus likely to doubt the vote of sheer self-confidence, and the vocal notes accompanying it, with which her next contracted Broadway remake for producer Ray Stark so vivaciously opened.

"Just Leave Everything to Me"

Such is the insistent refrain in the new number added from the stage version, by its composer Jerry Herman, to inject an initial volley of the definitive Streisand sound. Whenever the screen scene is left mostly in her hands in 1969's *Hello, Dolly!* all is well. Even the multitasking boasted explicitly by the opening song invades her effortless syllabification, with "thing" stretched in its twanged refrain ("thi-i-i-ING") to a kind of four-syllabled plurality in itself. And we are hardly asked just to marvel at the song material, here or later, in this old-fangled Hollywood spectacle, with each number unashamedly cueing the eye as well. Never so simply elegant as to curtail the comedy, the knockout costuming of the star is extravagantly good throughout, with Dolly's eye-popping copper-red up-do barely contained in its own flair by the secondary framing of flowered hats and other feathered headgear. Certainly things (as in "Everything") couldn't have started more propitiously—and this even before the star's entrance onto one of film history's most expensive sets: 1890s New York in a few square blocks of blockbuster reconstruction by a late vestige of classic Holly-wood backlot big-budgeting. Here and in later settings, in Streisand's unapologetically scene-stealing performance, there is plenty of scenery to chew.

Even earlier in the extended pre-credit sequence, well before "Just Leave Everything to Me" whisks Dolly away toward Yonkers behind the unsung orchestral version of title song and main titles, a high-angle aerial photograph of an 1890s New York street scene (the Fox set) fades through a faintly tinctured version of those color changes that paced similar vintage photos in the main titles of *Funny Girl*. The image mutates from green to blue to sepia, then gathering to full color just in the nick of time, when time-based imagery itself kicks in. For exactly at this point, in the upper-right corner, a slowly spreading and just faintly delineated iris-out on an elevated train car in motion, preceded for a second or two by the sound of its clanking progress, continues to open up the whole frame to the finally arrived establishing shot in the emphatic color cinematography and ambient soundtrack of a 1960s period pic. But it isn't just that the screen has "come to life" as a photographically archived past recovered. Emphasis has fallen, quite unexpectedly, on the mechanics of mobile presentation—as it will do again, next, in a sequence of literalized New York hoof and foot traffic.

Balancing off that initially released upper zone of the photographic shot—offering a motion picture in rapidly gestating embryo—now the bottom segment of the mise-en-scène is all that we get of movement, human or otherwise: only mobile feet and legs, with no human faces on view until Streisand turns toward us from the top of the circular staircase on a horse-drawn streetcar. First, there is the clippety-clop of the policeman's shod mount; then—as if to evoke a percussionist's drum brushes—the quick metrical strokes of the street sweeper at the curb; followed by the snap of a shoe-shiner's polishing rag as yet another pair of feet take up the steady beat. Next, as if in allusion to the accosted boys playing hopscotch at the start of "I'm the Great-est Star" in *Funny Girl*, we see a girl at her own sidewalk game this time, together with some jumping of rope. And then, only then, with the first strains of "Come on Dolly"—not just an invitation but an entrance cue—we see her dressy lace-up boots descending a front stoop and striding around a corner into full-frame action. But seen from behind only, again as at the opening of *Funny Girl*—until finally meeting our gaze in an unexpected tipping of the camera's hand. The whole quick-cut cross-sectional urban sequence—peaked as the "unacknowledged" star, her face still averted, traverses the grand set in that horse-drawn streetcar—is then capped, technique uppermost again, by a punctuating (and somewhat disconcerting) rapid long-distance zoom overlapped with a quick and much tighter reframing, as if to suggest a single camera movement.

Its target and goal: the first close-up as Dolly turns slowly to face us for the inspired opening number. So far, unlike the "transparent" treatment of *Funny Girl* once the colorized photo credits are behind us, we're watching an experiment in the technology of spectacle. And it happens four times more, even more surprisingly yet, with the unexpected freeze-frames that punctuate "Just Leave Everything to Me" by interrupting the receipt of Dolly's calling card—handed or tossed out at random—by Streisand's voiceover of its contents. Four times in a row, that is, the barely begun film brakes into mere optical image, in the performed reading of a printed text, and this within the artificial mechanics of the film's own exposed status, right from the start, as a visual imprint. One is tempted to think of these freeze-frames as optical puns on this already showstopping first number. And their effect is only further fulfilled by the rapid "dolly" that tracks the star's gusto straight toward the camera at the song's climax, just before she leaps aboard the departing train to Yonkers to activate both the plot and her matchmaking scheme: the star here, one more time, offering her services with a calling card in each ambidextrous gloved hand (fig. 11). In the buildup to this rousing pre-credit impetus, having spilled out into motion in the first photofilmic frame, the cinemachine has thus several times jammed to a halt in order to advertise its own title

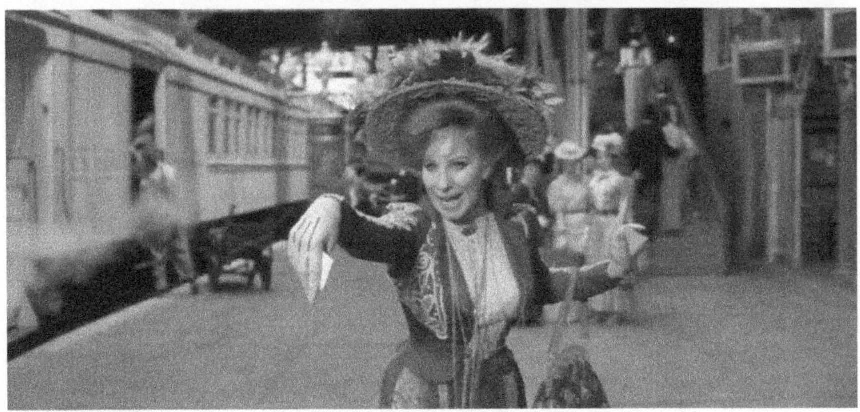

11. Ambidexterity (*Hello, Dolly!*: "Just Leave Everything to Me")

heroine. It does so exactly as she has announced herself in close-up with the song's sly first bars—namely, in the role of a woman who "arranges things," the vague grammatical object splaying out across three slightly different senses of the verb: "furniture, and daffodils, and lives."

It might seem negligible, this surfacing of mechanical technique in an otherwise transparent widescreen spectacle—first colorist photo montage, then sectored motion, next tricked zoom, then freeze-frames—especially since such techno flourishes disappear from the film from there on, which lumbers along in its mostly scenic framings uninflected by any such reflexive ingenuity. Certainly all this bears a striking contrast, rather than any deep or even passing affinity, with that same year's Oscar-winning freeze-frame editing of Raoul Coutard's neo-verité camerawork in Costa-Gavras's *Z*, nominated for the Oscar along with *Hello, Dolly!* as best picture of 1970. One might try chalking it up to a minor residue of late 1960s style invading a period piece, if with an effect more tentative and curtailed than the bled-to-sepia freeze-frames of *Butch Cassidy and the Sundance Kid*. (As it happens, the latter is a film whose Victorian sequences were shot just afterward on the same Century City backlot set, a film vying eventually for best picture along with *Z* and *Hello, Dolly!* in their collective loss to the more culturally with-it seriousness of *Midnight Cowboy*.)

Altogether, one might write off entirely the photo-graphism—the delayed animation effect, the elided zoom fade, and even the stop-action (after that action was so recently jump-started in terms of both image and full-scale moving bodies)—as mere retardations and distractions, never to be repeated in later camerawork. Just gestures, stylish nudges: helping the film to splutter, somewhat more knowingly than otherwise, to flamboyant life as dated spectacle. As such, these laboratory disclosures of the medium were ignored at the time and mostly forgotten since. Yet I recall them here for the way they keep curious optical company with certain camera reflexes later in Streisand's career—as well as harking back to the overt multiple imaging of superimposition and slow dissolve, respectively, noted at the close of her first two TV specials. For they do call up a minor strain of technical bravado and self-investigation, answering to the usual bravura of the star's performance, that next appears as a recurrent technological irony in the treatment of voiceover in her subsequent "old-time" Hollywood musical, *On a Clear Day You Can See Forever*. Differently manifested later under her own screen direction, whether of musical numbers or whole films (given her notable return both to freeze-frames and irruptive flashbacks), what surfaces here (from the very different directorial imagination of Gene Kelly) is nonetheless a cinematographic acknowledgment of Streisand's work in front of the camera. This is a tendency that threads its way through and beyond a movie-within-the-movie episode in *The Way We Were* into the technical self-consciousness of later films and concerts. It's hard to know what more to make, whether locally or all told, of these half dozen or so reflex ironies of screen mediation front-loaded in *Hello, Dolly!* But similar effects do seem to persist as something like their own mirror of difference in bracketing the audiovisual recording phenomenon of the star's outsize talent when framed for on-screen delivery—where any reminder that her performance is being mediated by an artifice of transmission only seems to enhance, rather than distance, the multichannel, multimedia impact of her "star presence."

One looks back on *Hello, Dolly!* always with the bittersweet sense that Streisand herself still famously undervalues her own achievement in this film, which in fact looks better with every passing decade. She is certainly spectacular to hear, as well as watch, in almost every scene. And never better (who has ever been?) than in the swagger of her one-woman parade down the middle of the train car in "Put on Your Sunday Clothes," with her unforgettable prancing delivery of "to town we'll trot"— and to a gravelly evoked "smoky spot" at that. It is a destination, as if approached in her own performing body, where—so she lustily, smokingly intones—"the girls are part of the view." The very delivery of that last key word suggests a tantalized fixed stare, rather than a distracted glance, in the prolonged note of her "vieeuuuw." The male gaze incarnate—channeled by a woman who is in on the fun. But the woman can sometimes take control of the gaze as well, answer back. She is certainly the cynosure of all looks in the climactic title number—strutting her stuff on the mezzanine of the Harmonia Gardens restaurant, and then showering return hellos upon the dance floor tables, unnerving her marriage-broker client and her own would-be marital target, Mr. Vandergelder (Walter Matthau).

But it is the next song that brings out the full energy of a younger Streisand in raucous womanly resistance to masculine (and masculinist) stolidity. Already addressing the standoffish male with a feminizing address in the very title of this "So Long, Dearie" number, Dolly goes so far as to symbolically unman him by seizing his walking stick—and almost incidentally his top hat. (Dolly already becoming the Vander*gelder* whose married name she aspires to?) She then drapes him with her boa in humiliating compensation for his lost prop (fig. 12)—before sweeping away in a horse-drawn taxi to the summarizing prolongation of her final belting "o" note. Slung (more than sung) in his face in this at first unfinished dismissal, the grammatically unfixed "it should have been so long" finds, when soon repeated, its true point in lyric wordplay. After a pause for the rhyming "How could I have been wrooonng?" comes a shift in the two-word "so long" away from the implied quotes of an idiomatic kiss-off to the adverbial backcast of a dismissal too long deferred. In those next three hefty

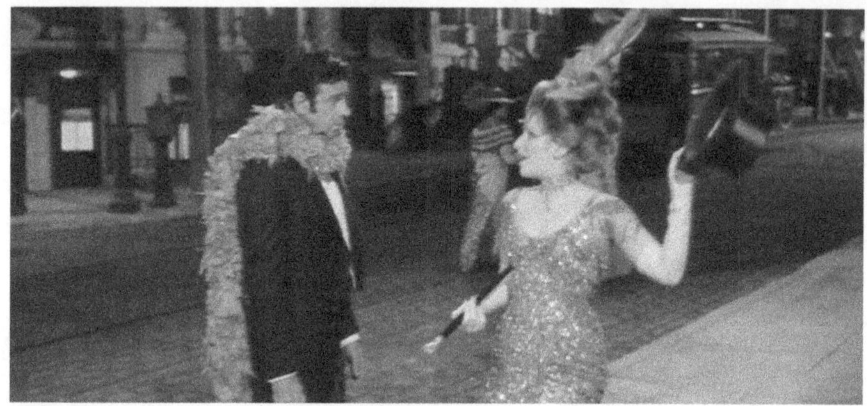

12. The unmanning goodbye (*Hello, Dolly!*: "So Long, Dearie")

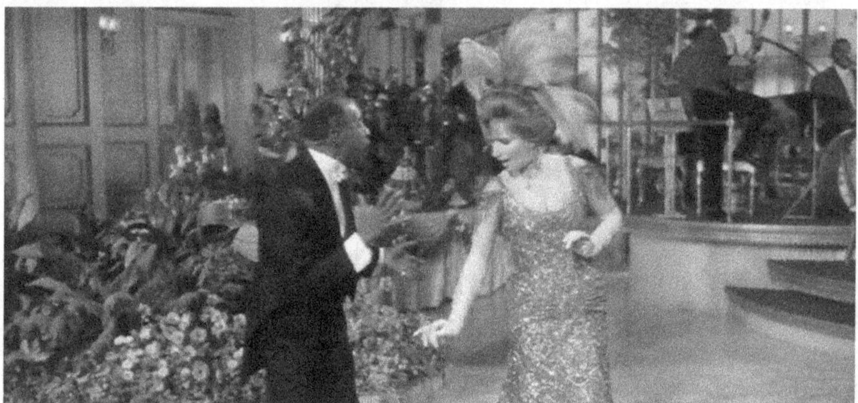

13. The true duet: jazz meets Tin Pan Alley (*Hello, Dolly!* title song)

breath-catching beats of "so loooong ahgohohoohh," the voice itself is heard leaving its exhaustive trail of supposedly expended desire. With Horace wrung dry by being sung virtually to death, the way the number leaves him speechless plays against the passing animated rapport between Streisand and her brief vocal partner in the previous title song.

In contrast to Horace hounded into silence, that passing exchange with Louis Armstrong is the film's true elating if fleeting duet, folded into the title song, where "Satchmo," fresh from his big hit with it, confronts Dolly for a few bars of throaty greeting. As they begin to parry each other with some scat-singing, his style is answered by the trombone slide of her voice as well as her mimic gesture (fig. 13), and then recapped, after the final chorus, with his classic demand for "one more time!": a lyric reprise to match this ballad of self-renewal for the wily widow. Surely this meeting on equal footing—not just of iconic talents but of two great traditions in American popular song, African American bandstand jazz and the heavily Jewish legacy of Tin Pan Alley—is one of the high points of the musical comedy screen archive.

Impossible to top by mere ensuing dialogue, but Streisand gives it a try. So permit me to digress into a pocket of personal favoritism regarding a brief scene that, apart from song numbers, I'd rather rescreen than any other dialogue bit in Streisand's comic backlog. This "desert island" moment occurs when—after her exorbitantly showy and comically shameless descent to the restaurant's main floor, greeting total strangers with buoyant noblesse oblige—she joins a nonplussed and disgruntled Matthau at table. Served up is a rapid-fire exchange-of-one, Dolly's take-charge barrage stupefies him into mostly mute objection to her every insinuating remark. Transcending the sardonic Mae West voice and often drawling pace that Streisand has previously deployed to age as well as camp her way into the part, even while sexing it up, the script now gives her a way to break out into full arm-flailing rapid-fire Streisand patter. After indulgently over-ordering on his tab ("Oh, dear no, I couldn't face a chicken, not a chicken. Bring a turkey, with all the trimmings"), she further steamrolls over him, while in fact salting his own side dish, with a counterindicated allegory of their going separate ways: "You salt your beets, and I'll salt mine." Anything following this with less racy pizzazz than boasted by the "So Long, Dearie" number would be a serious downhill plunge. These are just the sort of breakout moments, if more in firecracker rage than pushy connivance, that one cherishes in Streisand's next film as well, tucked between the musical numbers—but never again quite so magisterially on display as over her symbolic wing-clipping of that shared bird in *Hello, Dolly!*

Multiple Personality on Order

Clairvoyance, telepathy, reincarnation: these plot points—as more than just psychological figures, let alone fantasies, in an "ageless" love story—anchor the upbeat thrust of *On a Clear Day You Can See Forever*, with Vincente Minnelli signing on this time, instead of the equally legendary Gene Kelly, for the director's chair. Multiple personality disorder is demedicalized as metempsychosis even while turned ultimately, in Streisand's hands, to a mere metaphor for the performer's many-featured avatars: the variability per se—and timelessness?—of drive and talent. More than a comic case of paranormal fiction, this third Streisand musical gathers what weight it has as no less than a theatrical parable. Star acting as reincarnation, many selves warehoused within the same body: that's the inescapable trope of this musical comedy, on stage or screen, though in the latter case raised to a new star power (squared) by Streisand in the lead(s). On narrative offer, and almost marketed as such, are the familiar Barbra personae in the star's brandished multifaceted range, from goofy to glamorous, diffident to extravagant: a gamut in dramatic voltage from low to high that had already come to be recognized for the same breadth, if not quite the same unshakeable control, as her vocal span. Exaggerated in this one plot by a thematic of temporal dissociation and psychic break, it is the star's manic shifting of tone and vocal inflection, in dialogue alone, that had by then rapidly become the trademark of a Streisand "starrer."

But in this crowded film, her character(s) are worn thin in being put through their triplicate paces as a reincarnated British temptress impersonated in her upper-crust allure by a slatternly Cockney orphan from the early nineteenth century, each harbored—and ricocheting—within a 1960s mod New York ditz ball, one Daisy Gamble. Grating to the French psychology professor whose advice she seeks out (Yves Montand as Dr. Chabot, whose silent *t* gives her trouble right away), it is Daisy's period equivalents of today's "like" as filler between phrases—her repeated "I mean's"—that highlight for him the wordy pointlessness of her nervous remarks in demotic American English. In and out of his mind's eye, the deceitful bejeweled opulence (and itself faked upper-class accent) of her fabricated past life as an upstart femme du monde is in frequent montage tension with the myriad, if never iridescent, mood shifts of a contemporary "role" Daisy is trying to perfect, for her fiancé, by further normalizing herself. From this extrasensory layering of time frames, the sense is that all of human history may be just the restaging of separate performance agendas.

The switch here, though, the surprise within "type-casting," is that Streisand the multimedia heroine of difference personified, the bagel among the ordinary baked dough, is not in the role of Daisy fighting to redefine her possibilities but rather to disappear into some new quirkless stereotype as male appendage. Already a "go-alonger," as she calls herself, in an epitomizing anti-Streisand sentiment, Daisy wants to toe the straight and narrow by giving up her five-packs-a-day smoking habit. It's symptomatically "unnormal," she insists to her visiting hippie half brother Tad (Jack Nicholson, who quipped at Streisand's AFI tribute that he had "forgotten ever being in a Streisand picture"), even after he's pointed out that "no one knows what normal is." Later in this scene of confessed deviance, Daisy's uptight fiancé insists that her dress should be neither too high below nor too low above for dinner with the prospective boss and his wife. It is a bit of dialogue immediately useful in checking off the alternatives posed by the contrasting designs of Cecil Beaton's décolletés for the flashback sequences and Arnold Scaasi's high-necked mini-skirt ensembles for Daisy's current incarnation. The obvious synthesizing subtext: Barbra as the dialectical resolution of kooky urban life force and traditionally elegant looker. The charmingly divided persona, now warm, now sassy, that rocketed to fame in *Funny Girl*, and that next triumphantly suppressed its ingenue side in the ravishing quasi-matronly sprezzatura of *Hello, Dolly!*, has now been released—and realized anew—across the mercurial mood changes of an explicitly split-personality plot. And this time out, the mirror scene of "Hello, gorgeous" is replaced, after the heroine's supposedly final return from long-dead "hypnotic" temptress to her everyday Daisy phase, by a semi-perfunctory hair-smoothing check of her meticulous pageboy in the bedroom mirror—just a last norming pat—at the start of the scene debating the "unnormal." Under Daisy's current social constraints, the mirror should have only one fresh and wholesome face.

In the process, Streisand's personality profile, as the phrase has it, finds a new cinematographic rhythm as well. The single, almost negligible cross-fade brace of the flashback armature in *Funny Girl* is, as noted, easily put from mind in recalling the star-is-born arc of the biopic in its chronological momentum. Instead, such cross-temporal junctures make up the closely articulated skeleton of *On a Clear Day You Can See Forever*. Such flashbacks mark not a prolonged autobiographical reverie from the best seat in the house but rather, in the recurrence of their explosive bursts, the involuntary return of the repressed. The fail-safe, disaster-assured comic set-up with which the film begins will soon have led directly to the debate over "normal." An average New York girl needs to stop smoking to impress her milquetoast business school fiancé's potential employer, and audits uninvited a famous professor's class on hypnotism to see if rumors are true—and post-hypnotic suggestion might help. Backfire guaranteed. And it is our first clue to Daisy's witless directness that she doesn't even seem aware of the jokey phrasing in her own forked wordplay when looking for a method to "get rid of the addiction without getting something else, like fat, or nervous, or acne" (recall Dolly's more than ambidextrous grammar of "arranging" at once "furniture, and daffodils, and lives").

In the immediately preceding scene, Daisy is both hypnotized and even "regressed" secondhand by just sitting as interloper in the back of the classroom while Dr. Chabot demonstrates his mesmerist's technique with an enrolled student. Lost in her deep temporal sleep, Daisy suddenly springs to spastic life in the nasal kindergarten complaints of a whiny put-upon brat: in-joke and retro-self-reference, no doubt, alluding in particular to the actual "A Kid Again/I'm Five" number from *My Name Is Barbra*. No doubt? Need analysis go that far? When a "Streisand picture" expects her to pull out all the stops, some of them are bound to sound familiar notes. The question of intentionality may well disappear, as we'll continue to recognize in later films, into the very fabric of the persona and her cumulative repertoire. In any case, by the next scene in Chabot's office, Daisy has further disclosed not just her susceptibility but her psychic powers of second sight and premonition. At which point, by ironic reversal, the professor begins to "audit" this interloping student: listening in to Streisand's improbable backstory in song, beginning with the famously erotic on-camera panto-mime of inflamed desire in "Love with All the Trimmings" (no turkey, stuffing, and beets this time).

But before the flashback structure gains enough present-tense foothold for a mu-sical number, Daisy's unplanned recall erupts first by unwitting flashback assaults on her own consciousness, triggered by Chabot's hypnotism: shock insets of Melinda in blood-red ensemble at her capital trial for treason (judged a spy for her clairvoy-ance). With their sense of mortal trauma and involuntary recurrence, these volcanic blasts-from-the-past anticipate, in an entirely different key, the scarring sexual-abuse flashbacks Streisand will introduce later, as executive producer, into the storyboard for *Nuts*. Similar temporal ruptures, in the return of a repressed sexual violence, occur under her direction in *The Prince of Tides*. But they are notably shadowed in the former courtroom plot, as well, by psychiatrically fabricated implications (like the dark side of *On a Clear Day*) of multiple personality disorder. In the Minnelli-directed musical, by contrast, recovered memory is, from here out, more often romantic than threatening, as befits the musical comedy genre.

Hooked, the psychology professor probes further in continuing hypnotic sessions, whose episodes, highlighted by two musical numbers, no sooner smitingly unfold than they snap back from the passionately craving Melinda Winifred Wayne Tentrees to the only momentarily transformed features—the vanishingly amorous expressions—of the everyday, ill-spoken, Brooklyn-accented "patient." Her learned "doctor" is both ontologically baffled and sexually flustered, then increasingly frustrated. The pattern builds—in conjunction with the genre logic of musical communion—until his access is completely sutured, if disembodied still, to her erotic past. The first number, how-ever, "Love with All the Trimmings," sumptuously enacted at full imaginary distance from the present, has reached him as if by sheer osmosis. Driven up a tree by Daisy's "I mean's," he is, in contrast, transfixed by the lusty and silver-tongued Lady Tentrees. If we soon feel uneasy with the haughty Frenchman's ethically unhedged preference for Daisy's former incarnation as lascivious cheat, and find something decidedly more likeable, if less captivating, in Daisy, then we have entered the film's true subtext: a Streisand vehicle scrolling through the rolodex of her comic/erotic possibilities as embodied alter egos.

Dr. Chabot's first full "glimpse" into this everyday girl's seemingly lost but still har-bored eroticism comes, by montage retrieval of Melinda's doomed passion, with that first and most often excerpted "singing number": the flamboyant seduction over the banquet table at Brighton's Royal Pavilion. It is there that Streisand—fabulously tur-baned and draped (plunging neckline excepted) in sequined white by Beaton—speaks of her desire with eyes, chest, and silent lips, all intoxicatingly grazed by her unsipped wine glass. Speaks, that is, of such postponed inebriate bliss only in a silent telegraphing of desire, hence the quotes around "singing number." Rather, she communicates through an enticing form of body language (and voice dub) alone. With no song openly sung, she radiates a hope for keener satisfactions—other than the feast before and between them—to the rakish Robert Redford wannabe across and down from her on the seating chart. Here, in lyric and leer alike, Melinda's vaunted powers of clairvoyance are narrowed to the exploratory span of erotic instinct, where "every wish" will be, as if telepathically, "fulfilled before it's made." One may look back on this episode, not as Daisy involuntarily does, but in regard to the technical aplomb of its prolonged voiceover, as the most extreme detachment between actor and singer in Streisand's career. Yet its foreplay's every intake of breath, twitch of lip, and lift of lid serves to remind us, under constraint, of what it would be like to see her actually perform the song itself, rather than the pantomimed satiety it promises.

The genre tease is almost as tantalizing as the lyric, including its subsequent structural compensation. For while we itch to see again the fusion of the two registers, voice and body, it is a "wish . . . fulfilled" soon enough—as if it were exactly what the doctor himself has ordered. This comes through in the next song, when Melinda—via a hypnotized Daisy, and in turn via Streisand's actual vocal address—protests across time, bridging its gap, that her passion for Robert Tentrees can't compare to what, in its own way, she has come to feel for her hypnotist. Regressing from Daisy's flesh-pink chiffon-scarfed mini-skirted outfit to a matched-tone empire gown by Beaton at his elegant best, Melinda's reassuring "He Isn't You" is performed with high Streisand affect. The star is fluently blocked in her "lilting" moves about the room's gilded finery from divan to mantle and back—including an ornate mirror backing her at one point—as she sings forward into the present. The soft shift of lip and knowing glance, all part of the number's extrasensory delivery, are finally intercut with Montand returning Melinda's gaze, not that of Daisy, the latter slumped unconscious in front of him. To vary the hyperbole, Streisand's dulcet power could wake even herself from the dead. And then a final lap dissolve brings reality back in double image (rather than mirror repetition) from beneath its fading eroticism, Daisy coming awake, unawares, to dispel Melinda (fig. 14).

From that point on, the contemporary characters move into separate solos, their crisscrossed desires never really fusing into a duet. Chabot pines over the missing Melinda, whereas Daisy takes fire after discovering a tape of his snide regret over what the inexorable course of time has left him with instead, after recording one of her seductive throwback sessions. With the result that an enraged Daisy bursts out into the original

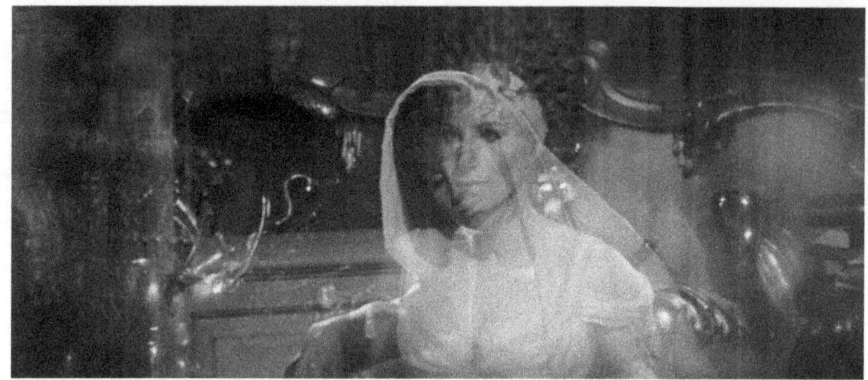

14. Telepathy on the cusp (*On a Clear Day You Can See Forever*)

show's biggest number, "What Did I Have That I Don't Have Now," the up-tempo Streisand belter we came for, this time blocked not in serene amorous languor but in a furious open-armed embrace of self loss. Before this, the only full duet achieved had been hers with herself—in the madly decorated floral arboretum of her bedroom—in intercut shots of her singing herself less to sleep than awake as she tosses and turns with thoughts of the one-too-many men in her life. But once infuriated by the doctor's secret contempt—and his agenda to penetrate to the hidden Melinda—she refuses to see him again, or answer his call(s), musically executed not only by telephone but even by his own telepathy.

Good riddance, we may agree. There has always been something too snootily patronizing about the doctor's attitude, the foreigner not calculated to be a full-fledged Streisand fan, fixated instead on only one facet of the mutable persona. He can't bear how all that fashionable elegance taking flight within Daisy's involuntary memories can return into the "caterpillar" before him, "this little nothing of a creature"—like a reverse time lapse, in contrast to fast-forward editing of the opening song ("Hurry! It's Lovely Up Here"). For that was a pre-credit number made able, thanks to Daisy's paranormal powers, to bring flowers from seedling to bloom before our eyes. The doctor, in a disgusted snit when she refuses to be experimented on any longer, complains about the ironies of transmigration: "Melinda's soul in your body: what a housing shortage." It's all a tad nasty as well as huffy, not to mention kinky—which Daisy is not slow to suspect. In fact, she beats him to an answer after her most defensive question—"What do you want out of me?"—by hearing the truth phrased right there on second thought in the prepositional phrasing: the extraction of Melinda in brief feverish reveries. And she won't let him have at her any longer. All of this has its own kind of intertext in musical-comedy history. At the first sound of Streisand's nasal cockney in her pre-Melinda scheming, we may recall Audrey Hepburn's similar efforts in earlier lyrics, as well as music, by the same Alan Jay Lerner credited with the present script. There, too, the fair lady within of the song sequences (mostly over-voiced by Marnie Nixon in the Hepburn film) is dismissed by the haughty professor (of linguistics rather than psychology) in his attempt to remold her speaking voice. Dr. Chabot, unlike Professor Higgins, finally gives up on Daisy in the hope of a pending return of Melinda for their next-century marriage—while releasing the current woman to a life beyond her broken-off engagement, as figured by a take-off into self-assertion with the closing title song.

Vocal Dissociation

Multiple personality in variably available incarnation: again a star parable, each new role a "comeback." But beneath this overarching level of narrative reflex churn two other self-commenting episodes, the second only now emerging in the plot sequence. Earlier, as lead-in to a song solo ("[There's No] Melinda"), the psychologist has asked himself out loud—still professionally dubious about having elicited any real temptress from the recesses of a previous life—how "a man who never existed" (her husband Tentrees) could "desert a woman who never lived?" And, with a further nod to our attention, he wonders especially why "hearing about it makes me so sad." He is of course asking about suspended disbelief in fiction, as only amplified by the cogency of mise-en-scène and real actors in screen narrative. But by the time Daisy refuses his, as it were, scientific advances, he's now wholly in the grips of the reincarnation claims, both as smitten man and as principal investigator in his newly well-funded experiment. Rebuffed by Daisy, who literally shuts her ears to his blandishments, first by hands, then bedroom pillow, then ear muffs, he persists in his own would-be extrasensory outreach—and via a second, this time technological rather than metafictional, stretch into screen allegory. At this turning point in the separation plot, whether from his office balcony or the top of the Pan Am building, wherever he thinks the signal might somehow go through, he sings out "Come Back to Me" in alternate montage with Daisy's defensive flight from his imperious appeal.

Here three figurative readings overlap: psychological, dramaturgical, and technological. As well as a lurking further irony regarding Streisand's star "presence" as its own kind of emotive ambience. By now, in narrative terms, it has been hard not to suspect the whole film as an extended metaphor for the latent charm and intelligence hidden inside an ordinary girl—when seen through the right eyes—and hence in turn a parable of star performance (in the anagram-like release of talent from latent). But this penultimate number also confirms its logic as a kind of technological irony of the musical genre. Psychologically and theatrically, the gist is this: that a hidden (in this case historically buried) beauty will out. Seen through the probing eyes of a man who knows better, a bland girl—who admits that on a vocational test she was rated as having no distinguishable "character . . . not even any characteristics"—can explode with a personality so multifaceted that it can sing its heart out in two centuries at once, flung between embodied "characters" in the deathless voice of stardom's own assertion and desire.

Psychologically, then, regression accesses the very sediment of possibility. Technologically, as funneled to our notice by the doctor's sung yearning for more of this access, telepathy (the projection of sentiment at a distance) becomes, when carried by song, emblematic. It foregrounds the essential ventriloquism of a post-synced musical genre, where all voices are displaced by dubbing. It is in this sense that his song—as if in a send-up of the whole Hollywood expedient by its past master Minnelli—is mouthed, through remote projection, by any stranger Daisy meets, even a jaw-snapping poodle as French as Montand. If the Doctor can mount his appeal even in a cross-species telepathic channel, it is no surprise that he is heard begging her to come back, in whatever mode of reincarnation: whether (as if anticipating the historical backcast of *Yentl*) "as a girl or a boy." In this complex montage of the "thrown voice," there is even a moment when his song, remediated, is piped through the lips of a TV news announcer at yet a second technological remove from cinema's own screen mechanism.

This entire episode is so comically unashamed about the shaping of lips to music in standard Hollywood production that one almost suspects a thru-line of deliberate mismatch in the film as a whole, hedging its own genre bets. A viewer, listening closely, might well have regretted the sloppy bad faith of post-synchronization in the opening number—where, with Daisy striding off unregistered to Chabot's class, the lingering last high note of "Hurry! It's Lovely Up Heeeeere" outlasts, on the always "here"-and-now of the over-voiced track, the moment of her plugging barely parted lips with a cigarette. It's a minor disaster of diegetic conviction. But over and above this local moment of over-voicing awkwardly laid bare, there is something more intransigent yet to ponder about the audio ironies of treatment in the doctor's imploring "Come Back to Me" number—with its importunate pervasive claim on attention managing to saturate narrative space, all but omnivorous in its very output. What Daisy can't bear in this pressing vocal demand of Montand's lone solo can read as a subliminal lampoon of what an unconverted listener may find aggravating in the wall-to-wall star numbers of a Streisand musical: the ubiquity of her vocal imprint, insistent, unremitting, not just over-voiced but overweening. So encompassing here, in fact, with her next and final number, that the clustered students in the closing title song, though deaf to it, are nonetheless neutralized by it as mere props—among whose canceled attention she strides forth demanding ours.

In any case, that initial gaffe of post-synchronization in the same campus setting, with Daisy's own body subordinated to the Streisand sound, can easily seem roped into the circuit of cinematographic irony that is more openly and blaringly laid bare in Montand's wireless but widely broadcast appeal in "Come Back to Me." But then, too, that first number, addressed by a girl named Daisy to her own fresh plantings, had begun, rather than ended, with a separation of voice from body so extreme that we only see Streisand's already famous tapered and manicured fingers pushing bulbs into potted soil. Playing on the then contemporaneous meme of "talking to your plants," offering the encouraging words they need to flourish, someone we only recognize so far as Streisand, not her character, actually sings them into a time-lapse growth. This accelerated over-voiced imaging, then, suggests a deep technological matrix for the coming plot in both its edited time travel and its engineered vocalism alike. All the while, figuratively, a voice so forcefully "organic"—sprung from the phrasal grafting of "Hurry! [up]" (to the "buds below") onto "uUhp is where to grow"—executes a further vocal mimesis (reaching out as well as up) via the widening intonation of "open up and spreeeahhhd out." Internalized by—or merely intersecting—the actor's projected body from an unseen power source, the Streisand sound on-screen is never quite contained by the actress-who-sings, a technological fact to be stirringly exploited a decade and a half later in the sound design of *Yentl*.

In Minnelli's film, though, Daisy may be both reincarnated and clairvoyant, but nothing in the plot explains this preternatural ability to speed up natural process—except the two figurative services with which its magic is associated: technically overmastered temporality (post-sync and all) and, in her own person, the educed surfacing of things "subterraneum" (her jokey rhyme with "geranium"). Captured from the film's first image as recorded (not yet embodied) song rather than any (other) paranormal superpower, Streisand's sense of timing locates the same vocal thrust that will, at the end, be charged with forging a path into its own future. For it turns out, the doctor has just discovered from tapping into what might be called Melinda's pre-conscious, that she indeed will "come back": that, in fact, they will both be reincarnated as a married couple in 2038. Romantically consoled by this marital prognosis, the doctor, in bringing her out of hypnosis, sings a few bars of "On a Clear Day" to the surprised Daisy. Like Streisand, she is a quick study, just by ear. Soon fully conscious (of herself) again, she picks up on the lyric briefly in saying goodbye, and then launches into the whole anthem of self-realization for the closing, open-mouthed, unself-conscious number amid student foot traffic and conversation on the campus grounds. It is there—or somewhere hovering above—where the famous "foreverrrrandeverrrrrmore" finish is matched (after her orange Scaasi outfit sails in hokey mid-flight superimposition over a flaming orange sunset) to an infinite graphic regress of self-reflecting screen rectangles for the closing credits, a slightly dated effect reminiscent of the *Vertigo* decade. This optical rather than psychic regress has a way of inscribing the musical genre signing off on its claims to contemporary impact.

But far more has been at technical play, as is clear, in the 1970 structural complexity of this film than is meant to find apotheosis in the clumsy techno bombast of its already time-worn closing graphics: at play, not least, and exaggerated in Montand's telepathic number, in the mobile soundscape of the screen voice in uncertain sync with itself. So the future the film really anticipates, in the context of any such study as this, is not of course reincarnation but a rethinking of vocal embodiment in the later movies over which Streisand will have more control. For this quintessential "recording artist," it is the craft, and finally the art, of recorded sound on-screen that she continues to manipulate and transform, so that films like *Funny Lady*, and especially *A Star Is Born* and *Yentl*, tend to double round on their own conditions of audial production in the staking out of new premises. Close listening, focused by the carefully framed gaze, keeps us alert to a technological evolution in the genre of screened song that is both spearheaded and stage-managed by Streisand's increasingly intense superintendence. And implied by the immediacy of her performance even when she has not been behind the camera in planning the shot. We see and hear this, this shearing slip between mobile image and inner voice, not just activated but flagged in the nuances of the famous title song from *On a Clear Day*, once Streisand has picked up the cue from Montand and run with it—out of his office and into the campus rose garden.

Floated in this closing song, at the level of reflexive performance rather than technology, is another inference as well. If the question "What did I have that I don't have now?" in the previous big number could almost seem to wonder aloud why the magic of *Funny Girl* wasn't quite kicking in, the title song's pep talk now waxes more explicitly metatheatrical yet. For if our heroine "should . . . draw back the curtain," the doctor is "certain" (in the song's launch) that "you'd be impressed with you." Montand has enough trouble in making the internal rhyme of "voodoo you can do" sound English in the verse that one can imagine good reasons for dropping many of the somewhat tongue-twisting lyrics from the stage number, including the cross-acronym pun about a wised-up world minding its "ESPs and Qs." But other more natural slides between words return in the chorus with Streisand's gliding enunciation, outdoors and running free, including, for this character able to hear telephones just before they ring, the song's reminder (rendered like an abstract intuition, rather than actual

ESP) of extrasensory audition. The self-affirming fact that you "can hear" a whole new world both "far and near" allows us, in Streisand's delivery, to hear already the hint of that proximity ("can [n]ear") in the very word for its audition: a version of telescopic phonics facilitated entirely by the exactitude and sometimes tactical slack of the star's always vernacular enunciation.

And all the more so, this overlap of word edges, as they finally open the topography of her voicing to the approximation of infinite regress at the peak and closure of the song—as internalized by Daisy in the move from the doctor's indoor rendition to her outdoor and finally aerial way forward. Timed to the lyric's own shift from the vocabulary of hearing to seeing, what happens next, in vocal more than visual terms, sweeps us up into the further lift from that (n)hear/near slant rhyme into a clearer air—and ear—that carries the lyric to its climax as if in one pulsing open breath of repetition. It is in this levitation, first, that "on a clear day" is lengthened out with the particularizing demonstrative (and self-demonstrated) variant "*that* cleeeaaar day," where in turn the throat itself is freed from prolonged exhalation—into its own exaltation. At such moments the sensed sound can disappear into the making of further sense. In this case, right after the move from "a clear day" in augmented restatement to the consciously opened horizons of that forcefully "clear(ed) day," the energized and clinging ear may suspect a further lexical moment exercised on the run (up) by voice. Within the widened contours of vocal execution, that is, the force of "endeavor" may well be heard, though unassimilated to syntax, traced across the split husk of "forever"—into "*and ever / and ever*"—so as to release a separate name for this new confidence. Like "cleared day," this is not so much articulated by Streisand as—what should one say?—heard in the mirror neurons of one's own inner voicing. This is how audition pieces out the sense from amid the sensuality of listening. In negotiating such phonic ligatures, ordinary language must often separate from the notes that emit but exceed it. So, again, is the "terrain" of voice made manifest as part of the audience's own somatic soundscape. Short of any such granulated legato half-puns as we've just intuited (clear day/cleared day; and ever/endeavor)—but still pushing beyond the contours of mere declaration—the second word of the iterated "and ever" is immediately remobilized. It is made to edge further ahead yet into the pulsional redundancy of "And ever . . . And ever . . . And ever more"—held as if forever in the effort, the endeavored stretch, of Streisand's long last "mooooOHhre" (ringingly familiar from the final two syllables of "My Man" in *Funny Girl*).

As often in her "big finishes," the terrain of sound is charted as having no end in sight. In the present case (but where does that locate us exactly?), the vocal cantilevering of just that last *for-ehvvverrrr-mooooOHrrre*—built of the three previous "evers"—has warped space into time: the vocal inverse of the time-lapse photography that opens the film with the floral imperative of "Hurry! It's Lovely Up Here." The last song is meant to up the stakes further, of course, carried on the vitalizing ascent of airborne image and voice. Whereas the film's soundtrack has previously operated in a kind of teasing playback with itself in the finesses and ironies of its oscillating synchronization (singing through a cigarette, lip-free telepathic seduction, remote transgender and even trans-species mouthing), the separation of body and voice here seems final. Certainly any need for studious dubbing disappears when Streisand all but does, her outfit accessorized by a matching superimposed sunset in that final take-off into the stratosphere. Yet this optical figuration for the "high note" is not just overexplicit but in a sense backward. The power of the inspirational lyric as musical comedy finale, now broken quite free of the reincarnation plot, is of course not to suggest, against genre parameters, that the body escapes beyond range of audition but rather that its tangible sounds open their deserved perspective within the throat of the expressive talent—the expansive personality—when attended up close.

Need it be said? Plot aside, on entrance and exit from this one narrative's fantasy of extrasensory force, and often in between, what is truly hypnotic in all this is, as always, the Streisand sound. And nothing in the way the film puts us on technical alert to its audiovisual construct of that sound, let alone to the voice's own risk of the overbearing—any more than with the reverse freeze on the marquee at the start of *Funny Girl*, or the tricks of cinematographic animation, shot change, and freeze-frame in *Hello, Dolly!*—is meant to reduce the enchantments of performance to some correlate in technique. Rather, and in ways we'll find variously ransacked and satirized in some of her coming comedies, as well as potently transformed in her later musical ventures, these cinematographic disclosures—linked repeatedly to formal questions of genre—keep us in mind, while the star operates so mesmerically before us, of her always mediated presence. From here out, the career effort is somehow to continue matching that magic, no easy feat, with plot material that doesn't close off unduly the scope of its promise for the narrower pleasures of a momentary entertainment.

INTERMISSION (1)

Genre Triage

Intermission is one word for it. Breather another. Or worse: refashioning. After three extraordinary musical workouts in a genre even Streisand's vocal athleticism and stamina couldn't finally rehabilitate for the box office, some time at least to regroup must have seemed in order. But something else seemed afoot as well when the abstinence from filmed song dragged on. Five movies in a row passed by without a real on-screen musical number, including only two title songs ("The Way We Were" [1973], "For Pete's Sake" [1974]) and two repurposed classics (a spirited and delicious version of Cole Porter's "You're the Top" for the credits of 1972's *What's Up, Doc?*—followed by a mannered snippet of "As Time Goes By" on camera later in that frantic romp). This was more than time off, time out, for some lighter (quieter) fare. It had the distressing look of a career makeover. Streisand had pressed the mute button on fully half of her star power. In an "interim" one wouldn't think to call experimental, exactly, only the first of these post-musicals—the formulaic (if quite likeably raucous) stage vehicle *The Owl and the Pussycat* (1970)—seemed a perfect lateral move for Streisand. This is certainly not the case with the frenetic retread of classic Hollywood screwball in *What's Up, Doc?* And, with the musical comedies behind her, if the downbeat fantasy of *Up the Sandbox* was a brave venture in stripping away the remaining lighter comedy from Streisand's dramatic persona, it was a miscalculated one. Same in reverse—in a further falling off after the romantic chemistry of the next year's Robert Redford teaming in the straight drama of *The Way We Were*—with the return to chaotic urban farce in *For Pete's Sake*. The pattern of all this wavering exploration, if not experimentation, almost as hectic as some of the plots concocted for it, is clearer now than at the time, where the films sometimes felt as if they were just punctuating an occasional lull between best-selling albums.

Intermission, breather: fair-enough names, on the surface, for this interregnum between high-powered assaults on the popular imagination in Streisand's war on the norm, her prosecution of difference as emotive power. A recess in the mission: another way to think of it. Genre triage: yet another. And not just in that medical term's original sense of "sorting," by kind or type. With the Hollywood musical comedy about to be taken off life support, there is, for the emergent Streisand, a resulting career emergency in the prioritizing of screen options. The subsequent script choices offered an odd combination of routinized and scattershot, a matter by turns of type-casting and overzealous departures, even at times within the same film. Although now and then disheartening for admirers turned "followers," the careenings of the career's first decade are in retrospect, misjudgments aside, one clear measure of Streisand's restless talent. After the international coup of her debut in the backstage biopic of *Funny Girl*, the subsequent big-budget musical workouts weren't in fact working out at the box office. As a result, expressive dualities were soon being partitioned rather than re-directed. With her recording career going strong, the actress-who-sings was looking to subordinate further that appended clause in the face of vanishingly bankable options in the realm of screen song.

In remembering the 1970s comic throwaways after the Broadway-tested success of *The Owl and the Pussycat*, it is not easy to square those screen choices with the vaulting ambition of the arriving star just a few years before—even when they do seem to capitalize on the ambidextrous (sometimes merely two-fisted) panache at the heart of her talent. But the horizon had been far wider once, incautious in its reach—at least in the recording studio. Not just in the mix of tempo and tone in her early albums, comic patter songs balanced against love ballads, there was a yet deeper instinct for twinning and doubling, even apart from the obvious comedic/dramatic split in her emotive range: a further attempt to maximize the flip sides of her talent's two-sided coin. A 2021 video interview with Zane Lowe reveals what we (if not she) can look back on as the ill-judged first flush of her ambition after her growing TV fame—an intended venture perhaps partly inspired by the frequent Nefertiti comparisons for her Semitic profile. For Streisand had wanted to play the most famous Egyptian of all, doing back-to-back TV versions of Cleopatra, Shakespeare's and Shaw's: a showcasing of, yes, differential verve that the studios understandably balked at. No high drama for this star. The actress-who-sings was already being pegged, instead, as a comedienne with a voice.

Coming right on the heels of *Hello, Dolly!* and *On a Clear Day*, her first straight comedy, *The Owl and the Pussycat* (1970)—presumed by fans a temporary departure at the time—was as refreshing a jettisoning of song as could have been wished. Especially in the way its screenplay exploited the wild variations, and intonations, of Streisand's comic vocal delivery. Says the heroine in self-defense at one point, after one of her roller-coaster tirades: "I don't shriek, I talk loud but I don't shriek." This is the fourth of her films drawn from a pre-tested theatrical success, and for the third time with a role inherited by her from its original performer. But it suited to a tee. The plot, or at least the point of its character polarity, is easy to gather (up) in a few sentences. In a pitched battle between mind and body, a book clerk and would-be writer (George Segal) is confronted by a part-time hooker and would-be "model and actress" whose taking money from male visitors he has reported to the apartment management. The confrontation that ensues gets them both evicted. In the 1965 stage production of the Bill Manhoff play, the casting of Alan Alda and Diana Sands added racial difference into the temperamental dichotomy. The whole concept is strenuously revised by Buck Henry's screenplay, beginning when Felix fishes a full-screen rejection notice from his mailbox while holding legibly in his teeth a paperback copy of Henry James's *The Art of the Novel*. Before long his prissily literate vocabulary will be infuriating the unschooled Doris.

When it turns out later, in stripping away his own pretensions, that he is really Fred, not Felix, it is only then that Doris—admittedly wavering from the start between "stage names," including Waverly itself, along with previous stabs at Wadsworth and Wellington—finally confesses to be being none other than one Doris Wilgus. It isn't this implicit shape-shifting multiplicity, however, that links her most directly to the Streisand star persona, nor her fiery volatility and erotic gusto. She has actually, besides TV commercials, *starred in a movie*. Not *Funny Girl*, but as a kinky biker girl instead, one of the eponymous *Cycle Sluts*. This boast of a screen role left uninterrogated at the time, it is a film that Felix (Fred) later discovers by accident in passing a poster-board in front of a sleazy porn theater. After his screaming in desperation at the elderly Asian man in the nearly soundproof ticket booth, to the amusement of the next man in line, "I want to see *Cycle Sluts*," we cut to his wincing through the S/M film—behind the moans of an elderly masturbating patron—as we hear Doris's yelps of sexual intimidation on the soundtrack without ever seeing her on-screen. We've already had that pleasure. Yet her lead role in *Cycle Sluts* isn't the true reflexive hook, either, in linking this proud "star vehicle" of Doris's to Streisand's screen manifestations. The true mirror moment comes with a quite digressive exchange between the "new couple," Doris and Fred, when they seek borrowed shelter together after mutual eviction.

"Like Two Different Girls"

Whereas Buck Henry's script has enhanced the comic jousting between the life of words and the flesh of deeds, lexicon and sex, and circulated it through the "adult movie house" in the process, what he preserves almost intact from the Manhoff stage version is the one telling exchange of metatheatrical dialogue—tactically repurposed as a kind of essentializing Streisand hat trick. "Do you think I'm pretty?" she asks Felix out of the blue, and when he says "I do," she returns: "I only make you think I am." As movie audiences were still reconciling themselves to the on-screen uneasy prettiness of Streisand's otherwise paradoxical "look"—her features both somehow commonplace and anomalous at once, rote and ravishing, and thus synthesized in a fascinating rarity of attraction—the scene already grabs our attention before its further and more telling turn into a theatrical in-joke. In the play, Felix anticipates: "In other words, you're not pretty—you're just a good actress." Broadway's Doris doesn't at first mean to be sharing the secrets of her sometime craft at all, we're to think. She's taken by surprise in the recognition: "Well—yeah, I never thought about it but it is—it's acting." At which point, in the play as well as the film, Doris demonstrates two alternate faces, pretty and its negation, now vital, now numb and blah. The stage direction for the second: "Doris lets her face and body slump into vacant stupidity." Felix, as audience of one, is politely transfixed: "That's amazing. Like two different girls."[1]

In the same terms, Felix is similarly impressed in the film with this profound Janus-face of performativity, but Streisand as Doris takes the lead in the explanation when asked how she does it: "It's hard to explain, it's kinda like acting, you know. You gotta act pretty." We do know. That's what we're here for: the disarming chameleon charms of this unusual new "eyeful" in the post-musical Barbra star turn. In this scene itself, Doris opens the curtain on its Jekyll/ Hyde duality from behind her raised, then parted hands, first disclosing her most poised and erotically enticing face in sultry Melinda mode, followed by the flaccid cancellation of all glamour, even all human presence, the persona relaxed into stupefaction. In the star's hands (and here emerged from behind them) is the reverse engineering of screen beauty as a willed concentration—as well as its maintenance otherwise as screen magnetism, always palpable with Streisand in playing however many "different girls." Even at the time, and more so since, it is a delicious moment for Streisand's self-mirrored recognition of her persona as a performative fiction. And Segal's slightly adjusted line is perfect too, shifting the simile "like" for her "amazing" display simply to "That's two completely different girls!" Which makes three, counting the star actress in front of him.

What's Up, Doc? is the next stop in this swerve from the musical genre—though in its own clownish mayhem it hardly ever stops long enough to take stock of its "diversion," or even pause for clarity. It is a film unrestrainedly directed by former film critic Peter Bogdanovich in his misbegotten homage to the screwball comedies of classic Hollywood, yet recycled here in the woefully cartoonish mode blazoned by its title. The star who shared, in an unprecedented tie, the Oscar for Best Actress with Katharine Hepburn is now supposedly taking the latter's earlier and atypical flighty part in such a comedy. This, at least, is the director's publicized fantasy: to bring to the screen an updated version of the most madcap of these comedies from the 1930s, the unhinged *Bringing Up Baby*. More than just headstrong and self-indulgent, however, like the Hepburn character, Streisand's Judy is a walking disaster. For all her fresh-faced cuteness—and confronted with Ryan O'Neal (rather than Cary Grant) under wraps as a clueless sex-shy nerd—Streisand's Judy comes off as an anarchic narcissist who causes traffic accidents by crossing the street whenever and wherever she wants and who turns out, in some quirky allegory, to be in this regard a direct offspring of the law: daughter, as revealed in the final courtroom scene, of the dithering, pill-popping judge.

Minority opinion here, granted—given not just the film's legion of fans but its status, oddly enough, as the *only* Streisand film lots of people like enough to revisit. In her "character," as Judy in *What's Up, Doc?*, if you could call it that, anything like genuine "difference"—ethnic, cultural, personal—is certainly all smoothed away in a lovely nondescript tanned glow whose only veer from the veneered 1970s norm is her maddening eccentricity and self-possession, hardly redeemed simply for the way it reveals Streisand's skill at making this, even this, vivid. Snippets of verbal comedy hardly redeem the mounting physical slapstick either. Early on, there is some punning phonetic banter in which Streisand as Judy (with an ear for the vocal syllable wasted on crackpot non sequiturs rather than song notes) completes the tongue-tied stumbles of Howard (O'Neal) in regard to his fiancée Eunice (Madeline Kahn)—whose place Judy is impetuously trying to usurp. But even the best of these verbal turns in *What's Up, Doc?* are more mechanical than organic. Objecting to one of Judy's outrageous interventions, Howard starts a frustrated complaint with "You" and Judy redirects with "Eue-nice," then answering his baffled "How?" (how in the world she manages to be hiding under a banquet table with him) a split-second later in introducing him to a third party as "How-ward." Write-offs, yes, they are still the best writing in the script. With an encyclopedic list of learned references at hand from her several college expulsions, Streisand's scatterbrained willfulness is certainly pitch-perfect in its flippant way—if often in a grating key—and, as usual, her timing couldn't be improved on. All of this freewheeling precocious bluster serves to fluster unspeakably (into mostly flummoxed silence) the uptight, absent-minded, easily baffled scholar O'Neal is trying to inhabit, who is forced to put it bluntly when he self-defensively tells her off, insisting that he finds her behavior "not even vaguely amusing."

"The Same as Those Who Aren't Different"

The improvement she promises to attempt is little more than a travesty of Streisand's own difference personified. The hero doesn't get it. Frustrated, upended, and as yet unseduced, Howard tries softening the supposed blow by adding: "I know you don't mean any harm, you're just different." For a viewer who joins him in finding not even the vaguest of amusement in her self-indulgent persona and its "Roadrunner"-style invulnerability, more slapstick than genuinely screwball, the next turn, if it were anything but silly and unactionable, would seem even more unwelcome: a further dumbing down yet of the true Streisand *difference*. Says Judy in ironically daft return: "I know I'm different . . . but from now on I'll try to be the same." The straight-faced sarcasm of her contradiction confounds Howard, who in confusion can only parry the paradox: "Same as what?" Only Judy, not Streisand, could imagine this goal: "Same as people who aren't different." This pivotal exchange with Howard about the scandal of difference, in respect to the absurd benchmark of sameness, is quite overtly reminiscent of the circular reasoning in Daisy's anti-abnormalcy campaign two years before in *On a Clear Day*. More oblique but hard to shake, we may have previously suspected another in-joke and career cross-reference: this when a presentably suited male in seeming control at a formal reception—misread by Howard as the rich philanthropist and would-be benefactor of his archaeological research—is obsequiously greeted. At which point the taken-aback server correctively introduces himself as "the waiter, Rudy"—quite likely a skewed nod to the head waiter role, by the same name, in *Hello, Dolly!*

If we are picking up on such potential hints, then we are continuing to play the game—begun with that matrix moment of "acting pretty" in *The Owl and the Pussycat*—whose coded allusions are almost inadvertently woven into so many of these early 1970s films. Beyond that tacit probing of the "Hello, gorgeous" trope in *The Owl and the Pussycat*—as the work of performance rather than self-presence—film after film is laced with allusions to Streisand's big musicals and ongoing record career. The unnerving specter here at the time: that Streisand herself, "unnormal" through and through, would be caught in this rut of recycled and continually resplit difference, robbed of impact by iteration. As we will continue to see, the intermesh of allusive self-reference in her films—in the lesser comedies not least, all of course with an increasingly layered backlog of dialogue and gesture to draw on—is part of the one-woman genre she seems cultivating by default in those years. And would have to find ways of rejuvenating.

Even the supposedly normalized "free spirit" of Judy Maxwell in *What's Up, Doc?* is a case in point: a woman more unlikely even than unlikeable in her reckless spontanei-ties, even when doing an explicitly Streisand turn. Not only is she full of literary, phil-osophical, and scientific citations from those many colleges she's been thrown out of, but in the ultimate tease regarding Streisand's musical stardom, she alludes to the star's discography when sliding into a few bars of "As Time Goes By." Even this, however, is a deflected allusion, since she surprises Howard by having been asleep under a tarp on a refurbished penthouse piano top, rousing her hardly sleepy-eyed self with an ad hoc Bogart imitation over the coincidence of finding Howard on hand: "Of all the joints in all the world." As she prods the musicologist to accompany her on the keyboard in the theme song from *Casablanca*, even there she is only doing a vamped-up delivery of her 1964 version of the song from *The Third Album*. Less palatable yet, in the matter of recirculated sexy affect across this phase of Streisand's career, she delivers herself of an exaggerated comic version of the fake come-on moves she puts on an upstaged Burt Bacharach at the piano on his TV special the next year. This was a semi-scandalous face-off that still strikes me (and this time I'm less alone)—though she was in unusually exquisite voice leaning over Bacharach's keyboard—as perhaps, in its simpering cutesy intimacy, the most sustained low point of her on-camera career: a tasteless case of what can only be called lethal flirting. But even the year before at (or on) the piano, under Bogdanovich's blunt baton, if Streisand the actress were merely surfacing momentarily her inner Judy, the risk of the frivolous as a new formula felt very real at the time—and not least because of the film's huge success. The monumental Streisand difference was being downsized to oddball, her unique beauty tamed to cute, even while more and more mainstreamed in its ever-more-contempo long-blonde style. A film like *What's Up, Doc?* seemed at the time in danger of trapping the comedienne, even when goofy, in little more than an "acting pretty" mode. What's up, Barbra?—one had begun to ask. She knew better, obviously, and wanted to try harder for something different—more urgent and challenging.

Testament to that effort, *Up the Sandbox* was, however, a strange downer: a low-keyed, charmless, and ultimately unengaging feminist fantasy. After two films already sheering off comedy from musical in Streisand's lighter turn-of-the-decade fare, this 1972 venture separated any real character from its schematic protagonist in a stitched-together alternate-reality montage whose episodes were schooled, unsaid, by the cultural weight of available Hollywood genres. Its forthright effort at innovation sadly fizzled, even though Streisand's own performance—of a thinly drawn, in fact barely sketched, urban housewife—was always convincing as far as it went. Or as the script would let it go. This was Streisand as Margaret Reynolds (whoever she in turn was): focused, determined, intensely concentrated, and wholly watchable in every scene—except, alas, in several of the grotesque daydream sequences meant to express her needs. It was as if the hypnotized flashbacks from *On a Clear Day* had become the spur to any number of vacuous flash-forwards, leaps into impossible tomorrows and alternate lives. The film's very funding and production were a kind of escapist fantasy in their own achieved right. Breaking temporarily from the stranglehold of her four-picture contract with producer Ray Stark, Streisand had pitched in to form a production company with Paul Newman and Sydney Poitier, called First Artists, as in Artists First, later joined by Steve McQueen and Dustin Hoffman. It was a consortium intended to give more say—and leeway—to stars in nurturing their own projects: in her case, a half-baked departure where even the sustained nervous energy and seriousness of her performance fails to replace either the music or the laughs of the musical comedy genre she still seemed trying deliberately, but here *purposefully*, to leave behind. Instead of the music/comedy negotiation, it was now, for her new heroine, the breached barrier between homelife and screen-fostered fantasy.

Home/Movie

Beleaguered domestic routine versus a psychic staycation in screen-based daydreams; apartment-bound homemaker versus cinephile fantasist; depleting chores versus ludic interludes—but with the dead seriousness of the latter episodes as far from playful as screen-primed imagination can get. And all of this is put into counterpoint—now reality, now fantastic fugue state, though often to be distinguished only after the fact—without the least explicit allusion to movie-going as spur, except insofar, by that most roundabout of routes, as we, in the audience, are of course supposedly taken out of ourselves by watching. Though barely—in this unengrossing narrative. That's one curiosity of this strange project. *Up the Sandbox* is a film in which radical difference, the flight from routine, is to be accessed for the urban wife and mother only through overheated reveries of a defiant, violent sort, rather than through comic or romantic interludes—but without any of these escape valves being pegged explicitly to the heroine's screen experience. These inner movies she moves to, to escape her life, are meant to be self-generated, for all their genre clichés. The film seems inclined to stage some kind of unresolved dialectic between maternal domesticity and a compensatory dream life, though the latter—unlike in the comedies just before and after it (*The Owl and the Pussycat, What's Up, Doc?*; later *For Pete's Sake*)—are never specifically linked to any kind of dream-factory fantasy or Hollywood screen backlog, porn stardom or otherwise. Except—and a big exception it is—by the plot's interpolated genre misfires in each case. But with *Up the Sandbox* in particular, everything is a bit oblique, even when blatant, in this low-keyed and over-earnest dud. The director, Irvin Kershner, looking back for his DVD interview, calls it a "period piece"—one for the archives—and not just for capturing what he calls the "PC" moment of equal-opportunity parenting (the film's redemptive climax is the husband giving the wife a day off by taking the kids) but also as a milestone in Streisand's career: her acting, he thinks, never better. Certainly never more disappeared into a role until then, never more "Streisand"-free, even with very little character there to develop in compensation.

In *Up the Sandbox*, the role is so serious that Margaret Reynolds almost never cracks a smile. Happily pregnant for the third time, loving motherhood but worn to shreds with chores her professor husband has no time for, her only relief comes, almost involuntarily, from a set of imaginative syncopes that glide into and out of plot with inconsistent road signs. We never quite get the hang of the transitions. The main plot is so under-realized that departures from "reality" can at first go unmarked. And they are many, right from the start: first when her pushy mother arrives unannounced and unwanted, breaking through her apartment door chain with an outsize metal cutter; then when a female colleague admits blithely that she's having an affair with Margaret's husband on a convenient closet cot in the department; next at a crowded press conference given by a South American communist dictator (a bearded Fidel Castro lookalike). This episode expands under the force of its own absurdity. Preaching women's equality in regard to military skill, the dictator is interrupted by Margaret with a counterargument about feminine tenderness and nurture. In response, she finds herself invited to his hotel suite. There, when they are alone, he strips off his beard, opens his uniform, and reveals his secret femininity—in a bizarre breast-baring anticipation of *Yentl*.

Accidental career foreshadowing aside, even apparent retrospective allusions in this film, faint as they are, may be perhaps unintended. In Margaret's first scene bathing her infant boy, she lifts him dripping into the air, before we've even seen the star's face, with "Look at that face!"—title of the rousing number she had sung in comic profile to an anteater in her first color TV special when she was still making tongue-in-cheek fun of her own nose. Later, in one of the film's rare light-hearted (if hardly inspired) moments, we find Margaret comically fending off her husband's advances, forbidding him to cross an imaginary line on their bed, objecting finally, before reprisal, with a tight-lipped "Ya Touched Me." Comic homage to her rapturous ballad "He Touched Me"? Planted for recognition or not, that sort of thing is about all the fun there is for Streisand fans, except for one explosive rant after a party whose tedious festivities were interrupted in midstream by a make-believe cosmetic repair. It was there, jealous of her husband's fascination with a busty academic in a low-cut dress, that Margaret, queasy with morning sickness over the third pregnancy she hasn't yet divulged, has gone upstairs to the bathroom and into a fantasy in which her belly, suddenly swollen, can be manually depressed in order to pneumatically inflate her breasts. After this lowbrow departure from any feminist playbook of the period, her subsequent explosion on their way home, over the husband's suggestion that she should "find something more to do," triggers her fury as she storms through a litany of daily chores, obligations, and challenges as a "mere" stay-at-home mom. This is the explosive "Barbra moment" that, grown almost formulaic, is already at peril of becoming a cliché—yet that never ceases to fascinate, down through *The Guilt Trip* (2012), when she bursts into flame at her patronizing son.

In the plot of *Up the Sandbox*, with Margaret's hands so full, the spells of lurid alternate realities can't help but take their toll on her as well as the audience. The convertible Castro scene, communist feminist exposed only as secret female, is not even the nadir. The rest of the shapeless interludes anticipate, not the transgendering of *Yentl*, but the kind of dopey slapstick variants of genre options to be checked off later in the yet more trivial farce of *For Pete's Sake*. The desperate respites in *Up the Sandbox* involve alternatives to Margaret's life that are just as unlikely as are their options for Streisand's talent: an espionage attack on the Statue of Liberty with a cohort of African American terrorists (trashing her uplifted gesture of solidarity with the sculpture from "Don't Rain on My Parade"), followed by a dreary African safari sequence, actually filmed on location and built around exotic pregnancy rituals. But complicating this racial nexus—as an unsettled subtext of downtrodden solidarity between women and Blacks in the film—is the earlier appearance, alongside her and her children in her apartment elevator, of an angry and threatening African American man (phobic fantasy or not, one can't quite be sure). What this episode seems further to precipitate in her mind, in any case, are exactly those coming flashpoints from alternate screen genres (the thriller turn to domestic racial terrorism, the documentary impulse of African ethnography) that gather into no cohesive through-line even in her unconscious. Maybe that's just the joyless point, for this woman stretched thin in every direction—but it doesn't make for much of a screen narrative.

In contemplating this adapted novel (of the same title, by Anne Richardson Roiphe) as a psychological study in search of a movie, it can't be an accident, despite the lack of specified Hollywood references, that the longest and most decisive of the plot's digressive—transgressive—illusions involves a literal film-within-the-film. This is an annoying home movie shot at a large anniversary gathering for Margaret's parents by an obnoxious relative with two glaring lights mounted on his camera, blinding the group with his invasive camaraderie as he circles the dinner table. Only when the light level returns to typical cinematic treatment—and to stable narrative framing, rather than hand-held panning—does the real fantasy kick in. It begins with Margaret slamming her mother's face into the celebration cake in rage over her leaking the news of her new pregnancy in front of a husband she's been afraid to tell. In answer to this, in a final scene soon coming, we arrive at the film's most effective lighting and framing by renowned cinematographer Gordon Willis. A flickering shot of Margaret through the poles of a merry-go-round on which her spouse is doing kid-duty finds the wife coming in and out of stroboscopic view after announcing her positive pregnancy test—in sutured response to which, with each turn of the spooling ride, reverse shots catch the husband's reaction settling from astonishment to acceptance to pleasure.

Here is an effective evocation of the cinematic apparatus—rather than a looting of its established plot forms on the escapist heroine's part. As such, this intercepted axis of rotary motion completes a tacitly meta checklist of alternative realities in *Up the Sandbox*: betrayed wife melodrama, Cold War political intrigue, terrorist sabotage, exotic African exploration, even chest-enhancement comedy. And finally an abortion clinic nightmare, from which Margaret is shoved on her gurney into slow-motion escape. Her flight through the air from multibed ward to a soft sandbox landing is another of those rare cinematographic liberties that one tends not to associate with the look of Streisand films, early or late. But hardly aura-bursting when they do tactically appear. We've noted before their contribution to cinema's acknowledged technology in the realization of star image. Along with numerous allusions in her films to date in the matter of self-image—references to acting, performance, and the multiplied personalities of either reincarnation or daydream—these adjacent gestures toward the cinematographic apparatus of illusion and adjustable motion never feel extraneous to the Streisand persona. So thickly concentrated at the start of *Hello, Dolly!* in its attempted jazzing up of the Broadway hit, such disclosures of mechanism continue to keep the projected and variable screen manifestation of Streisand's stardom (along with the genres that might, or might not, plausibly environ her energy) very much on the viewer's mind. Genuinely perplexing this time, however, in tone and intent, the interesting thing about *Up the Sandbox*, once slotted into the Streisand filmography, is that the unflinching dead seriousness of its realist heroine (apart from the violent radical firebrand that emerges in one of her film-like fugue states) may be preparing us, by Streisand's own workout, for her most successful film of the early 1970s. Certainly one of her indisputable career highs is her role as leftist campus radical, passionate FDR supporter, and (later in the House Un-American Activities Committee years) outspoken Hollywood gadfly, one Katie Morosky, in *The Way We Were*. Unlike the domestic divide between home and movie-like escape into political commitment, racial exploration, or outright domestic terrorism in *Up the Sandbox*, Katie's acknowledged "double life" is at the self-aware heart of her failing marriage to her screenwriter husband in the film's second half. Her estranging new Malibu home is in fact movieland itself, where she is sidelined to a stay-at-home wifely role. In this context, it is only unprofessional movie footage per se, home-screened, in contrast to commercial filmmaking, that ends up marking how far her ideals have lapsed.

Scattered Pictures

This beloved 1973 romantic drama is the signal exception to her roving and rifling through comic possibilities during this transitional period. It is a film in which her varied emotive performance, paired with the veteran scene-stealer Robert Redford, fuels audience interest from its lively college-campus start. Thanks to the vivid performances of this star pairing, we're carried across some lesser filler moments, with their uprooting from Manhattan to Malibu, to the equally effective finish at their famous accidental meeting, years and a divorce later, in front of the Plaza hotel, her eyes staring off into the distance (of the past itself, as the score comes up) in their final embrace. But the real title scenes—the marked renditions of "the way we were," not as nostalgic ruminations but as explicit doublings and projections—come earlier, one having been left on the cutting room floor, one on the release print screen after having been recovered within the plot from amateur celluloid memorabilia. Yet these two brief episodes converge on the DVD as a diptych of political commitment and its surrendered energies. Under pressure of this convergence, what comes forward from the Streisand undertext, as so often in the comedies as well, is a compound reference to finding one's place: here, not just in Hollywood, as wife, but within its preformulated screen molds, as star in search of the right narrative hybrids and transformations.

Streisand fought fiercely with the director Sydney Pollack to leave the deleted scene in. Agreeing about its relevance and power, he claimed it slowed the film down too near the end—in its rapid move through the maternity ward separation to the later chance meeting in New York, where Katie has recovered her political fervor and is aggressively leafletting against the bomb. But without the earlier debated scene, Streisand was—still is—right to think that the rather precipitous divorce rendered Katie too much the victim of the both conservative and philandering husband's needs—and his feared industry repercussion from her leftist politics. The scene she fought for was meant, as she saw it, to right the balance—a moment of recognized loss in regard to her own desire in retrospect, a reminder of the sell-out her marriage has become, in part by stifling her protest against the Hollywood witch hunt under McCarthyism. In an earlier and heated confrontation with Redford's frustrated Hubbell, Katie shuts down discussion by insisting on a political predication for the self: "People *are* their principles." If remembered by us later, her emphatic dialogue has foregrounded a verb that puts continued pressure on its own lamented *past* tense in the film's nostalgic title. The deleted (but fortunately not lost) scene has her stopping in her convertible next to a quad at UCLA where, before a clutch of dubious and lightly heckling undergrads ("Who does she think she is?" we overhear as the group disperses), a female student is passionately calling on her peers to support faculty resistance to HUAC in its plan for mobilizing on-campus informants. All Katie can think of, in projection, is *the way she was*. Intercut shots of a tearful recognition (fig. 15) make clear her own realized loss in her married life, implying in her unfought divorce that looking forward as well as back—to the way "we" might (again) be—could constitute an act of recovery.

That UCLA scene is, in effect, the only extended moment in the film in which Katie appears alone (except when famously on the phone to Hubbell)—if at the same time doubled by the undergraduate avatar of her former political self. And it answers to an earlier brief episode, one of the few in which she doesn't appear at all—though ghosted there by her on-screen double, this time by celluloid projection, in yet another version of the title scene. This is a case of others in scrutiny of the recorded *way* she (in particular) *was*. This past is newly appreciated in a home-movie screening where Hubbell and his preppy college pal J. J., along with the latter's wife and former mean-girl co-ed Carol Ann, look back on an early scene, in *our* film, that we may well not have noticed was being filmed by J. J.'s new portable camera. This found footage gives us again Katie on the hustings, a dyed-in-the-wool FDR leftist, slowly galvanizing the student crowd with her appeal to a protest against Franco's violence. We see only the lucid fire of her peroration now, in this home-movie clip—not the way she lost her cool over a nasty pun appearing on the flip side of the five hand-held P-E-A-C-E placards behind her on the outdoor stage: ANY / PIECE / BUT / KATY'S / PIECE. Until she overreacted, she was going strong. She had star power, the representative Hollywood types all now agreed, both magnetic stage (and hidden camera) presence, but, as Hubbell has told her before, she was too serious for the job. In retrospect, J. J. voices the power revealed in his own screen footage: "She was a spellbinder."[2] Adding: "She was really getting to those people. Take a look at some of those faces." We don't see them on the

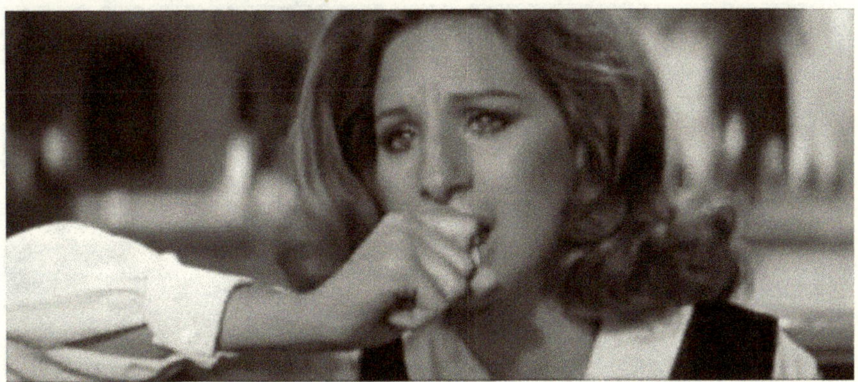

15. Her way lost (*The Way We Were*: cut scene)

screen-within-the-screen, just the three old friends looking on from their shared sofa. We don't know what unlikely panning of the student gathering the low-resolution camera may once have recorded. All we see is a more closely framed black-and-white image of Katie and the mic in medium close-up (fig. 16), intercut with a slow dolly in on Redford's present face—as, by now, the only relevant audience of the way she was.

Two screen rectangles of different ratios here gloss each other: the inner image flanked, in the dark, by figurine lamps with their own arms functionally raised to support bulbs and shades. Katie, instead, brings her own glow. With the print streaked and spackled by an artificial aging (in years before this familiar effect has become an easy Photoshop affordance), the visual logic of the scene, however, is not just a technological regress (about how it was recorded for posterity), nor even an optic metaphor for the degradations of time. What emerges, as if in a Necker effect from its own recession, is an inset framed inference regarding dramaturgy and genre. The effect marks this one plot's distance from the captivating stage presence of a spellbinding microphone star who has (in the present film) submerged her musical and comedy fame in an unwavering seriousness of performance that manages, driving the drama, to work a new spell of its own. The pointed—poignant—difference between our movie and the movie within is, of course, that in the straight dramatic success of this hit film Streisand has expanded and refined her actorly range, while Katie has narrowed her activist one. In losing the battle over the missing scene of Katie's slackened political will, as Streisand never will again in taking more directorial command of her projects, her own self-determination only increased. And there is a nice incidental symmetry to boot, exactly a decade after Katie's later pamphleteering for nuclear disarmament. In mounting a private fundraising protest for Democratic senatorial candidates in back-lash against Reaganite Cold War escalation after the nuclear disaster at Chernobyl,

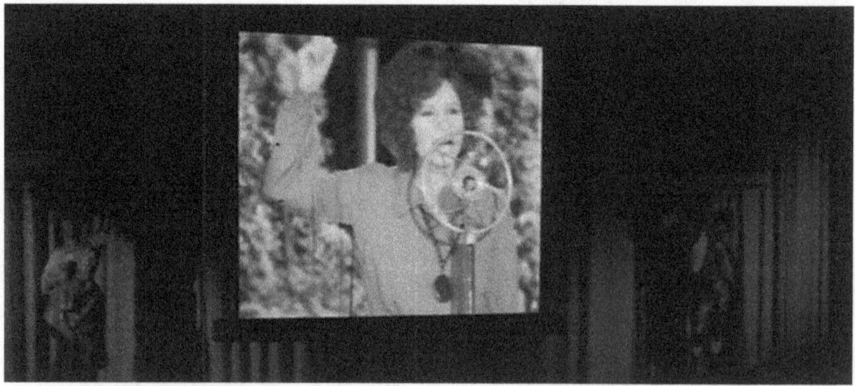

16. The way she was (*The Way We Were*)

Streisand doesn't just deliver the mandatory "The Way We Were" but pairs it, in her famed *One Voice* concert, with Harold Arlen's "A New World" on the way to the FDR-identified "Happy Days Are Here Again" finale. Both in *The Way We Were* and later, Katie's slump helps mark Barbra's rebounds.

For the Love of Pete!

In 1974, as last and least of the minor comedies, and especially so in the immediate wake of the hugely successful *The Way We Were*, comes *For Pete's Sake*, a movie no one could like for long (at most for the first ten or fifteen minutes), let alone revere. If, under the rubric of "Home/Movie," we saw how cinematized inward fantasy was hived off from domesticity as a saving (if dreary) escape valve in *Up the Sandbox*, here, in this joyless farce, a young wife's similarly overstressed role in helping to make Manhattan ends meet has an even bolder recourse to various genre modes of Hollywood production as absurd real-life choices. As if trying to capitalize on the commercial success of *What's Up, Doc?* and its cartoonish buffoonery, this film actually begins with a cartoon. In spare skittish graphics, a busy wife is projected in her daily chores to the accompaniment of Streisand's bouncy title song. Eventually, credits over, the almost abstract female figure approaches her apartment window and the reverse shot, from the view of her husband on his curbside motorcycle, closes in on a no-nonsense short-haired Streisand looking out in live action, bringing the film (we are to think) to whatever comic life it will boast.

From this frame-within-the-frame as at first a cartoon effigy, nothing in the plot—after its funny first few minutes of nosy characters, from loan officer to grocery clerk, urging further austerity on the part of the struggling couple—nothing, not one episode, even begins to let the star escape from the stick-figure role she is stuck with. After mistakenly borrowing from the mob to finance her strapped husband's scheme for getting in on "pork belly futures," Henrietta (the lightly regendered "Henri") is bound up, like some more typical male character on the skids, in a series of Mafia contracts. These propel her, in one different mode of performance after another, from at-home-alone call girl (an allusion to her previous Pussycat, but here in actual near-miss scenes with on-screen clients), through criminal bag-woman in tacky blond wig, to delivery girl for a truck of stolen cattle being smuggled into an undisclosed Brooklyn location. In all this we're watching, perhaps without recognizing it, or at least being meant to, a send-up of versatility itself, however flubbed in each case. As Henri's contract shifts hands, its price always bid up by a thousand bucks, she is cycled through all the genres sensibly closed off to Streisand otherwise, especially mob action flick and western.

The film achieves in this way the reductio ad absurdum of the tacit cinematic pressure points in all these early 1970s films—from the recycled screwball aspirations and *Casablanca* allusion in *What's Up, Doc?* through modal variants of a fantasy and action thriller catalog in *Up the Sandbox* to private film documentation in *The Way We Were* and back to alternating and incoherent genre parameters in the almost self-dismissive title of *For Pete's Sake*. Now, in the last, the reflex pattern finally takes the form of a commercial movie screen, with Henri making the kind of literalized breakthrough Doris might have dreamed of with *Cycle Sluts*. Henri has chased her small herd of bovine stolen goods as they follow their bull into a literal china shop and then, just after, into the back of a movie theater—only for them to charge out from behind the shredded screen in, yes, the middle of the film's own projected stampede down a western main street. The live-action herd is seen snorting up the aisle toward the exit, to the delight of one effusive patron, looking over his shoulder at another: "Now that's what I call real." Hardly. The nub of this particular reflexive satire is the problem with the whole film—and with the starring role. None of it feels the least bit real. But nor is it just a run-through, as with *Up the Sandbox*, of certain diversionary charades in the coils of a routine-routing imagination. This is Henri's only putative world, not some movie-juiced alternate reality. No passing verbal joke can save it. If we are to think that her husband's ultimate success in pork bellies mixes metaphors with his counting on a bull market in commodities—an unsaid cliché awaiting only real cattle on-screen—it's too silly for (even these) words. If there is a sense of "taking the bull by the horns" in Henri's final rodeo marathon through the Brooklyn streets, it has no more narrative traction—or comic kick—than that same bull in the china shop. There is nothing in her role as cattle-rustler, nor as bomb-toting blonde mobster, nor even in the metatheatrics of penniless wife submitted to kinky parts in one role-playing prostitute hook-up after another—nothing in any of this, even as just another breather between serious screen performances, that Streisand can breathe life into. After another merely goofy girl, it is time for a genuinely funny lady. And for songs she can sing.

Act II

CALLING THE SHOTS

A STAR IS CLONED

This chapter's title may sound at first, mistakenly, like a critic's dig about Streisand's controversial remake of the Hollywood warhorse and former Garland starrer—a revisionary take that is almost everywhere, regarding both conception and execution, seriously underrated. Still less is the title a sideswipe at Streisand's late doted-upon dog Sammy (for Samantha)—who toured with her in the early 2000s for an occasional on-stage appearance—before being notoriously survived by two more of herselves via genomic duplication. At stake, rather, when regarding the transitional innovations of *A Star Is Born* on the heels (previously dressier and higher) of *Funny Lady*—at a decisive turn in Streisand's "evolution" as both actor and especially on-screen singer—is the way genealogical as well as genre lineage comes readily to mind. Certainly, in these terms, the notion of cloning is so little a pointed barb that it is meant to point straight to the wellsprings of energy that characterize the inimitable star's persona(e): in precisely the capacious self-multiplication of her performer's gifts—yet with each screen character, at least when the part is right, harboring always the Streisand within. The vacillating comic and romantic genres of the five previous films—sometimes shuffled into either flaccid or antic differentiation from within a single plot, as we've seen—amount to a wager with imposed and artificial variety whose real risks are, in these years, a leveling of the star's embodied difference, the core force of her talent, on behalf of worn but recognizable plot formats. The first two chapters in Act II now mark a course correction that returns her to the on-screen musical on its own redefined terms, the star gradually taking up a position behind the director's lens in what can best be called the cinematographic orchestration of her own songs. And it is a position she retains even when executive-producing the very different stage and screen, concert and dramatic, material brought into comparison in Act III.

It's hard to deny the uniqueness deeply coded in the DNA of Streisand's talent, with its continual dodge of expectations—even from note to note in her vocal delivery. So ingrained is the unflagging expressive variety tapped in her best screen performances that her stardom could be thought "cloned" at a given career turning point only if such a phenomenon is understood as part of the fundamental originality she already constitutes. When the films really work, it is a case, put differently, of talent redoubled. In the second song from *A Star Is Born*, in fact, a variant of this genetic trope caps a list of "I'd likes" that add up to the titular "Everything" for which the singer shamelessly yearns. This includes—if it's not "too much" to ask—the dream of a "perfect twin": an alter ego "who'd go out" exactly when, as the rhyme seals the timing, "I came in," where that latter verb is couched in the lingo of either stage or song entrance as well as genetic duplication. Twinned in the reflection of her own difference, the star would be continually reborn to her own possibility. Such is the sung fantasy. Embedded there in that passing metaphor of tandem manifestations—as if to be actually performed in medley at the end of the film—is that mode of duet-for-one often emerging as a solitary trope for the star's stand-alone talent.

In moving as Streisand did, long deferred, from *Funny Girl* to its eventual sequel *Funny Lady*, and from there, just a year later, to *A Star Is Born*, the identifying talent isn't superficially replicated in the first case, nor wholly reimagined in the second. Rather, across the genealogy of these singing parts, and on the way to *Yentl* (as one can now see in hindsight), Streisand's particular species of emotive genius does seem genetically mutated from within, the stardom adaptively repurposed, the talent not just retooled but deeply renewed. What casual fan, put to the trivia test, might not guess at more than a year's distance between a prewar period piece in a revisited musical comedy vein for *Funny Lady* and the pop-rock epic of *A Star Is Born*, in other words between the soft retro curls of a matured and cynical Fanny Brice and the galvanic frizz penumbra of an eager and unshackled Esther Hoffman? Almost all that unites the two films—about a seasoned Ziegfeld headliner, now strapped for bankrolling in the Depression, and the lead singer of a post-1960s club act rocketing to arena, LP, and TV fame—is the widely undervalued originality of Streisand's contribution to each: a new and very funny plumbing of star hauteur in the one, a wholesale rethinking of her screen vocals for the other. Yet it is this rapid transition between these adjacent screen narratives that amounts to the bold cloning of Streisand's screen dominance in the musical genre. It awaits for Yentl—for *Yentl* the film, that is, along with its heroine—to survive erotic setback in driving for the expanded ringing horizon of other desires. In this cloning of the star as a source of incarnate vocal invention, marked in part by her passing in and out of cross-gender trappings in each of the three films, we see how the shifting quotients of difference itself—manifested as the stamp of creative fecundity—are released as never before.

So 1975 first. In that year's answering bookend to *Funny Girl*—that beloved film where it was mostly the musical numbers, and an occasional comic one-liner, that count in one's memory—who could have expected the different weighting of song and script in the sequel? The surprise is definitive. The sharply played episodes of testy dialogue *between* brand-new Kander and Ebb numbers (following their lauded success with the film version of *Cabaret* three years before) often ask as much of Streisand as do the composers' breakout song solos. One proof of this surprise is the widespread failure to notice, in many a cursory review, the wit and bite of precisely these dialogue encounters—which is what drew Streisand, at first dragging and kicking at the idea of a sequel, to the script. As foil to the imperious new Fanny, James Caan is quick and amusing in the loud, obnoxious bits, and in between as the Jewish schmoozer and instinctive con artist—although to the disappointed lover he brings only a kind of limp petulance and no chemistry. Omar Sharif is so unnervingly aged, and so wrong for the posturing vanity he must display, that we see through him long before Fanny does. Besides Streisand, only Roddy McDowell is perfectly cast as star minion: all-purpose dressy factotum and Nick-infatuated gay confidant. He has replaced the self-effacing Eddy from Keeney's in *Funny Girl* so as to stand in, at the same time, for the gay following that has congregated around Streisand in the years since. Snippy rather than witty in himself, he is the mere sounding board for Fanny's irony, an audience of one for her privately enacted star turns. And more importantly, the embodiment of every fan's dreams: there at various rehearsals and recording sessions, listening in, watching it happen, in on the act. Yet the music he's often privileged to superintend up close, silent like the onlooking audience he embodies, is a good deal more uneven in shape than was the tested Broadway score for *Funny Girl.*

The film's musical-comedy dimension opens cleverly with the Yiddish shtick of "I've Got a Blind Date," an aptly imagined signature number in the Fanny Brice mode—and in an overt ethnic register new to Streisand, one she was eager to try out. But once Fanny meets James Caan as Billy Rose, and signs on in desperation as headliner for his dubious new ensemble spectacle, the character begins digging in her heels against his vulgar overproduction. Definitive here is the "five and ten cent store" number, where Streisand, in white male tuxedo, celebrating "his" titular "Million Dollar Baby," ends up coughing out the lyric in mockery of the smoking and crumbling cheapjack set. So far so good, by way of send-up. The seasoned Ziegfeld star, tastefully knowing about production, is meant to be always right. But the ensuing comic battle between her and Billy—engrossing enough in the self-sabotaging let's-put-on-a-show format—is meant ultimately to be redeemed by a seriously mounted and supposedly rousing showstopper, "It's Gonna Be a Great Day," an original Billy Rose hit. Yet in the film's treatment, this number is in its own right as overproduced, in its glitzy deco chic, as are the rest of the boffo bits—and far less ingratiating, given the racist exoticism of its White Goddess aura, with Black slaves dancing in celebration of Streisand's biblical trumpet summons. This is a pity, given that the song's peak is so quintessentially Streisand in its prolongation—"Angels in the sky-y-y-y"—that it locates them as in fact "sky-h-i-i-i-gh." Despite the deco pizzazz of her costuming, here is one of the very rare moments in Streisand's career where a song performance is better listened to than watched. Another such, more damaging yet to the arc of this ironic romance, soon follows.

That big "Great Day" number is only meant to be the apogee of the comic plot's show-on-the-road adjustments, high point of "Crazy Quilt," not *Funny Lady*. In a more pivotal letdown, the encompassing film founders on the sluggish visual pacing of its own *offstage* big number, the Kander and Ebb "Let's Hear It for Me"—after its promising start in Fanny's charging down the hotel hall after a final literal kiss-off of Nick Arnstein in his stolid, tedious vanity. With the heroine's spirited commitment to reuniting with her waiting husband, though via a lyric couched in the vocabulary of defiant self-assertion, the number comes off as a contrived allusion to—and, as filmed, a pale recollection of—the legendary "Don't Rain on My Parade" from *Funny Girl*. That number's upbeat juggernaut of romantic commitment, propelling Fanny from speeding train, through taxi, to horn-blaring tugboat, is replaced now with a cautiously driven Rolls Royce convertible taking her from the Malibu coast to the nearest airport for a slowly launched biplane flight back to Billy at last. At last but too late. The letdown en route isn't the song's fault—or the singer's. The lyrics are expert and ironically pertinent in their every turn of diva revival. The figurative comeback number begins with a lead-in talky bridge, where, still on exit from Nick and her hotel room, Fanny, strutting her stuff toward the camera, delights in being for once the one who "walked out." No problem yet. Ever since Streisand running from the Ziegfeld troupe after Nick's boat to Europe, there is never anything better in the dramaturgy of her song staging (as *Hello, Dolly!* showed again, and *Yentl* will remember) than seeing the singer emoting in full stride, in railroad stations or old-fashioned railroad cars themselves, Manhattan walking paths, hotel corridors, or Central European parks.

The lyric soon arrives at the inveterate Streisand onomatopoeia for the song's upsurge at "Sou-OW-ow-und the trombones," that first single word not just sounded out but bursting out of its own monosyllabic borders. This self-achieved call to big-band confidence is followed by the metatheatrical lines about a renewed marital self still envisaged as a star, but this time in her own life, "strictly SRO." As a lyric idea, and certainly in its unhedged delivery, it is the perfect token of fame's entrenched vanity—even as it explicitly updates the lead-in to the "Don't Rain on My Parade" number, triggered there by her insistence on the phone to Ziegfeld about needing a "personal life too," since "you can't take an audience home with you." By the time of the sequel, Fanny has become her own audience, and you can hear Streisand savoring every double-edged line of the lyric, its vanity riding for a fall. One's regret over the pealing delivery of this "Let's Hear It for Me" appeal, a would-be amorous bounce-back still wryly phrased in terms of star chutzpah, is that the drag of its montage pacing makes its aptness feel half-hearted.

The sluggish climactic "staging" of this promising Kander and Ebb number was widely recognized to let Streisand's vocal gusto down. But reviews were surprisingly deaf to her own machine-gun timing of the ironic dialogue in a script by the rare (in the period) female scenarist—and notoriously stinging wit—Jay Presson Allen, fresh from *Cabaret* and sharing screenplay credit with Arnold Schulman. It was a script that appealed to Streisand for its acerbic break from the Fanny of *Funny Girl*, and that winningly paces her through three early meetings (hardly "cute," but very funny) with showman and songwriter Rose. She first encounters him when he is characteristically showing off his skills of memory in Bernard Baruch's office, where she has come to check off her Depression stock losses—with Billy's shorthand allowing him to deliver back her every sarcastic remark, as well as price quote, in exactly her dismissive cadences. With no interest in any further connection, and no knowledge of his theatrical ambitions, her ironic lapse into talent-scout lingo is nonetheless symptomatic: "There's an act in there somewhere" (spoken almost under her breath, as so many of her reactions are, to her gay sidekick Bobby).

In *Funny Girl*, the closest we come to genuine "biography" is one shot of Fanny in her Baby Snooks outfit, from Brice's most famous bit. Mostly the performance was just Streisand as Barbra. It was the chance for another "take" on the character that finally convinced Streisand to accept the later *Funny Lady* role: to venture a part, other and tougher, and openly ethnic in its stage numbers, that wasn't just a retread of Barbra incarnate.[1] What seems to have taken critics by surprise, less so fascinated audiences, is that Streisand in the sequel is indeed playing an aging stage and radio star quite different from her own persona. The script, the line readings, the accent and timing: all are geared, though fictionalized through and through, not to an older Barbra but to an imagined older Fanny, born Fania Borach: not just a Jewish comedienne but a sharp-tongued Jewish wit, a funny lady in that particular sense—always ready with an edgy comeback. Yet what happens in the process is a curious circling back through the contours of Streisand's own stardom in this Brice role, indeed her own doubleness. A familiar oscillation persists: romantic versus street smart, stylish but down-to-earth, as these incompatibles get off-loaded—or further cloned—onto the two men in her life: the husbands she thinks back on, separately, in the montage sequences that bookend the film: first Nick alongside her in clips from *Funny Girl*, then Billy displacing him in the present film. The contrast in male alternatives isn't subtle: Arnstein the refined Jewish gambler from the Upper East Side, now a jet-setting, polo-playing lothario from Beverly Hills, versus Rose the sloppy, vulgar hustler, tasteless even in his moneymaking instincts. His garish pajamas violate their train-compartment honeymoon, while in Fanny's final rejection of Nick, after he has remarried for money, she realizes that she had fallen, in the first place, for his designer toothbrush set—and, more to the point of contrast, in love mostly with his delicately monogrammed pajamas. But this collision between refinement and chutzpah, Arnstein and Rose, is the star's own cultivated dialectic, of course, Barbra's more than Fanny's. It involves the one-of-a-kind Jewish superstar (but unlike Brice, with only the first name changed) who has—from her first low-rent club dates, maximizing her finds as a thrift-shop maven—invented a new kind of stylistic magnetism by transfiguring the everyday. And then by layering on the studied glamour ever after.

The script knows this too, since it has Billy shoot back—to Fanny's honeymoon train car diatribe against his bad taste in pajamas, in their most violent marital spat—by asking where in the world his fast-talking, no-nonsense New York City bride "gets off" (both senses potentially) reading French fashion magazines. We know the answer—even without having seen a famous Paris photograph of Streisand, in her own self-designed leopard jacket and hat, man's tie included, sitting alert in the front row at a Chanel show in 1966: unapologetic arriviste with her own style to show for itself. Now lavished with tasteful finery in *Funny Lady*—off stage and on—by designer Bob Mackie (previously famous for Cher's svelte glitz), even in this film, however, she finds an opening to play against type. She does so on the way to her recurrent unisex fashion in *A Star Is Born.* Varying the quick-change finery of her low-cut fashion-plate out-fits, twice Fanny appears offstage before Billy frocked in dressy men's suit jackets and hats: beginning with the close-up on her in a gray felt fedora for the gripping "More than You Know" run-through in the recording studio. Then later there is a yet more mannish navy-blue suit with snappy tie—when she intercepts Billy, unannounced, as he seems about to plunge into an affair with his new swimming star. The point of the cross-dressing is never castration, just refused subservience. But they still can't make their marriage work. As she puts it, in theatrical metaphor, "My timing was always off with you, Billy." And with no vocal timing at that.

"A Perfect Duet"

Fanny and Billy never really sing together, except under each other's radar in the con-trapuntal "monologues" of "It's Only a Paper Moon / I Like Him / I Like Her." By genre format, in musical comedy lives meld in song. But in the "backstage" variant, singing isn't just a mode of being but of career, a gesture of performance as well as self-expression. They once laugh at themselves in the mirror after dousing each other with face powder, but other moments of mirror reflection frame a different picture. To begin with, later in the same dressing room, Fanny, having spotted the wedding ring on Nick's finger in an unexpected visit, moves immediately toward her makeup table to peer at his mere (and receding) image, rather than at the man himself. The room's large semicircular mirror soon frames the gloomy goodbye kiss on the cheek in his guilty exit, all at one remove from direct eye contact. As at the end of *Funny Girl*, just before he leaves the dressing room—and leaves her to the irony of the "My Man" number—the framing is emblematic. In both films, there is no looking at her offstage losses except through the always waiting—and hardly protective—panes of her stardom.

Whereas the fracturing triptych mirror from *Funny Girl* had its way of suggesting the woman and the star at odds with each other, here, at Nick's exit, the single reflection of the arched mirror would show to the twice-deserted Fanny, were she to look at herself rather than her departing hope, only stardom's unified chilling surface. And we don't need to see this for ourselves any longer: just watch her looking from here out in a smoldering scene of self-disillusion. At this withering pivot point, the film waxes ferocious in the tracking of her despair, where the cosmetic mirror frame, no reflection now necessary, will delimit otherwise the constriction of her world. The ensuing scene, later on this bleak opening night of her new show, finds Fanny, slumped despondent and more sarcastic than ever, in front of a fancy console Victrola, with a bow around it, in which her new two-sided hit came wrapped by the record company. This is the pressing finally achieved from the truncated rehearsal version we've seen in the recording studio, where Fanny in high spirits gulps in wide-eyed exaggerated chagrin at a slightly off-key note (fig. 17). The redone and finished product has reached her just

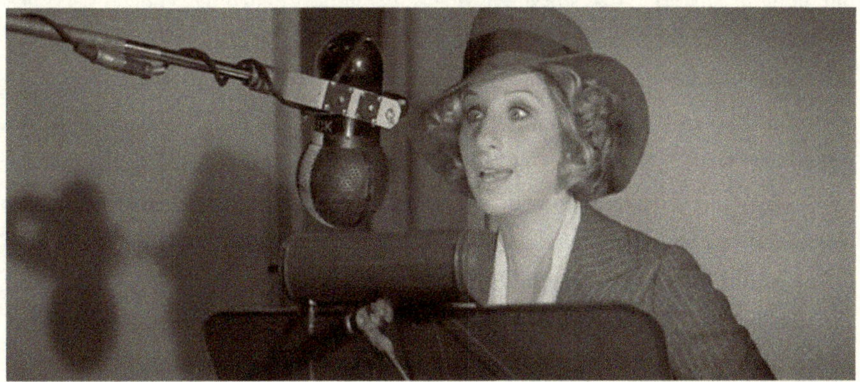

17. "Oh how I'd cry" (*Funny Lady*: "More than You Know")

before the news from Nick about his marriage, and, far from recovered, she tells Bobby and her maid to go along ahead of her to the opening night party. When they've left her to the sound of her own recorded voice, right when the song swells across the line at which its recording session broke off earlier—"Oh how Iiiii'd cry" (if her man ever "sai-eh-eh-edd goodby-eye-i-i")—she scrapes the needle in disgust across it ("Why don't you just shut up!") and flips to the upbeat B side.

It is only here that we can finally appreciate the structuring halves (not sides) of this recording, first executed in vivid audiophile close-ups in the studio. On the one hand, there was the electric moment of production intercut between Fanny's explor-atory delivery of Billy's lyrics and its vinyl tracks being laid down in close-up under a dusting brush—where, all the while, we thrill to its optical sound recording passed out through high-powered speakers into the movie auditorium. On the other hand, heard later—in this deferred completion of the song, from the actual impressed disc—is the ambient sound of its old-fashioned tinny playback in her suddenly oppressive dressing room. Until she can bear its romantic blather no longer—and snuffs out the torch song with an effacing needle this time, rather than the originally recording one. But the flip side of the studio-gifted single is even less consoling, motivating an even more aggressive recoil. There is no prose description of what follows that can capture the scene's laconic, then frenetic, irruption, where Kander and Ebb outdo themselves in fiercely dramatic song-writing—and Streisand in the kind of joyless gravelly rage she no doubt wanted to revive for a number like "Rose's Turn" in the failed *Gypsy* project forty years later.

Yet composers and star are not the only heroes of this sequence. Beginning here is a five-minute sustained triumph of cinematography by maestro James Wong Howe, in this his last (and tenth Oscar-nominated) film. Streisand is at first seen sitting again in front of the arched vanity mirror, punctuated by warm cosmetic light globes spaced out along its curvature—as she shreds one of her almost matching yellow roses (Nick yet again) in an accelerated he-loves-me-he-loves-me-not charade, twirling the blos-som faster and faster as she mutilates it. After the chirpy self-congratulations of the recorded ditty in the background, "How Lucky Can You Get?"—rhyming the re-peated title word "get" at one point with its persona as "personal pet" of the one she loves—the camera begins gliding up and around the mirroring arch, timed to the line about circling the "globe" with the singer's "circle" of friends. It is at this point that Fanny begins humming along snidely through her just-lit cigarette. And then, after the camera has completed in effect its 180-degree arc going nowhere, it follows her toward a champagne bucket for her quick hit. There it captures her twice: in person but also reflected in a narrow and slightly fogged rectangular mirror—near which she

is standing, oblivious for once to the reflection (blurred around the eyes themselves)—
when she breaks out, in a dissonant minor key, to over-voice the song's further infuriating rhyme ("get . . . pet") in "We're a perfect duet!" It is a finely compact moment:
the star singing against her own recording in the absence of the celebrated "one that I
love." With only the viewer made privy to the optic duplication—and psychic split—of
her image (fig. 18). Between singer and narrow reflection is generated an inner and
reverse depth of field, a clouded one at that, to match the sarcasm of her own vocal
doubling—Fanny bleating out her line without being aware of her duet "shadow" in
the mirror. But a more resonant deep focus is about to explode the scene.

A painfully disappointed Fanny is seen shutting off the lights in (and on) that sad
mirrored chamber of cosmetic presence, then moving out, the record still droning
perkily away, onto a darkened and empty opening-night stage. She is soon accompanied by the overlaid murmur of a dragging percussive thud on the record's stuck
groove—"how luck, how luck, how luck"—rubbing in the galling syllable. This hurdle
is overtaken by eerie dissonant strings as a bridge to the star's sour strutting of her
stuff—as she moves from the back of the stage toward the vacant orchestra pit, having
taken over the lyric in her own bitter delivery with a travesty of the song's insipid bliss.
Continuing the cinematic motif of circularity even in this dogged diagonal progress,
with one swat she sends a hanging security-light into a spin that lasts almost until the
end of the song. In the entropy of this rotary motion, neither the stark naked bulb nor
its centripetal trajectory serves to figure, let alone illuminate, the larger "globe" of the
vain singer's vaunted international celebrity—but only to cast a cold light on Fanny's
narrow stage world. With the song soon over, and the star storming off through the
exit door, the light fixture is slammed again into its pointless tapering spiral—not
unlike the graphic pattern on the deco screen [below] when the record first started

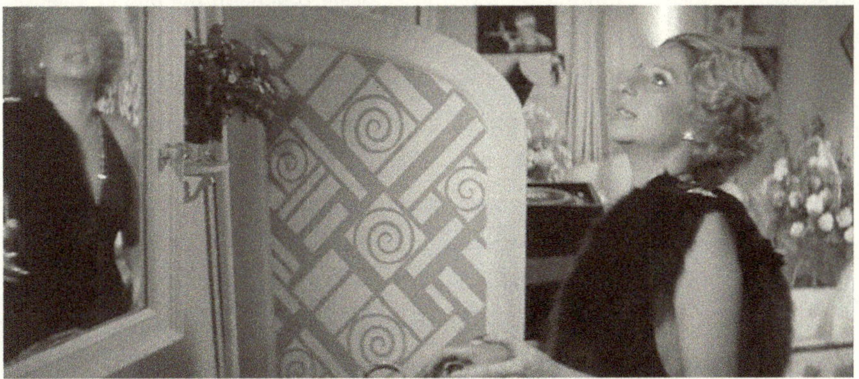

18. Mirroring's "perfect duet" (*Funny Lady*: "How Lucky Can You Get?")

spinning out its luckier-than-thou bluster. But in between these two effects of raw diegetic light, Streisand as Fanny has gone to the control board and flooded the stage with colored spots, the snarl of her irony gravitating toward the hot-pink glow, stage front, for the song's "bed of roses" contrast to her present emotional state. And as she stalks toward the camera in this deep-focus mapping of her grudging vocal terrain and its escalating ferocity, with her protective boa over her arm rather than around her shoulders, her painful self-exposure renders her even more naked than does her backless décolleté.

Fanny soon regurgitates the previous film's opening (mirror) line with a "Hey there, gorgeous," doing so in building toward a final rhyme of "get" with the "haven't run into him yet" of any man who would leave her. With Nick's second exit, first from one marriage and now into another, what's she's actually run into is her own emotional dead end. All that's left is for the world-weary rather than globe-trotting belter's sarcasm to strike out against the dim-witted giddy optimism of the recorded song, turning the now spat-out acid of her "gee, whiz, wow" from an overflow of high spirits on vinyl to a nauseating lie stuck in the artist's own craw. In what we might call the acoustic mirror of the song's climax, and its phonic overlay, we can chart again the granular contour of Streisand's voice—here as sheer revolted prolongation, as of course only she can keep the sounded pain still syllabic. Listen as she drags the stentorian "wow" halfway toward a sheer scream at the final return to a stuck-groove repetition: that roaring inner howl at "*How* lucky, *how* lucky can you geheheht?" In the power of her vocals, and with the focal length of Howe's camerawork measuring the depth of her isolation, Streisand has filled the empty stage with desolation personified.

Whereas Pauline Kael once feared that Hollywood would fail in finding musical roles for this unique singing actress, who performs character through music, in response to *Funny Lady* the testy critic deserts just such a continued effort on the star's own part in a blanket and tone-deaf dismissal of her singing in the film as a whole. No distinction is made between numbers: "Streisand is in beautiful voice, and her singing is terrific—too terrific. It's no longer singing, it's something else—that strident over-dramatization that turns a song into a big number."[2] No immediate examples are given, though implicitly included here would be the review's justified opening regret over the "Great Day" staging, that diegetic showstopper whose grandiosity stops the film's credible comedy dead in its audiovisual tracks. But the critic's contempt is more sweeping. Kael also, as we later find, has in mind the motivated stridency of "How Lucky Can You Get?" with her complaint about the voice's icy sheen, so that her missing the point seems all the more glaring in the lament that "attention is directed away from the music and onto the star's feat in charging it with false energy. Streisand is out to knock you cold, and you get cold, all right" (112). Certainly this is the dramatic import of her role as the jaded Fanny: the lurking chill at the heart of the character's ego, disappointment, and solitude, now turning shrill in privately vented distress, now arch and snarky in defensive dialogue encounters.

Kael, though at first Streisand's most passionate champion, picks up on Fanny's line about the marriage to Billy ("I fell in like with him") to deliver her own sea change of heart, wholly subsuming the caustic role into the star herself: "I fell out of like with Barbra Streisand" (118). The singing star's attempt to imagine a Fanny beyond her own contemporary persona as the world's most ingratiating funny girl is a performative effort that repulses Kael in page after page of diatribe, all under a title, "Talent Isn't Enough," that seems deliberately echoing the "talent is beauty" keynote of her "Bravo!" review of *Funny Girl*. "Streisand's performance is like the most spectacular, hard-edged female impersonator's imitation of Barbra Streisand" (112)—including in what she characteristically derides, in this almost luridly gay-baiting review, as the "fag-hag" style of "How Lucky Can You Get?" (114). Along with passing snide sideswipes at the reactions and remarks of "young men" in the audience, such a negative gay touchstone becomes a motif of Kael's infamous screed, with costume changes claimed to resemble those not of a glamorous star but of a "transvestite" (115). And on the knockout punches of the singing, there is the ultimate phobic inference of gay bad taste, an attraction to schlock and camp alike, in Kael's hyperbolic charge of niche marketing: "When you hear Streisand shout 'Come on, kids, let's hear it for me!' you know damned well who the kids are: the song is destined to be juke-box favorite in every gay bar in the world" (115). Even while Kael's failure to distinguish star from character is surprising in itself, and certainly distracting in critical terms, the whole phobically presumed closed-circuit of a gay adulation—and parody—looped into Streisand's stardom has never had a more symptomatic outbreak. What Kael goes blind to, deaf to, is the exacting effort of the actor and singer—with no trace of Barbra left (except for interludes of romantic pleading)—in imagining the downside of an ascendancy like Streisand's own, including in part the risks of repetition, the very rut of self-imitation.

Going Solo

Linked to the smoldering vocal sneer of "How Lucky Can You Get?" is an easily forgotten finishing touch to the purgative fury of this "perfect duet" with self, not even secured by its obvious allusion to a comparable debut moment. What in *Funny Girl* first lifted Fanny's private drive to public notice—in a similar on-stage pseudo-private soliloquy ("I'm the Greatest Star")—here testifies to a personal implosion over Nick that leaves Billy's erotic interest nipped in the bud. The residual moment is only briefly glimpsed at that, after the savage last strokes of "How Lucky Can You Get?" Just as a young Fanny was watched unawares from a shadowy corner of the empty daytime music hall by her eventual friend Eddy (the gay Bobby's neutral predecessor as talent aficionado) in the supposedly unseen self-affirmation of the "Greatest Star" number, so she is under surveillance here as well. This time the now-established star's contempt for a mythologized limelight, in the vacuum of her personal fantasy man, has been watched from a side aisle of the orchestra by Billy, realizing all too well what has sprung her anguish. And the sting of recognition has left its lasting mark. It's what he means when, artificially grayed like Fanny in a much later reunion, he sings a few bars of his hit "Me and My Shadow" to her in the closing scene. He does so before explaining that Nick was the inspiration for that lyric, the unshakeable hovering rival. In this final gesture toward a strictly professional reunion, Billy has visited Fanny in L.A. years later, not for another try as a couple but—true to the real zing of their partnering—for another big stage extravaganza. She promises to think it over, and the film ends with an image less of consideration than—completing its pattern of mirroring across the plot—of pure inward reflection: all singing for the first time (with anticipations of *Yentl*) gone inward to reflective monologue in front of her entry-hall mirror.

Before she sees him to the door, Fanny and Billy have echoed each other's lines in relaxed, self-mocking ethnic cadences, laughed at themselves and each other again, and on exit he barters genially over the "billing" she hasn't cottoned too: "Rose and Brice, Brice and Rose, Rose and Brice, whatever." After his exit line's "Make it Yes" off-screen, she gazes contemplatively for a long moment into her empty living room before (and then after) turning off the light—staring as if into something more metaphoric about what has always furnished her world. Shades—and shadows—of the dressing-room lights-out before the vacant bravado and unprocessed loss of "How Lucky Can You Get?" The most ironic line in that number, certainly in regard to its tone of toxically repressed lament, was that "You can spare me the blues," since "I don't sing in that key." Every feeling, every mood, in Streisand's voice, does indeed have a key, and here at the end the etymological conjunction of melody and its mellowing comes again to mind. This low-wick finale is certainly "no fun," but what cinematography and score collaborate to figure is hindsight as insight. The camera finally gentles in on a gargantuan widescreen close-up of Fanny's eyes, reflecting pinpoint star-shaped highlights—and this at the same scale that opened the film with the opening of those same eyes upon an inner *Funny Girl* montage. But this last frame in *Funny Lady* has been preceded and rooted by three intercut shots of Fanny's underlit image already internally contained in that large hall mirror, with stage lights and lens flares gradually animating the frame in the triggering of key flashbacks from this sequel, memory flashes set now to music, all disappointment subsumed to a slower, less brassy reprise of "Let's Hear It for Me." At this serene plateau of a no-longer hungry career, the mirror is all rear-view.

Sequel/Equal: Queen to Be

In briefly refreshing one's presumed memories of *Funny Girl*, song by song in their solo variations, I had wanted, in chapter 2, mainly to stress the successful template—in the "backstage musical" tradition—that Streisand later returns to, in ironic dismantlement, in *Funny Lady* and then purifies further, under her own control of the musical numbers, in *A Star Is Born*. In this new pop-rock mode, all singing is now either transacted in tentative half measures between the singer-songwriter couple in laid-back romantic episodes—feeling out melody, lyrics, and themselves together—or performed separately either in the recording booth (a very one-sided duet, to be sure, in Streisand's near-solo on "Evergreen") or in separate career trajectories on stage. This is the film's innovation and its liability at once: to concentrate music as live-miked performance, and thus, in giving its stage presence over mostly to Streisand—here in a realist mode later superseded by *Yentl*'s suffusing interior monologues—inevitably to downplay narrative development as a kind of filler between concert footage. But what a recompense for paltry dialogue: the live recording (pioneered for the last number of *Funny Girl* but never previously sustained across the whole course of a big-screen musical) filling the theater as never before, with this the first film to avail itself of the newly invented system of Dolby Stereo. The resulting impact contributes to inverting rather than just revising backstage genre conventions, turning story inside out to a punctuating breather between numbers. But numbers sequenced in a melodrama all their own.

As the film opens, Esther Hoffman is a small-time club singer at a modest roadhouse, fronting a trio with two Black backup singers, a group called, yes, "The Oreos." We learn as much, by an in-house male-voiced introduction, just as a fading hard-rock legend, fresh from a stoned, barely phoned-in concert, quite literally stumbles upon her act. This is a two-song set to which the viewer is also treated in its overtly paired feminist gestures, satiric and aspirational by turns: the asserted right of the woman to want anything and "Everything," preceded by a song registering her defiance of the man who would dare get in her way. That opener is a complicated patter song by Rupert Holmes called "Queen Bee," stressing the woman's "sting" from Nefertiti to Cleopatra and beyond. Its flaunted desire for the expansion of an intrinsic female power is couched as well, via an in-joke regarding Streisand's two sequential Funny Women, as the dream that someone would "write me a sequel," or in other rhyming words, "give me an equal." The rest of the song, however, is steeped less in cinematic self-reference than in a feminist verve. Whereas "men got the muscle," it's the "ladies got the hustle." And we're about to get a case in point.

When the burnt-out John Norman Howard—after entering the bar, only to be immediately besieged by fans, and thus distracting from Esther's song—is shown a table down front, he only makes things worse by bickering with the waitress over keeping his own paper-bagged bottle at the table. Esther's frustrated response—coinciding with the closing line of "Queen Bee" about giving the man the final "lovin' sting—Zap!"—is to step off the modest stage and shove the microphone straight into his drunken face in time for his pathetic grievance to the waitress: "What are you gonna do with my bottle?" All Esther needs to add is that "You're blowin' my act." On either side of that ad-libbed line, in these first two songs, is unfolded in embryo (no deference to men; no ceiling to female need in "Everything") almost the whole agenda of the film's programmatic 1970s feminism. Here and throughout, it is the musical numbers that do the dramatic heavy lifting, both by design and often by default, given a certain slackness in early repartee as well as in later pained dialogue.

Not exactly meet-cute, this collision of the principals. But the exploratory small talk and eventual candlelit sex to follow fill in that gap. After spoiling her act, the rock legend tries to join it, one on one. Spontaneous music-making soon becomes the medium of their connection in a shared number, with John Norman extemporizing lyrics to her piano tune. For the next song, we see them in the recording booth, still in character as performers, for what seems like a test run of the film's #1 hit "Evergreen," goofing off in the half-hearted effort to turn the mezzo aria into a duet. And from there we jump-cut to the heroine's second on-stage appearance, Esther forcibly thrust into the spotlight by John Norman at a benefit concert he can barely drag himself through. The number the band has up its practiced sleeve is again a feminist rallying cry to which the audience slowly warms as her own vocals heat up. The film's true drama only gains traction in these musical segments—less interludes than tethers—because singing is what Esther and John Norman have, first in common, then (given her surging career) coming between them. The mere over-scoring of the eventual marriage and honeymoon montage is without interest, its non-vocal music too impersonal to count as anything but the arpeggios of an amorous dream-come-true. All the couple's relevant music, and certainly all their singing, is on camera and often in company, if never as full duets. This is how far Streisand's instincts have come since the vestiges of musical comedy in *Funny Lady*, and how far they will go in another considered direction with *Yentl* seven years later. If you're going to sing in a pop-rock musical you'd better be a singer. Or otherwise song must be completely reconfigured, as in *Yentl*, to figure something else.

In *A Star Is Born*, the problem comes in trying to integrate the at once buoyant and aggressive feminism of certain big numbers not just with the compensatory love songs but with the first rom-com, then melodramatic, dialogue in between. Joan Didion and John Gregory Dunne, responsible for the script, did not serve Streisand as well as did her songwriter collaborators, since neither lead character comes across with much personality—except their own imported and quite different Hollywood charisma. Their erotic chemistry is more than persuasive, but their musical styles and vocal ranges are too disparate for any vocal catalyst to emerge in actual performance, and no dialogue really galvanizes their bond. Certain genre conventions remain hampering, as well, for the actual sound design and its editing. Oddly enough, the film runs momentarily aground when it tries departing from realism with even the least little segue of "internalized music." The audience reaction was odd but telling enough to note in a review of mine at the time—which is why I remember it here. Before their first love scene, Esther is playing a tune on John Norman's piano, for which he is testing out some impromptu lyrics—even though she's doubted it could ever be a song, since (self-challenge in the making) "no one could sing that high." This extemporizing is to bloom fully as the song "Lost Inside of You" (cowritten by Streisand and Leon Russell)—and is being tried out here well before John Norman seeks suicidal relief with its album version at full volume on the last track ever of his car stereo. In embryo, this early tentative duet between instruments, piano and voice, is an intimate partnering that fades over into sex after he has gotten caught up twice on his falsetto improvisation of the double entendre in "till I came . . . inside your life." Through their embarrassed laughter, Esther is touched by the music and the man both—and lifts her own hands from the keys to reciprocate the gift of his lyrics, to cup and caress his face, as she will do again in leaning over his corpse. Here's where a musical's received conventions can trip themselves up in a period of genre flux. After a brief moment, the keyboard sound starts up again—and the audience titters as if it were suddenly a player piano. Popular response, at least every time I saw the film, was collectively allergic to this hoary liberty: the well-legislated shift from diegetic sound to the track alone. It seemed to me at the time a surprising, almost daft, reaction, but a litmus test nonetheless. So clearly has this film been cemented in the realist tenets of a backstage or home-studio genre that it has surrendered even normal screen leeway and poetic license.

In any case, the intimacy figured there between the couple—and the internalized blend of their music—can't last, since what John Norman thrills to in Esther's voice is what quickly drives a wedge between them as his career continues to tank. The downward spiral climaxes in his stoned disruption of her Grammy acceptance speech, where he stumbles to the podium insisting that she has no one to thank (but herself) for her success, and where she whispers this time, varying the personal pronoun in her long-ago first line to him: "You're blowin' *your* act." After his subsequent brawl on the stairs with an aggressive DJ, when Esther drags her coke-addled husband into a nearby bathroom, we see the two of them reflected in the wall of mirrors above the sinks. But varying the long-standing motif in Streisand's films, soon to be ramified further in *Yentl*, it is only John Norman—in this long-held two-shot—who is inspecting his own reflection, looking into what he's become, while she searches his face, not hers in the mirror, for some hint of what's wasting him. For once it is not the heroine's own image, as rising star or otherwise, that focuses her anxiety. And yet if she looked sideways at her own reflection she might get some answer to her point-blank question about "what's wrong with you?"

One answer is of course that their "acts," whether "blown" or the opposite, are quite separate—and thus in their own way narratively divisive. Barely in the role of Esther at all, Streisand is out there on her own in the main performance numbers, carrying the show on its feminist tide as well as on the lift and punch of her own vocals. And in service to this, in what amounts to her unheralded debut as virtual co-director, she is aptly and amply credited in the end-titles, not just with costumes sourced from her own closet but with the design and execution of the "musical concepts"—all of which are indeed tightly conceptual (and certainly tailor-made). But one danger of her take on 1970s feminism—well worth running, of course, but tricky in the particular male-effacing storyline of this inherited plot—might make the suspenders and pants of the opening numbers with the Oreos, or the later-on stage pant suits, seem an unabashed castrating force in the diminishment of her undeserving and self-indulgent man in his own perpetual bronze-chested décolleté.

Hardly the case here, though. The real narrative trouble—thanks to the script, in a dialogue often rather shapeless in its play between cutesy and confrontational—is that Esther is asked to wax too softly nurturing and maternal in order to shelter Kristofferson's feckless John Norman: a minted Barbra persona more down-home and unaffected than a hip divorced Esther as L.A. singer-songwriter might be expected to display. In terms of star aura or residue, there is only a brief and oblique ethnic evocation, immediately deflected, when, well into their early exchanges, John Norman (he of the fussy two first names) finally asks her name—and immediately queries "Hoffman?" Not for the extra Jewish signaling (beyond the name Esther to begin with), nor for its less than fast-trackable stage oomph, but because, amid all the groupies, she's the only woman he's met in a long time, as he explains, who has had a last name at all. In these early scenes, one of the most credible lines is left on the cutting room floor along with her guitar strumming of "Evergreen" (discussed in chapter 1). The telltale lack of calluses on Esther's (let alone Streisand's) fingers, almost an in-joke in itself, opens the script to one of its definitive switch points between musical and erotic drive: springing the wasted rocker's sense that his role—both as guitar coach and would-be troubled lover ("We'll have to do something about that")—is inevitably to harden her for the plot ahead.

The Woman from the Moon

But first, he would be her proud Svengali. Though Esther is dressed just for bystanding in a gray flannel suit, John Norman sends her out alone to the auditorium stage after his own botched star billing, and soon surprises her with her backup singers joining in on a line about the "little sister" to whom the feminist verses are directed. This first song the band has ready is the rousing anthem "The Woman in the Moon," where the hairdo as well as the suit, wild curls against tailored lines, makes a combined statement about a force of nature and its formal constraints in the belter's art, the curls a burst of sheer assertion even before they become a star corona and (later yet) a crown of thorns. When not performing, just recording, the curls are tucked in, the effect softened, for the "Evergreen" number, but it is in immediate jump cut from that elating studio session that we arrive at her unwilling shove into the limelight—and the backlight—with the bold halo offering an apt aura for the lunar lyric as well as the stellar performance.

With the star-in-the-making being stricken with nerves at first, this onset of a public triumph recalls the early tense moves of the "I'd Rather Be Blue" launch from *Funny Girl* (fig. 19). Like Fanny, Esther shyly faces the audience and ekes out a few hesitant notes—with the difference that, unlike Fanny in her lucky-break debut, the already professional Esther is not just scared but also furious with John Norman for thrusting her unrehearsed in front of an audience clamoring (in fact stomping) for the kind of "rock 'n' roll" only he can deliver (fig. 20). But in another seedbed moment for the uprush of the Streisand sound, we watch, as in *Funny Girl*, a public space laid claim to by the reach of voice alone, both found and delivered. After her clutched first syllables, it is as if Esther lets her increasingly backlit hair out rather than down in a blaze of self-framed confidence. The elegant semicircular pan and return, just before, in the unedited shot of the recording booth for "Evergreen," operated like a rapturous "dance . . . unrehearsed" of the wheeling camera itself (Streisand's superb luck with cinematographers continuing here with Robert Surtees). The effect is contrasted now, for "The Woman in the Moon," with a different deployment of the same 180-degree measure: across rather than around, marked by dramatic reverse shots rather than a swooning close-up two shot. The "musical concept" is matched perfectly with the lyrics and their

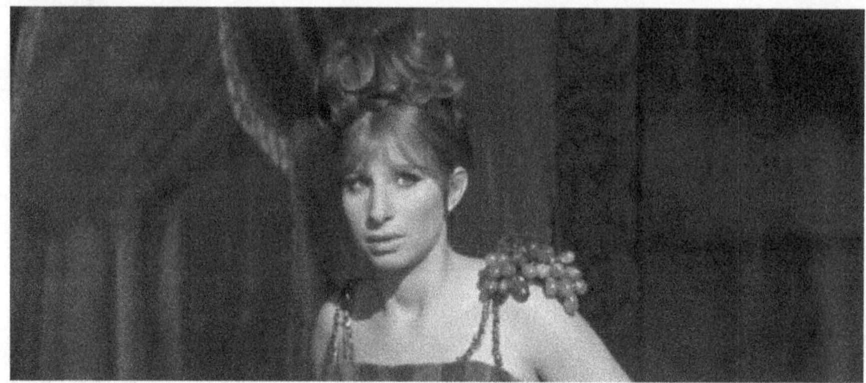

19. Finding a voice (*Funny Girl*: "I'd Rather Be Blue")

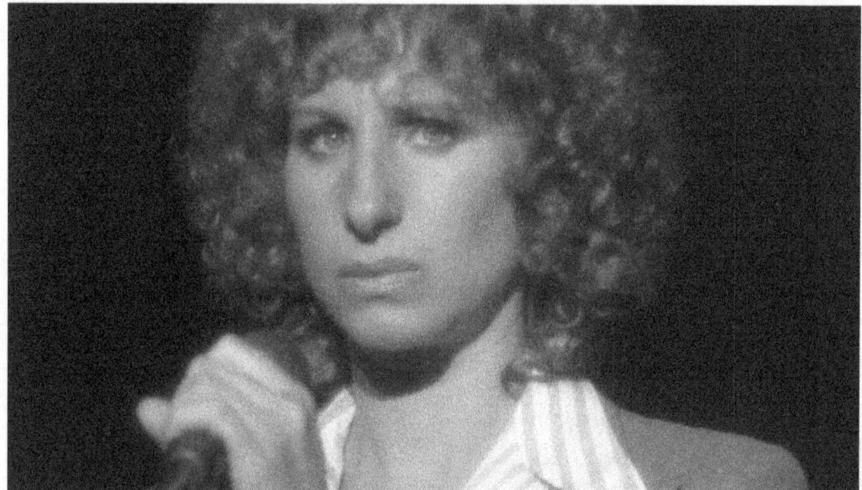

20. Reasserting the voice (*A Star Is Born*: "The Woman in the Moon")

vocal reflexivity. And not least when the first huge note of her gathered confidence seems timed to silence the audience still calling out for "rock 'n' roll": citing as her song does, even in beginning to override it, the tired warning to "save your time and trouble"—and not "misbe-haaaaaaaave." The size, and embrace, of her sound has, in effect, corralled the antsy, disaffected clapping into a rhythmic counterpoint instead, a collective "backup."

Whether the rock crowd feels chastened or not for their previous misbehaving, now she has them—and can further ventriloquize their initial naysaying: "They believed," like others before them, that "strange" was "a word for wrong." Certainly "not in my song." The past tense of "believed that" is phonetically indistinguishable on the run (the dramatic run-up)—even with a sense of diction as crisp as

Streisand's—indistinguishable, that is, from "believe that" in the present tense, which is exactly what the sneered slur, then rasp, of her delivery is getting at, building toward. They *did* believe that, always have, still do. Phrasing rightly makes no difference. Among the many phonetic ambiguities into which we'll have tuned in the course of this study, here is an indetermination, a prejudicial continuum, that only the song's feminist drive—with its own asserted difference—can put behind it. In the previous line about a worn-out "soaahhng," that sung note wears itself out for a long half dozen seconds of defeated force. This time around, the eager negation of such a false cultural melody ("nauaut in *MY-aye* song")—the rejection of any such enforced repressive concord—is delivered in those two last dismissive monosyllables: a "song" meant instead to break (and then traverse) new ground, again new vocal terrain. Hence the necessary caesura, the literal cut, from the singer shot from behind on the one line, the audience receding out of focus in front of her, to a sudden reverse close-up of her eyeline look. It is a look directed across the wrenched 180-degree axis—as Esther leaves behind that dated but lingering hurdle of normed performance where all "strangeness" is policed. The result is a gaze that scans the crowd until finally looking straight into the camera, in mesmerizing complicity, for the audience-enlisted line about how "You and I-i-i-i" have set about, and here if not before, "changing that tune." It is with exactly this sense of participatory energy that the title of the song, "The Woman in the Moon," locates a sub-stellar trope not just for an idealized femininity but for a stardom removed and untouchable. Yet the two symbolic feminine bodies are caught up in a trick phrase ratcheted into a new understanding by the furious final iteration about never being able to "hold the woman"—and then an iterated "I said the woman"— back. Which is to say "in the moon" after all. The slamming last phrase operates only under momentum from the shove of what precedes, *releasing* Woman from some distant abstraction, some myth, some archetype of lunar moods and tidal rhythms, into an embodied drive that is here surging forth in voice.

The opening lines have spoken of early lessons refused, the likes of "not to act" in any way "too strong, girl," to keep the strange under wraps, wholly at bay. The eventual marriage to John Norman does come off with an explicit dismissal of "the honor and obey part," but it doesn't work out, the attempted equity or the partnering. Esther wants desperately for them to go on tour together, yet everyone around them, including the rocker himself, knows that his public participation in her career can only endanger it. In this vein of cross-purposes between private and public commitment, there is one genuinely arresting scene. When John Norman interrupts a photographic session to tell Esther that he can't do the tour, her looks of suspicious recognition and then open disappointment—at one point with her head thrown back in profile to take a deep frustrated breath—are captured with congratulations by the photographer with her power-drive camera. Life is uninterruptedly fed upon by commercial art so as to be converted into a dramatic glamour still—in a scene that ends with his knowing ironic response to her fear of "going public" without him: "You already have"—as if right there, a moment before, with those soulful publicity shots. It's a further swift irony that one of these shots is prominent among the enlarged photos of rising-star Esther that surround her husband at the recording studio in the very next scene—another case of the film's apt editing—as he hears that his band has gone on to new success without him. That partnership is over, indeed every collaboration for the faded star, and the marital duo is, by his own self-abuse, doomed as well. John Norman Howard has nowhere else to turn professionally. The next and last time we see him trying to make any contact with his talent is the bleakly credible scene where his efforts to write a quiet love song, "With One More Look at You" (based—as the character is of course not supposed to know, but only the film—on the exit lines of the two previous Norman Maines in earlier versions of *A Star Is Born*). But he is continually interrupted by telephone calls for his exponentially famous wife. It is a fine film-historical homage, and an admirable song, and it has, climactically, its own posthumous life within this one plot.

Lost in Her Music

Too soon he will be taking, silently, that one more look, at Esther still half asleep in bed—and driving to his death in a red Ferrari that has been carefully set up as a token of Esther's energy. When first sitting in his black Cadillac limousine, she joked that it was the kind of car people get buried in, asking him in a later scene, "Where's the hearse?" Instead, he is proud of his red speedster, license plate "WANTED," a race car that he says "reminds me of you . . . fast, but not my lady." In exactly such acceleration now, after a final unacknowledged parting with Esther, it becomes a death car—if not quite a ceremonial hearse. And as he pushes the speedometer to 160 mph across a waste of desert road, this man—whose band, the former Speedway, has ousted him under their new name of Freeway, and who is now going (in the words of his greatest hit) "faster and farther than I've ever gone"—is listening to a taped album of Esther's, not his, voice. Looking back repeatedly, in the rearview mirror, on the abstract dwindling of all he is leaving behind, he has initially plugged in a cassette of his own hit song, "Watch Closely Now." But just after the ironic line about the chimeras of stardom—asking, as if of lovers and audiences alike, if they are a "figment of my imagination," or instead "I one of yours?"—he has replaced it with a cassette marked "Esther." So in an irretrievable sense is he "lost in the music," as the song sings (in those words he originally improvised for her before that first love scene), when finally driving over the fatal hill into invisibility as the last lingering strains of the cut die out with deadly timing. He gave her those words at the piano, and she in her greater vocal artistry gives them back to him in a displaced *Liebestod*, her last silken lyric thinned to oblivion. But the song's emphasis on reverse internalization ("your entering of my life has meant my self-abandonment in you and yours") has one more stage to go, where the more radical loss of internalized death must be purged. And one more stage performance is required.

But first, the excruciation over his found body. So minimal and inward is Streisand's performance here, in its terse agony, its almost feral despair, that the rhythm of delivery, even beyond the spare script itself, feels almost ad-libbed in the choked-back panic of its devastation. Yet everything answers to earlier moments in the film, negates them, across the run of a steady close-up of Esther over John Norman's laid-out corpse, leaving off-frame both the upended Ferrari and the helicopter she arrives in, recalling the one that first brought her along to his indulgent performance at Sun Devil Stadium. Also off-screen after his fatal accident, in a voiceover yearning to turn vehicular suicide into a photo op while police are fending off these unseen bystanders ("It's all over now"), one of them (fan or press reporter or rubbernecking motorist, it's all the same at this point) asks for "just one shot, please." All Esther wants by contrast, in the trauma of the moment, is that no one but her should have this last look. In close-up camerawork hardly calibrated to respect this privacy, her performance is almost too painful to watch in its abject bafflement and grief, Esther appealing to the corpse finally for help. In the camera's own long-held version of "just one shot," her now-vestigial wedding diamond, near the bottom edge of the frame, glints against the inconspicuous gold ring in the dead ear of the man who will never again hear her sing. Nor hear the least word of her current whispering grief. After she stares at and caresses in tears the inert face—as in that first physical contact at the piano—this time, in lieu of a kiss, she licks her tissue to clear blood from his beard. "He needs a blanket," she has said, half mad in her shock, after feeling the cold corpse, and then pleads, in her cramp of pain, for his rather than her privacy: "Could you please not stare at him now . . . please" she mumbles to the hovering medic. All this vetoed watching will be inverted again, two scenes and some indeterminate time later, in the memorial lyrics of incorporation, acceptance, and forging on that—in some combination of the psychological and the narrative sense—make for closure, where the blank face of devastation is brought back to life in vocal close-up.

In the Garland version, Norman Maine was delighted to have "the original belter" in the flesh, and on his honeymoon turned off her hit song on the motel radio to have her sing it in person. As he walked to his death in the ocean after taking the obligatory last look, Garland was singing quietly in the kitchen. The idea of the hero's suicide softened by the voice of the heroine is therefore not new, but its reciprocity is—for Streisand's Esther is allowed to work through her own loss in song. After John Norman's death she is shaken from her silent grief by hearing that tape he made, interrupted by phone calls for his wife the star, while trying out the lyrics of "With One More Look at You." It has been turned on accidentally by a workman in their mansion at the point where John Norman is answering the phone, and she half thinks, through the preoccupation of her grief, that he may somehow be alive there, and even, as the tape plays on, still making music. Which of course he is, in his preserved song to her. She first listens to the tape in tears and rage, arguing back at his recorded voice, calling him a "liar" for the cheating optimism of the lyrics, as well as his other promises about their future. Yet she goes on, in the next, last, and climactic scene, to debut this song for him—and to blend it in medley with his signature hit, which he had only been able to stagger through in truncated form in his previous drunken and drugged concert fiascoes. She dresses for this memorial concert not in black but in white, and again in a mannish three-piece suit, her performance being both in her husband's honor and in his stead, begun standing stock still and ended in a Jagger-like swaggering fury, purging her rage, filling the void of abandonment with a voice under audition within the locked look of the cinematic frame. The transition to this last double number has been exact in its shift of geometry. Cutting to Esther in jeans and a beige sweatshirt, sunk to a seat on the steps of their mansion's sunken living room, the camera dollies in on her washed out, tear-lined face until, beginning to shred the tape in her anger, she catches herself and moans an apology to its dead songwriter. In a markedly slow dissolve that frames her fading mistake (fig. 21), the ghost of her desecration is about to be repaired. For her slumped image is quite tightly framed on disappearance by the rectangle of a backstage door that her manager opens as she enters, under equally tight facial control of her own, to the concert stage behind the curtain—on the way to the framing camera's own longer, tighter-yet constraint and release.

The star must be reborn if she is to "go on" in either sense, and this she manages by reincarnating her lover in his own music. It is her half, in person now, of the *Liebestod*, with an elegiac urgency meant to transfigure the love-death into hope for continuance, however impersonal. "Star" itself becomes a resurrected metaphor, not a dead one, when she promises in his lyric that the "constellations" will "paint your portrait too." It is without doubt a spectacular performance of the self as performing spectacle, with audience long forgotten (as at the end of "My Man" in *Funny Girl*): a single

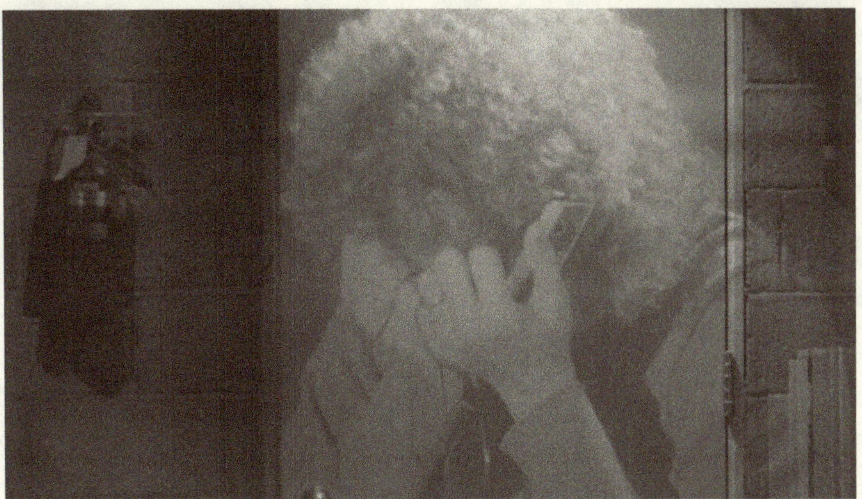

21. Elegiac cross-fade (*A Star Is Born*)

scene-less, set-less shot, setting off a knockout effort of lyric will. The camera, holding on her tear-stained face, is struck immobile for the seven unalleviated minutes of these two dovetailed numbers—as Esther delivers herself from quiet anguish into an orgiastic invocation of a gaze beyond the grave. A "musical concept" of such bravado knows full well the wagers it is running, the dangers, and looks them fully in the close-up face. What shackles our attention is the irresistible cinematographic trope of vocal *expression(s)* made *visible* in the very features of delivery.

Fixed Frame to Freeze-Frame: With More Looks than One

In the earlier manifestations of *A Star Is Born*, grief left the rising stars virtually speechless at the end. Streisand knew better than this. She knew by instinct what was missing from the other versions, both in their statements about female suffering and in their wasted chance of emotional alchemy: an absent flashpoint of recuperation that turns strength itself into art, art into strength. By way of "conceptual" architecture, the blueprint of the narrative's previous song segments has taken us from interrupted solos through impromptu or partial duets to a recorded song at the moment of suicidal escape, then another taped song mistaken for a resurrection—and then on to this final unyielding number, the star lost in the solitude of her solo's unanswerable appeal. In Esther's earlier TV rehearsal scene for "The Woman in the Moon," reminiscent of Streisand's own Emmy-winning specials in the middle 1960s—especially the cantilevered staircase finale of *Color Me Barbra*—Esther is literally put through her paces on just as tricky a set, preventing her from putting the lyric across with its proper deliberation and emphasis. The figurative need to "memorize your lines" while moving "as directed" (that countervailed imperative from the lyric itself) is, in effect, just what she is being told to do. "It comes at a very important part of my lyric. Why can't I just stand there and sing?" As of course she has done in the concert debut of this same song, and will get another, sadder chance to do—stand and sing, in an even more fixed stance—with the "one more look" apotheosis, and many more than one, at film's end: looks searching, nervously self-differentiated, emotionally flayed, almost preternaturally intimate in their mood shifts.

The cloning of the star that carried her from alternating comic songstress and romantic belter in the Depression-era vaudeville of *Funny Lady* to pop phenomenon-in-the-ascendant for the next year's *A Star Is Born* requires now, within this closural workout, her further cloning—across the heady suspension bridge of this medley—into rock diva. But of course as Streisand still, always that *same difference*. Miming the found first-person lyrics left by her husband, Esther is neither quite here nor there—but all *on*. As she struggles her way through the forlorn audiovisual ironies of this call to (and for) a disembodied reciprocated looking, the resplendent density of Streisand's voice keeps us on edge with every cliff-hanging effort of her high notes. This last extraordinary aria may read as bravura in a theatrical vacuum, but it is a vacuum much like that at the end of *Funny Girl*, planned to be ravishing. And making good on its sound design. Again, as in the closing number of Streisand's first film, the performer's effort grows inward to such an intense node of privacy that it banishes the fiction of an audience altogether. It closes un-applauded upon stop-action silence, followed behind the credits and the long-held last image of the star, by a voiceover reprise of "Evergreen"—equivalent of a concert encore—with that song's faith in love's perennial vitality. And with the freeze-frame on "Now" figuring just that power to "sail above" mortal "time" that love is credited with in the climactic high notes of the returning lyric. Esther's head is flung back on the last pounding beat of "Are you watching me now?"—so that the atemporal punch of the frozen screen image, which so many commentators of the period had noted in other films as a visual metaphor for death's stoppage of time—is here clearly meant as a flight from time into the thrilling fixity of art. Esther's draining performance pumps life into a posthumous rendition of John Norman's song about his own drugged, boozed-up cynosure, all eyes for so long upon him. Her tightly framed lyric delivery, tapering into the stratosphere beyond high C, climbs the mimetic reach of her borrowed (and fulfilled) question "how high can I go?"—which, in his own performances of this rock hit, had degenerated into a question of how high he could be and still go on, still make it to the stage. Her own reflexive version of this elevated note answers instead, along a different thematic axis, to the "you and I-i-i-i" in that long-held high note of direct address in "The Woman in the Moon."

With the self-destructive subtext associated with John Norman's worn-out hit redeemed in the film's final pairing of songs, Esther's medley aspires to a kind of mortuary mind meld. The dream of interchanged last looks across an unseen space beyond the grave ("With One More Look at You" / "Watch Closely Now")—a fusion beyond ocular suture—requires just the expressive gauntlet performed across the troubled surface of Streisand's prolonged delivery. In this restive, then febrile threnody, inching its way, over precipitous risks, to the highest of flights, the hoped-for defiance of time in the sustained "Now" seizes upon a swollen moment of beauty won from ruin. In the process, the triumph can't mask the structural problem, only escape from it. It is, both deep down and right there on the surface, a genre problem. Like dance in the traditional musical, song can't always be solo. But here irreversibly, its potentially figured bonds—sexual and communal—are no longer operable. What is left must be reconceived in process—as Streisand so valiantly attempts. But a duet for one, even in an honorific medley, will always be missing something in genre terms, even if that something would end up being—and here is a point well worth stressing—less than what we get instead. There is a publicity picture of Kristofferson and Streisand singing side by side, in fierce rock vehemence, in front of their tandem stage mics, as Bradley Cooper and Lady Gaga actually are seen doing on-screen in their otherwise quite close 2018 redo. But the earlier shot is a misleading collage—never achieved by camerawork or montage in the film itself. The newer film gains its main charge not just from music held in common along with the lovers' bodies but from on-stage collaboration. Not so in 1976. Never in Streisand's musicals, as we know, is there a real full-blown duet—even when, in *Yentl*, she co-stars with an accomplished stage vocalist in Mandy Patinkin. This may perhaps explain in part her thirst for such duets in so many recent albums. Even in TV specials, singing with the pale-voiced composer Burt Bacharach or later Ray Charles, it's always her voice that counts. In the case of the Bacharach special, the real duet is with herself in a series of shifting superimpositions in the medley of "One Less Bell to Answer" and "A House Is Not a Home." Again, the cinematography of self-difference made explicit.

As in a sense happens when Esther takes on John Norman's own material, makes it rise again in her: Esther singing *for* (in the double sense) rather than with him. Structurally, this closing medley has a perfect dramatic logic. But it achieves this at a familiar cost: the star's uniqueness, her singularity, serving to queer the communalist genre that her talent would otherwise seem born for. She is working instead not so much to renew the musical format as to invent a new one. And the invention here is relentless, line by line. The breathy words "I want (w)one mohohre" (a far falling-off from Esther's original "I want everything" in the opening set with the Oreos) are whispered, almost gasped out, eyes closed, then opened for a tearful stare into her desertion—rather than her rapt theater public. At which point the fabled vibrato comes to the rescue on the translucent yearning for the distilled and distended near echo of "looooook at youuuu." But the sound (if not the hope) is immediately shaded into a lightly rasped "Are" by a precipitous drop in tone for the choked throes of the gear-shifting segue: "Are you watching me now?"—as she launches, finally throws herself, into his rock hit, where it is the survivor alone who is now to be watched (fig. 22). The see/saw reversals in the ocular logic of trauma and therapeutic performance are as elusive as they are luminous in execution. The failed and faded rock star, no longer demanding the stare of the arena crowd, has with his last recorded lyrics wanted only to look, not be seen. And in her willed and willful appropriation of the lyric from the found tape, Esther has assimilated both the surrender and the desire as her own call to the dead, reviving in the process the rock drive of his squandered stardom: the "cover" not as a further shroud but as an elegiac gift—and a personal purgation.

In Esther's transferential internalization of both songs, his career-making hit along with unrecorded draft lyrics from his last days, the question "Are You Watching Me Now?" pushes through to a self-fulfilling temporal prophecy, as noted, in the film's final freeze-frame after Esther's pulsing "nowowowow": a kind of pain-dissipating synesthesia in evoking the holding action of the voice itself, if nothing more. And it's not just the reiterated "now" of such present-tense lyrics that bear—while trying to bury—the

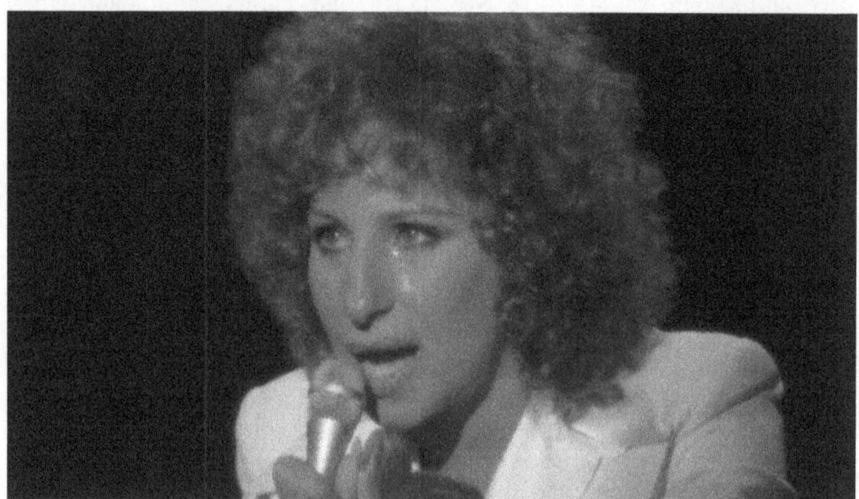

22. Camerawork's "one more look" (*A Star Is Born*: "Watch Closely Now")

pain. When Esther channels John Norman—most notably in the muted piercing reach of "How hIGH can I go?"—she is completing the previous assonance entailed in "rid-ing" the cresting passion "ar*i*sing ins*i*de me" with that final exploratory "I," after which that long *o* of "go" shades off, darkens, to a groan. The question enwraps its own lament for the very need it worries: "how high can I go-ohohoh?" In rhyme with the forces "urging me ahahahn," the vow to go "faster and fahahrther" than "I've ever *gahahn*" (a reflexive nod to Streisand's "hard rock" venture here) finds the last word curtly growled out, in defiance, even while sustaining the *on*-warding rhyme of its syllabic envelope ("on"/"gone"). Yet again, for all the wit of her dialogue line readings, the true malleable imprint of Streisand's genius—on-screen and off—comes through most immediately in the timing, modulation, and affect of the syllable's own drama in song production. It is there that the unique grain of voice she commands lays claim to whole territories of surprise, whole new strata of probed emotion. And at the close of *A Star Is Born*, all of these phonic features may be said to play directly across Streisand's face in this tour de force of acting-out—and working-through. Italicizing the eye contact she can never make again with John Norman is the void gaping between them—where the audience once was. The hope of being able to "refresh" her so visibly "tired eyes"—in the first half of the medley—is now renewed as the incrementally sounded dream that the couple might "love and live, love and live" (a repetition protesting too much in its own flexed prolongation) in the time-defying lift and trailing phonetic reverb of "for-rrEVVVERererer." In that limit-fraying enunciation, distending any operable syllabic border, the iterative flutter within the stretched word carries voice's self-furthered eleva-tion in the mode of sheer wish-fulfillment, with Esther's torqued head and shoulders ro-tating their way through the spring-like release of this wild-eyed, wide-toned overreach.

The inflected, edgy, tension-stressed vocals that have worked their way up to this apogee of forced enunciation have been subsumed in large part to the dramatic logic of soliloquy. Unlike anything Streisand has done before or since, here—for the honorary member of the Actor's Studio, too young to enroll when she tried back in her Brook-lyn days—is an endurance course of (and master class in) Method Singing, the vocal answer to her disappearance into, or beneath, character in her morbid monologue over John Norman's corpse. For it is in this interpenetrating emotion of his posthumous song to Esther—now sung back to him in overlap with his earlier hit—that the griev-ing vocals, unrepressed and in mounting control, pursue their unleashed way across the stark arc of her catharsis to its searing if momentary (optically braked) relief in that cinematographic freeze. Well beyond anything circumscribed by genre, the transfusion of music and drama is complete. In all this cross-mapped "looking," you can't take your ears off Streisand, nor finally, all sound gone inward, your eyes.

The idea of an elegiac finale in song, and its live miking, is openly borrowed and revamped in the 2018 remake, but without the ballast of Streisand's enacted emotion. In her version, every feeling knotted up in the braiding together of the two numbers is read off from the knitted brow, heavy eyes, welling tears, and winces of lyric identification—matched to every subtle twinge of voice—that passes between Esther and the unseen posthumous gaze. The remake knew enough to end with a song, and an effective one in "I'll Never Love Again," but Lady Gaga's inexpressive stare—and the strain of her high notes in monochrome boom as the only mode of emotion—must send the number reaching for flashbacks (brief amorous insets punctuating the number) to underwrite the pain in the form of a fleetingly recaptured loss. Nothing could contrast more with the fixed-frame lock on Streisand's nuanced marathon of emotion, where we're made achingly aware of the camera itself as the instrument of a looked-for watching. With the triple-octave range of Streisand's face as well as voice, Esther has—across the ricochet of symbolic looks—turned the pathos of this inspection (in the "Look"/"Watch" nexus) into a radical introjection. She has done so, that is, not just by annexing "Howard" to her "Hoffman" (as introduced for this elegiac number) but by becoming, in the racing heartbeat of performed communion, exactly the surcharged part of the other that can live on in and through her. In Streisand's version of female mourning, riding every lurch and undertow of the inferred emotion without self-pity, the only time she averts her face from the microphone, but then swerves quickly back, is to wipe—and swallow—away tears that can actually be heard in an extra nasalization of her voice at its peak of feeling.

The whole extraordinary descant is like nothing ever heard—or seen—on-screen. And an anecdote from the last-minute rush of the film's production history only helps magnify the effect as we have it. In releasing a new version of the film to Netflix (not DVD) in 2018, with restored footage from the initial "concept" of this scene, Streisand explains that, although there were intended to be cutaway medium and long shots of her hard-rock moves toward the end of "Watch Closely Now," pounding out her pent-up stress, there wasn't time to edit them in before early test screenings. In the upshot, the reaction of preview audiences to the unbroken long take was so positive that she settled for leaving well enough alone. Good for them—and her. Precisely with no editing, just the camera's clenched stare at her features as they struggle through the release of the lyrics, a music of the ultimate reciprocal look has found its perfect cinematographic realization.

Writing of all places in *The Hollywood Reporter*, academic culture critic and feminist firebrand Camille Paglia has favorably compared Streisand's film to the previous three versions, and, pulling no punches, to the one since. In summing up, over the course of its five-film cycle, the dimming of male luster in the glare of the rising-star syndrome in this screen cycle, Paglia's distaste for the "misogynist" sidelining of the female role in Bradley Cooper's version is unremitting. At the same time, she finds that Gaga's "bellowing" without nuance in her character's star-making high notes helps lend just the historical perspective that the 1976 version deserves—and not least, we might add, in contrast to the one-man-woman fetish of the "Never Love Again" ode: "In retrospect, we can now fully recognize Streisand's *A Star Is Born* as a feminist landmark."[3] One final marker of this for Paglia, besides the personalized mannish wardrobe of the star throughout, is her introduction at the memorial concert as "Esther Hoffman Howard." If dimming any militancy, this gesture does serve in "rejecting the previous films' female erasure" under the subsuming name of "Mrs. Norman Maine." Announced in this fashion is the moment when Esther in mourning "reappears for an operatic solo of grief, defiance and transcendence." And more than this, we might add: reappears in white, not widow's weeds, struggling out of her mourning to wash away, rinse clean, the crippling misery, to push past it. Can it be an accident if we seem asked to remember that Streisand's first lines in the film—as she rises slowly into the frame which, in the last number, she never leaves—celebrate a "black, black widow" whose symbolic snare and sting (all she'll ever "give you") is never "gonna outlive you"? As the widow in white, Esther's "gift" is of a different order. For in that final memorial concert she takes, at least briefly, her husband's name (hyphenated or not) in order to take on the work of returning to him the fame of his signature song, transformed, made her own, and so carried forward, "outliving" his defeat. About the grandstanding of the two-song single shot, and its self-affirming afterglow in the end-titles, certainly Paglia is unapologetic: "Streisand takes the audience prisoner in this almost unendurably protracted single take, a raw assertion of female ego and power. Then the credits flash with her multiple roles, starting with executive producer. Streisand was setting the terms for the new frontier: women in Hollywood seizing control of their own creative universe." Next stop: *Yentl*.

Once stars are born, even if partly made as well by will and publicity, they have a hard time being made over into mere characters. And I mean Barbra here, of course, not Esther. Once beyond any angst associated with the fear of here-today-gone-tomorrow, the agon of major stardom isn't a matter of not finding work, not finding the parts, but of not finding room in them for variety without an undue curtailment either of or by the given. Even when, as in Streisand's case, the iconic status is already anchored in a shape-shifting self-origination—a mercurial variety within a wholesale ethnic departure and empowered gender redirection—the specter of repetition and stall-out looms. Despite the initial burst of differential momentum in Streisand's unique career, the inertial charge can still seem to dissipate in lesser projects, as we've too often had occasion to note, the roles as if running on the fumes of fame alone, never exactly lazy—far from it—but stripped of grip. That's where, by contrast, the metaphor of cloning has come to mind. Authenticity must be retained in any vital departure. A biological figure for this mirroring within difference arises in doing justice to the active remaking of manner and mode that has carried us in this chapter across the genuine redoubling of star impact from *Funny Girl* to *Funny Lady*—and on then, in a rethinking of musical "concepts" themselves, to *A Star Is Born*. In this spread rather than splintering of invention, a cloning entirely performative rather than genomic still bears traces—and traits—genetic and generic alike. In *Funny Lady* as female self-sequel, Streisand's persona mutates back, in the biopic framework, to a more openly ethnic delivery; in the next, forward, to a first screen embrace of pop-rock. Every instinct in the star's Hollywood ambition would no doubt welcome, in the initial move from one to the other Fanny Brice, Felix's happy compliment in *The Owl and the Pussycat*: "It's two completely different girls!" Same as Brice becomes Hoffman, while still Streisand, let alone Yentl Anshel—in that next and extreme case, an ultimate performance of gender as mirror inversion, with the star her own fraternal twin.

YENTL'S LYRIC CINEMA

The plot of *Yentl* is angled to reflect a newly extreme mirror of difference exacerbated by the film's gender and ethnic slant. In *A Star Is Born*, Streisand is credited with "musical concepts" that are even more emphatically reconceived here as well—in a true genre skew. Instead of live miking, two graduated modes of its opposite: the star's vocal sorcery oscillating in its own acoustic mirror-play between song and interior monologue. The signal innovation of this "Film with Music" is as much a stroke of luck as of inspiration. As gleaned from the Director's Cut in the film's DVD release, what seemed like setbacks were actually lucky breaks. These blessings should be counted from the start. One can only be grateful, first, to the Czech director Ivan Passer, who thought Streisand was too old for the role at twenty-five, when she wanted originally to make it as a "small European film"; and then to another Czech director later approached by Streisand for the project, Milos Forman, who urged her, so strong was her vision, to direct it herself. Thanks go as well, for once, to the industry moguls who wouldn't fund the forty-something star in the role, whatever other reservations this might have involved, without musical numbers. Under duress, Streisand set out with a lengthy treatment of the Isaac Bashevis Singer story when it was conceived without songs, and—before reworking the script herself in collaboration with the British playwright Jack Rosenthal—began marking in the manuscript the points where songs might naturally arise as emotional outlets. With eventual lyrics by Marilyn and Alan Bergman, music by Michel Legrand, this further version of the Singer story has been "put to music" in the sense of being put to music's test—with a supple score whose alternations take the variable pulse of the heroine's desire across episodes both lyric and dramatic. Until we can no longer easily tell the difference.

Even the most rudimentary plot summary can begin to suggest how songs become part of the narrative armature. In this adaptation of the Singer story, Yentl's father Rabbi Mendel (Nehemiah Persoff) is her only link to the tradition of Talmudic scholarship that has nurtured her mind, until his death severs this connection. In order to continue the learning in which he had secretly tutored her, Yentl must go forth, her long brown hair chopped short, in the disguise of a male student, eventually taking the name of her dead brother, Anshel. Having met a band of young scholars on their way to the Yeshiva, and befriending one of them in particular, Avigdor (played by Mandy Patinkin), she soon signs on as his study partner once she is invited to become a Talmud student. She is also subsequently invited as a frequent dinner guest to the table of Avigdor's extravagantly pretty fiancée, Hadass (Amy Irving), and her family. It is shortly discovered by Hadass's parents, however, that Avigdor has made a secret of his brother's suicide, and for this familial stigma of melancholia in the blood he is deemed genetically unsuitable as a marriage partner and potential father of Hadass's child. Devastated, he cajoles Anshel into marrying Hadass instead, to keep the latter as near to him as possible. To which an agonized Yentl accedes only to keep *him* near *her*. Alone with the bride on their wedding night, Yentl, still dressed (and still in male garb), convinces Hadass, who is obviously eager to consummate the marriage, that the religious law prohibits it, given the wife's abiding thoughts for another man. So, pledging Hadass to chastity and patience, Yentl seals the vow of this odd coupling by spilling wine on the sheets to suggest defloration. But when it gradually becomes clear that Hadass no longer pines for Avigdor, but loves her husband more after all, Yentl decides to reveal herself to Avigdor at last, hoping they might forge a new life together. But he is horrified at Yentl's long deception. Even when placated by her confession of love, he rejects out of hand the idea that she should continue her clandestine studies, insisting instead that a woman comes by all the knowledge she needs through the intuitions of sheer biological destiny. The next day the irreconcilable friends part, and months later we see Yentl writing to Avigdor and Hadass, who are now married, wishing them well as she leaves Europe for a new sphere of possibility, by obvious implication America.

In a very different version of the plot, Singer's Yentl/Anshel—in a confession of emotional androgyny, an incapacity for marriage of any kind—has explained that "I'm neither one nor the other,"[1] arranging instead for Avigdor's reunion with Hadass. Singer's misfit protagonist, beyond the androgynous *neither/nor* of that spoken disclaimer, is actually more like "mis-assigned" to a girl's body. Enter instead, though with ultimately the same narrative result, Streisand's famous differential persona as the undelimited *both/and*. At just this point in the original story, however, the Yentl/Anshel figure—sexual border case and go-between—disappears from the plot without further mention, a mere function(ary) of sexual difference and its negotiations: a catalyst evaporated by the chain reaction s/he has set in motion. Her only trace is the son of the new couple, a child who, to the community's general astonishment in the story's last sentence, is named "Anshel." This birth becomes the plot's incarnate principle of a normalized regeneration: a symbolic second start for Yentl as an unequivocal male, a full-fledged inheritor. It is, by contrast, the essence of Streisand's film that the heroic energy should not be tamed or redomesticated by patriarchy but only continue to invoke it in the call for posthumous validation: "Papa, can you hear me?"

Behind the film's opening caption, "Eastern Europe, 1904," is the shot of a single feather floating down a narrow gulley of groundwater that we see stepped across by the indifferent feet of a few locals in low-level shots. All tightly preconceived by the director, as she explains on the DVD, this mere topographic squiggle begins to etch out a through-line for the story as a whole. It represents an autonomous forward motion symbolizing the natural course, and eventually the empowered emotive flow, of a forward momentum that we next, in this same opening sequence, see running down through the market town into a creek loud with children swimming. A similar body of water will appear later, broader, when it comes directly in Yentl's path: the current widening there into a full stream for crossing by ferry, later again for student bathing, then afterward into a major river for bridging, and then an oceanic expanse for transatlantic navigation. Streisand's DVD voiceover explains how she had to have her crew artificially dig that initial narrow trench to initiate the pattern she had in mind: amounting to the mobile hint of a narrative lifeline, at first little more than a tentative but natural trickle, widening over time through and beyond the narrow confines of her gendered world. Or rather, genetically conceived: a kind of fluid umbilical cord tying origin to destiny, rabbinical parentage to feminine possibility, as later captured by the stirring Bergman lyrics to "This Is One of Those Moments." It is by then, through hard-won deception, that Yentl has matriculated at the Yeshiva as the promising young Anshel. And it is the falseness of this masquerade that nonetheless serves to draw out, for her, the deeper authenticity of her lineage. She finds she can "now be a part" of exactly the "ongoing stream" that, by cultural as well as phrasal chiasm, "has always been a part of me"—a symmetry only highlighted, in Streisand's liquid enunciation, by the smaller-scale phonetic cresting of the chiastic str*eaeam*/*meee* echo built into the texture of this celebration. It is typical of the interplay of image vector and melodic drive in this film that such an early visual emblem—that feather-bearing runnel, become forded waterway—would find itself spelled out in the swelling of a later lyric.

Back in the opening scene, after a third, bluntly gendered reprise of a bookseller's hawking of "picture books for women, sacred books for men," Yentl is first seen wandering into the market square to a fishmonger's stand from which the transgressive possibility of sacred reading immediately distracts her. What ensues at the market stall, however, as the camera returns to it, secures a model of comic dialogue to be played out across many later episodes—and eventually linked, through the split consciousness of its wordplay, to the abiding tensile spread between audible song and silent lyric transmission. Alternately, in an original conception for Streisand's entrance, testified to amid the DVD's deleted scenes, Yentl's first appearance would have ended in a pratfall from a collapsing woodpile next to the synagogue, where she has climbed to spy yearningly on, and mouth along with, as otherwise forbidden to women, the men's sacred sonorities (fig. 23). This exclusion is seen by the camera through cross-barred mullions that partially occlude and subdivide her eager look, as well as through the glass that baffles (in the acoustic sense only) her participation in the solemn vocals, silencing her for us as well as for the men inside. As a prologue to the star's coming vocal arrival onto the musical track, it is as if, in a genre reflex, what we would have been seeing there, in that planned first scene, is the tease—by technological in-joke—of a Streisand song number not yet filled out with its post-sync vocal dub.

Double Hearing, Double Entendre

It is instead with the star's actual entrance in the release print—even before the soon-established pattern of vocal cross-fade between open-mouthed audial expression and inner song, inner longing—that the related two-ply model of dialogue is set in place. When asked at the market which fish she would like, Yentl, preoccupied instead with the books on offer across the square, is momentarily thrown. "Pike or carp?" The non-answer—"Yes"—is lodged as if unconsciously refusing to split an inconsequential difference. Snapped back to herself, and paying attention again, she next takes control of the dialogue by logical reversal. Having just inadvertently fudged a disjunction (one fish or the other)—and now in an open sarcastic wordplay that typifies

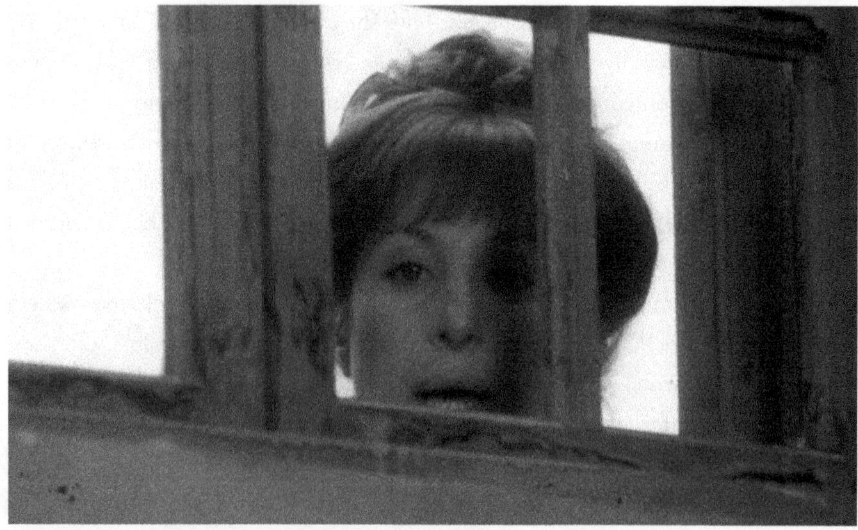

23. The barred voice (*Yentl*: deleted opening scene)

the verbal nuancing that will soon, in male dress, make her such a deft Talmudic hermeneut—she is heard wedging open a distinction where none was intended. She's been asked abruptly by a friendly if officious local gossip, "What's this I hear about your getting engaged?" It's news to Yentl, as only a deleted later scene with the village matchmaker could fully explain. Cut loose from that association, and thus in a way that isolates in advance so much of the script's wordplay to come, what we encounter here—as if the whole film were already New York bound—is something like Yiddish stage comedy *avant la lettre*. "I don't know" is Yentl's first answer. That won't do. "Well, did you or didn't you?" Parried: "What, hear about it, or do it?" Lexical schtick: Yentl's typical sardonic crutch from here out. Equivocation of this sort will become her characteristic hedge against all questioning approaches. It is just this semantic vacillation that grows subtly cognate in its structural switch points with the split-level song structure, ambient versus internal, its verbal flips in dialogue sometimes directly overlapping with vocal transits between these alternate modes.

It is in this spirit of repartee's light irony that one follows the recurrent glitches of distraction and missed cues running as undertext from scene to scene, where the gap between social context and private focus—sometimes foundering on covert double entendre or anxious self-correction—is at other times linked to a breach in the protected music of internal monologue. Double *entendre* in its own double etymological sense: *hearing* otherwise what may be alternately *intended*, whether with the melodic force of a private lyric impetus, to which we are uniquely privy, or in comic banter meant two ways at once. In the commentary, Streisand makes no mention of these twofers in her script. But they speak for themselves—with the flick of a recurrent forked tongue. The most obvious of these moments, in echo of the carp/pike choice an hour earlier in screen time, has Yentl's corrective redress not just leap across, but attempt to seal, the border of an inner song monologue—and this by way of voiced dialogue. Alone with Hadass in the "No Wonder" ("he loves her") number, Yentl's melodic stream of consciousness chimes her awareness of the girl's "silky hair" and "milky complexion"—both "nice" but "not that distracting" (unlike, it is implied, the preoccupying challenges of learning and debate that s/he and Avigdor share instead). But in fact "distracting" they are, causing Yentl, behind the Anshel barricade, quite literally to have "tuned out" for a moment, relishing the satire of her own internal rhymes during this teatime tête-à-tête. So that when of-fered either lemon or milk, Yentl, first responding with a pointless "yes," then opts instead for "milky"—before a quick double take as auto-correction. The tiniest jolts of this sort measure the narrative's deeper structural clefts. The contrapuntal inter-play of such rhythmic, fugue-like moments can become almost a proverbial fugue state, out of which Yentl must be snapped by the demands of Anshel's substitute (and subterfuge) reality.

In another such example of slipped gears between monologue and dialogue, Yentl in male gabardines asks that her tailors, to their surprise, leave the room while s/he changes for the nuptial fitting in the "Tomorrow Night" wedding montage—one of them called Zelig, as it happens, his name a fit riff on the shape-changing Woody Allen hero. Alone, Yentl reels with anxiety about the eponymous pending date. Realizing that, on her current collision course, she'll be wed to a woman "without a doubt" by the next night, she rhymes that inevitability, unguarded and out loud, with a panicky "I gotta get out"—at which outburst her tailors burst back in, wondering what's up. By quick segue and add-on: "Out of these clothes," she ad libs in alibi. Then, too, earlier in the plot, before Hadass's broken engagement with Avigdor—and at the level of dialogue alone, rather than leaked song monologue—a deleted scene has Yentl writhing in discomfort as Avigdor wants to indulge in dorm-room guy talk about Hadass's erotic charms. He's only reached "chapter one," he insists, and could go on all night. "Don't!" she bleats out, then regroups for a less emotional suggestion: "Don't you think it might be just physical attraction?" From negative imperative to naive interrogative: such is the bailout here, where the extemporaneous maneuver of a double take, rather than some full double entendre, is her characteristic default setting.

This pattern of ambiguous split references, lateral dodges, jiggered slippages righted on the run, or simply the format of overridden alternatives (as in a distracted "yes" to "carp or pike"/ "lemon or milk") may well owe a suspected debt to rabbinical hairsplitting gone slack. Yet it is rendered all the more notable as a linguistic equivalent of the film's pervasive narrative doubleness—between apparent man and resurgent women—by the appearances of such engrained comedy even in outtakes cut for length under studio pressure. And there are further links implied by these dialogue tics not just to Talmudic scholarship but more broadly to the familiar rhythms of Jewish interchange: the ambivalently answered question and its opposite number, the queried statement. This association comes forward when Yentl as Anshel, doing schoolroom recitations in a deleted scene, is asked why his response has so deliberately (in this most characteristic turn of a secular ethnic patois) turned a statement by Maimonides into a question. In its more demotic Jewish forms—as a kind of street-smart-aleck version of sacred hermeneutics in answering one question with *another*—it's what one may well remember from *Funny Girl* as the grammatical rhyme, between moments early versus midway in the plot, that plays "Can *I* roller skate?" off against "Can *I* watch with no expression at all?" In *Yentl*, the spirit is pervasive: interrogate everything, with the result that (from the held outreach of a gleaming high note in the

"One of Those Moments" lyric again) there is not just "more to question" but also, in consequence, "more to belieeeeve"—the latter word stretched in its sung last syllable toward a far horizon of eventuality. But, even more frequent than Streisand's vocal querying, as in the first and explicitly titled "Where Is It Written?" number, are the comic shifts in consciousness that texture the film's dialogue. Time and again they expose Yentl's guarded stance, in the disguised person of Anshel, between unstable roles. In this way they more sharply delimit the social border from which Streisand's singing in this film must typically beat its musical retreat into soliloquy. In bolstering this overarching sound design, the ongoing pattern of broken-back dialogue—as much as a cracked and halved mirror image rendered emblematic at the film's first narrative turning point—helps maintain a pervasive foothold in the twofold.

Singer Sung

The first two musical numbers both begin as pseudo-prayers, first to the "Heavenly Father," then, after his death, to "my own Father, who art in Heaven"—respectively, in these paired interrogations: "Where Is It Written?" and "Papa, Can You Hear Me?" Prayer is activated by the film as that sole form of sacred or liturgical utterance not proscribed for women. Yet each of these early appeals (in prayer's etymological sense of "entreaty")—the first sung while Yentl's ailing father has gone to bed for the night, the next after her transvestite flight following his funeral—modulates from the authorized voice of one-way sacred *converse* toward a more secular, questioning, transgressive *song*. The opening number must negotiate this transformation through a self-conscious interplay between over-voiced and synchronized lyrics, between stream of consciousness and soliloquy, as the embodied force of the differential wording passes in and out of the father's potentially disturbed earshot. Thus begins a marked alternation that generates across the whole length of plot a motif of stifled fervor versus expressed yearning. And just as the texture and execution of these earliest vocal numbers bear directly in this way on *Yentl*'s relation to the particular generic shape of the musical film, so too are they arranged to highlight even more generally the nature of film narrative at large, both as specular medium and as star vehicle. Such is the deep cinematic reflex of Streisand's conception—manifest most fully in vocal execution under the camera's mobile gaze.

Opening its partial release valve for the repressed female voice, the first song is begun in the "stage whisper" motivated by the proximity of her sleeping father. Standing before a candle and a mirror, about to wrap herself in a Tallit—the ceremonial white prayer shawl, striped with black, extended momentarily to its full width—Streisand as Yentl begins to intone the first words of her prayer, call it her recitative: "I'm wrapped in a robe of light." As stressed by this metaphor, the whole mise-en-scène now becomes cinematically reflexive in precisely the fabric's slow effacement of the mirror. It is an optical irony of *screening* that is as important in figuring the film's own projective mechanism—a kind of hypnotic industrial light show—as it is in fixing the terms of private devotional craving from this point on in the narrative's musical interlace. The very act of internal framing just before (reversed image-within-image in the mirror's initial plane) has markedly situated its star in the symbolic field of self-regard. But next backlit by candlepower, then silhouetted in turn behind a spread scrim that, in a slow tracking shot, eventually meets the lateral edges of our own (indeed originally white) plane of perception, the full performance of the first song will now have to emerge from this unmistakable screening-within-the-screen. Such is a passing effect that divides audience from vocal source and, for once, from the character's own mirror image—but that also mediates her privacy, magnifies it in shadow play as occluded visual field. Here, then, is the heroine in an iconic parable of her own screen presence. Not only will this scene of mirroring replication (enhanced at the start in secondary shadow duplicate against the prayer shawl) be many times repeated in the film, but the dovetailing of voiced song with interior monologue that ensues sets up exactly those alternating currents of expressive vent that constitute characterization itself in this plot-long performance. Then, too, this variant of the musical comedy norm helps to edit as well as editorialize the narrative, frequently tracking the heroine across space and time. In so doing, these shifts in vocal register offer a mode—and model—of intuitive continuity in its own right, now flashing forward in imagination, now looping back into the present, then again traversing real time to here another room, there a new locale. Voiceover can thus provide a means of passing over, a transition, a momentum.

"Where Is It Written?" this first song asks: where is the scripture that forbids Yentl's desire for learning? And the question ends up being wrung from her again, without being allowed to ring out, in the song's shift of scene to the upstairs women's gallery at the synagogue. Always this wavering between song in solitude and, by contrast, a subliminal *strain* in company: the agent of longing everywhere on edge because in fact tensely repressed, checked on the very cusp of voice. In neither private nor communal space can "where is it written?" become a viable (voluble) inquiry—in the form of a demand—that the protagonist can aggressively set forth, only a question to sequester. And this first musical scene puts in place the scaffold for recurrent later ramifications of this melodic constraint. Streisand's lips move in articulating the lyric query, and later words to its effect, only when alone, with her mouth instead tightened to the silence of a merely interior if still urgent yearning whenever she moves (in this matrix scene's establishing pattern) into earshot of her sleeping father—or at the song's close, of the women in the temple gallery. Both this latter end of the opening song montage and the previous blocking of its initial mirror shot are so crucial to the complicated audial template of the film that they were separately worked out in California video run-throughs with friends as well as collaborators (as we learn from Streisand's remarkably interesting DVD rehearsal commentary). Only then, and once actually filmed on location, could they be brought together in bracketing the final conception of this establishing song arc. The interior wooden framing of the window that would have closed out Yentl's voice in her deleted first scene outside the synagogue does in a sense return here, in the interior gallery shot. This time it serves to bar her quite literally, by a wooden railing, from the space of sacred interchange, behind which her vocals subside against the backdrop of chattering women—a white noise, or more like gray, coming into audition as the musically scored inner voicing fades off into this murmurous hubbub of drowned-out private sound.

But listen again to that moment in the opening musical number when Yentl's lips must first resist her song, when she first strategically decides to hold her words unshaped, her voice in abeyance. This happens when she must leave her private space of inquiry to tend to her father in the next room. Until that point she has been singing in unguarded close-up, her expressive image only restricted, naturally, by the forward limit of the screen. Though her voice of course flows over into the auditorium, into the space of audition, there is a kind of matte finish to the recording at this point—intimate and vivid, as always, and in Streisand's unique continuum with normal vocal enunciation—but not drastically different in resonance from the preceding dialogue on the soundtrack. The first lyrics, in other words, are still framed credibly within the precincts of the narrative space, part of its "ambient" sound—until Yentl's voice can no longer be permitted breathing room within that space, that social diegesis. For the remainder of the song, gone mostly interior, but sometimes given throat, the recording technique switches to a pronounced but subtle reverb. It thus takes its place more openly within that studio sound of which Streisand has been so gifted a manipulator in the preceding decade and a half of her pop recordings especially (though this and later dramatic transitions in the *Yentl* score are smoothed over, normalized, for the remixed soundtrack album).

At this point in the first number, Streisand's singing is all of a sudden illogically, psychologically, enlarged, markedly amplified on the Dolby soundtrack, filling the theater more completely, pressing on us, circumambient. We are asked to think of ourselves no longer as listening exactly but receiving, immersed, and what is more, this transition is never to be reversed. Streisand's film draws in this way upon, in order to exaggerate and mobilize for theme, a "sonic model" of "close-miked" voice reproduction that film historian Alan Williams, well before *Yentl*, had stressed as borrowed in turn, by the musical genre at large, from the "particular technological norms or codes of the American recording industry."[2] From here on, whether the sung melodies are dubbed or over-voiced, synchronous or entirely interior and autonomous, they are recorded more or less with this same aural resonance and just slightly artificial reverb. After the first recitative as prayer, what Yentl is therefore felt to utter, even when articulated by her lips as music, are never quite just songs but rather expressive impulses conveying their own private fiber and vibrancy, motions of the mind with whose pulse we are meant to find ourselves in sympathetic vibration. And not least by analogy with the thrall of the Streisand sound on record. We don't eavesdrop, we are granted access—or better to say we are plugged in.

Technology in *Yentl* thus stands in a multiple and curious relation to psychology. The distancing effect overcome in the live recording of *A Star Is Born*, but risking at the same time a displacement from storyline to recorded concert, is cocooned instead as internal monologue in *Yentl*. In this one musical film at least, the dubbing, the synchronous "duping," is never meant to dupe us. This is because the songs, when voiced rather than just superimposed upon a narrative space by the musical track, still represent only the outer limit of the mere *will* to voice, available to us solely through a privileged vision and audition. Incarnating the very paradox of sound on film, in its never more than fictional convergence with the gestural body on-screen, Yentl is a character consciously seeking a match between body and voice, striving to motivate the unexpressed exactly through her own physicality. By what convincing logic, though, do we hear her when she is only straining to hear herself? The very raising of that question is the film's deepest ingenuity. The songs, through their subtle reverberation, seem not finally assumed to share the narrative space with her but rather to open an alternative space. It is our listening, then, that lends the latter its shape and definition, its terrain and its craving horizons alike. We might think of listening under these conditions—an exaggerated case of that *listening in* so often elicited by the Streisand sound—as the acousmatic equivalent, again technologically figured, of mind-reading. To do so is in its own way to recall the telepathy motif not so much of the romance plot in *On a Clear Day You Can See Forever* at large but rather of its transference to the dynamics of post-synced vocals in the attempted distance-closing "Come Back to Me" number. In *Yentl* too, the immersive, the circumambient, as I've characterized its volumetric sound, might seem to some resistant ears swamping, engulfing. If that's its liability, it's also, in narrative context, its power.

Moreover, the diversified echo effect, the variably heightened sonority, though never canceled entirely, is dramatically increased—an aural code for the close-quartered reverbs of interiority—when Yentl is hiding her vocal energy from characters within her narrative vicinity. That this code of internal echo is thereby most pronounced when she is farthest from announcing out loud her own desires only binds the effect more tightly to the soundtrack's central conception. By the inverse ratio of a subjective dispensation—constituting the film's deepest poetic license—its heroine, and through her its star, its recording star, is most with us when she is held at the greatest remove from others within the scene, most ours when she is most exclusively "herself"—that is, incarnate as the Streisand sound personified. The technologically finessed histrionics of stardom are in this manner recuperated as period psychology. After the first few sung lines, Yentl's voice does not invade the theater as if from behind the screen, and does not, as in most films, even pretend to. Rather, her voice occupies our own space as if from within, a kind of phonic intersubjectivity between star and audience opened out on the topographic playing field of that sound's own textured extension. Once again somatic, almost haptic, in its intimacy, the magnitude of this voice contrives effectively to stand for Yentl's amplitude of spirit, however dampened or constrained within the plot's historical and cultural context.

When the orphaned heroine is encouraged, in the scene following her father's burial, with the bromide that "life" must "go on," the unstated crisis is not a mourning for the father only but a melancholy incorporation of lost possibility for herself: the life of the mind he both embodied and nourished. When next assured by the neighbor woman promising to house her that she'll be kept so busy she "won't have time to think," the sting of the idiom is registered as a tiny convulsion—Streisand at her most intuitive—on the otherwise blank mask of Yentl's numbed grief. Distilled cause and its precipitated effect: in order precisely "to think," to have contemplative "time" for herself, her image must be remade in the world's eyes. The funeral scene's fade-to-black, followed in dissolve—past a grieving optic drapery—to the liberation of the shrouded mirror, directly prepares us for Yentl's part in a mournful rite of passage in the ensuing scene: the funeral of her father's daughter in rebirth as a male agent. In an adjacent room, she now removes the mourning cloth from her own smaller mirror: this one melodramatically cracked on the diagonal. Yentl's having a piece of her lapel ceremonially ripped at the gravesite, just before, can thus appear in its own right "mirrored" in what happens next within the frame of this fractured looking-glass. For in front of this second and baldly symbolic mirror, wielding an oversized pair of sewing scissors, Yentl now slices through her luxuriant tawny locks, dividing herself from herself across the split of that same fissured plane (fig. 24).

Streisand reports that she "didn't intellectualize this" but felt that it just "seemed right" at this point, that crack in the mirror: in unaddressed effect, seemed right to

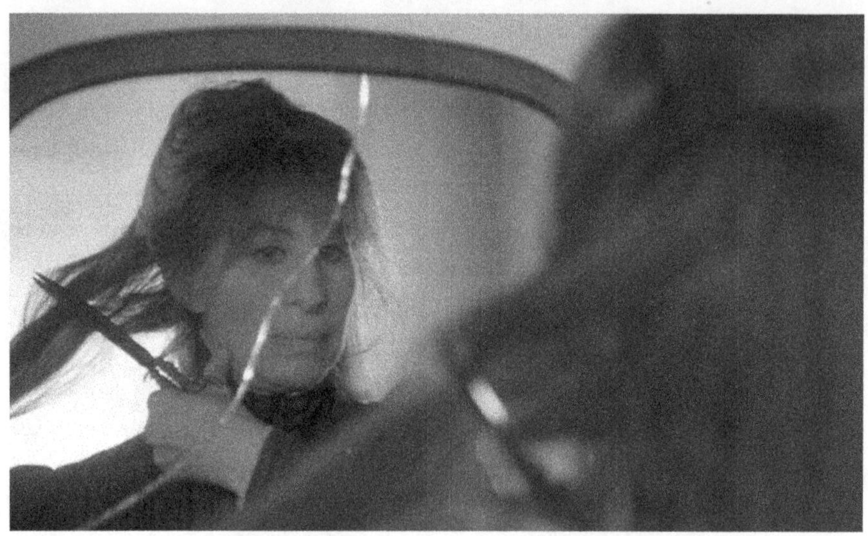

24. Split image/gender divide (*Yentl*)

have Yentl sliced in two, in advance, along this angled axis immediately before its flawed surface would next reflect (if the camera were to hold on it) her duplicated self-image as short-haired boy. But the camera doesn't hold. Cut on the cut. Here, already bisected on the bias, *the mirror has two faces* well before Streisand's own film by that name. And with cause flipped immediately again to effect. Matching the jagged glass fissure with the scissor's own angled slicing, it is on the sharp third clip of this denaturing tool that editing responds with the film's most abrupt jump cut: to Yentl setting out in male garb on the road the next day. In this film, and its uniquely radical mirror of difference, self-image is yet again the motor of plot. Intuition, not intellection: really? Is Streisand low-balling it? Even regarding this fairly overt symbolism of a skewed and cloven psyche and its splintered desires? In any case, what we'll find reflected, deflected, and multiplied in the film's subsequent mirrors—only a few of which (three in the tailor shop) Streisand alludes to by comparison at this early point in the DVD commentary—renders moot any distinction between gut feeling and a strategized linchpin of narrative development. For here is a pattern at least as definitive, this nexus of looking-glass imaging, as the forded-water motif.

We now follow the ghost of Yentl in the "figure" of Anshel, the dead brother and double, to her first night alone on the road, a disguised female picaro seeking shelter in the forest. Here the second song ("Papa, Can You Hear Me?") begins again in a prayer that is voiced but invisibly received. And that reverses direction in the lines of sight: "I see a million eyes," Yentl sings, alluding to the twinkling specks of starlight above, asking "Which ones are yours?" The song is sung out loud, but half to herself, half to an unseen spiritual auditor. Translated from its theological status as prayer to the dead, this is the secular nature of musical expression in the film: a melodic, pre-conversational monologue that must ordinarily suppress its intent and intensity behind closed lips. Only when alone, as in this second number, can Yentl discharge her energy without fear of detection and reprisal. Yet played by Streisand, it is the figure's exact situation before the rapt gaze of the camera, as well as the italicizing of the mise-en-scène by the lyrics about "stars" and "illumination," that turns this second song setting into another parable of the cinema: of its rectangular robe of light, its specular basis, the special aura of its star performances. The supplicant is overheard in song (and ultimately from overhead) at the center of an omniscient 360-degree shot (the star's coveted good left side foregone, as in so many of the "denaturalizing" shots in this film, as if the less flattering angle, as she herself suggests, were the more "masculine"—or at least the less She). As a single wind-fluttered candle casts light on her from a makeshift tree-stump altar, this musical setting comes once more into manifest alignment with the cinematic projection that materializes it. The scene even closes with an overt effect of cinematographic processing: a dissolving close-up of Streisand superimposed over a withdrawing reverse zoom that dims and distances a second image of her to no more than a single glimmering dot, a point of light indistinguishable from the candlepower that discloses her in the first place. The optic parable is hard to miss. An expressive presence alone in the dark, illuminated by a single flickering source of light, stared upon by a "million eyes" out of the impalpable blackness past the zone of the image: this is the cinema staging its own conditions as unrestrained star vehicle, even as its heroine remains a self still held in reserve by the narrative.

When Yentl as Anshel goes public, the solo voice of elegiac address must enter the world of secular study and exchange, of intellectual and erotic competition, and must enter not as song but as conversation. In its transition from covert prayer to this new mode of utterance, the "Papa, Can You Hear Me?" number cuts away again to "Anshel" on the road the next morning; in a vocal practice session, she is trying to lower her speaking voice into a credibly masculine register. It is as if the insider's pleasure at having DVD access to those rehearsal tapes has for a moment been offloaded onto the film itself, with Streisand caught practicing her part on site: the equivalent of the vocal exercises the singer has often said she has no patience for. "If I am not for myself, who will be for me?" the disguised Yentl quotes from her illicit spiritual reading, a recitation then deepened in gruffer macho repetition; yet "if I am for myself alone, who am I?" Identity is of course the troubled nub of the whole transvestite venture. Having called out unanswerably to a lost (but internalized) origin in the previous scene, she labors now, out loud but unheard, toward some middle ground between self-communion and community. She will not be alone again in song until she has begun to recognize her passion for Avigdor—and has secluded herself to let her feelings out. It is only then that, before another mirror, she temporarily removes the bandages that have flattened her breasts—as if to heal the injury of her gender as a disability in the search for learning. Yentl has by this point already compared her short-cropped hair to the opulent curls of Hadass in the latter's dining-room looking-glass, another of the film's self-divisive planes of inspection. The viewer of such secondary viewing is certainly cued to recognize—maybe even "intellectualize"—every duplicated image as the uncomfortable source of potential disidentification and emotional displacement. But by just the checklist so far, we have overlooked more than one secondary reflection en route: fleeting mirror shots that help set up the emphasis of the rest.

Mirror/Mirror\Mirror

The easiest mirror to forget, certainly, with no song attached to refigure its introspection, is one missing link so far—appearing during Yentl's first (and last) night sharing a bed with Avigdor. While he's enthusing about his engagement to Hadass, Yentl looks at herself quizzically in a small wall glass over the boarding-house dresser, asking "Is she pretty, this Hadass?" All the while she is being sliced in half, on the bias again, so to say, by another diagonal: this time not a crack but the beveled divide between image and the rest of her disguised and out-of-frame gender truth (fig. 25). She'll soon have occasion to decide for herself about Hadass's looks, and by contrast again with

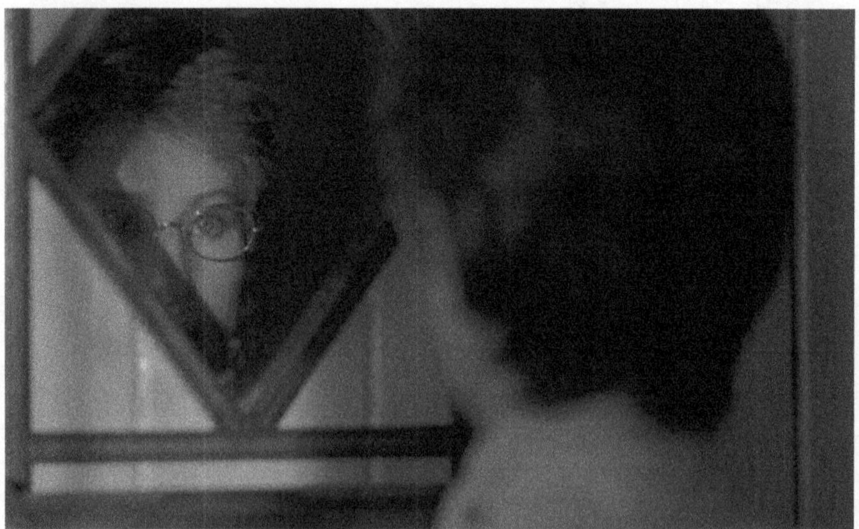

25. Off-frame desire (*Yentl*)

her own distorted male image, in the former's own dining-table mirror—with Yentl there touching nervously the loose ends of her shorn hair, straggling beneath her man's cap, as she stares at herself, chagrined, past Hadass's extravagant perfumed curls. And that by-now fifth mirror scene follows directly as a check upon her delight in being hugged by Avigdor in front of the full-length dorm mirror—after a brief perfunctory fuss over their dress before setting off, by joint invitation, to Hadass's formal dinner table. In perfect symmetry, this momentary mirror shot, over their own shoulders, is a reverse match cut—almost its own mirror reversal in this sense—from the capstone gesture of the previous rousing musical montage in "This Is One of Those Moments," where Avigdor gives Anshel a sideways hug for scoring a point (even in a correction of him) with the rabbi. It is in that song montage, played out under compression and lyric elevation, that every charming glance from the rom-com playbook is deployed in the celebration of an exhilarating homosocial warmth between study partners: Yentl inflamed with banked heterosexual love, Avigdor smitten with his younger boy's infatuated admiration and wicked quickness.

In the buildup to this moment, where Anshel has sheepishly corrected one of Avigdor's own Talmudic answers, an over-voiced "Yentl within" sings out (while still holding in) her joy at being at last able to "listen to the lesson of the leaves"—with its acoustically suited slant rhyme (*lissn* against *lessn*), as well as its pun on textual "leaves." She has indeed come to inhabit, in serial montage, exactly "one of those moments" she's dreamed of, with "certain things" achieved that "no man can take away." But that momentary feminist confidence sweeps forward into a fuller litany of the inexorable. Once even clandestine female ambition is ignited, the lyric juggernaut takes over in this reverberant escalation of pleasure and pride. It isn't just that such energies are impervious to patriarchal interdict. No man can steal away her triumph, but, as the lyric builds, nor—in a run of metaphors for unavailing onslaughts against this newly secured sense of self—can wave wash away, nor wind blow away, nor tide turn away, nor fire burn away, nor time wear away. All these threats are dismissed in the defiant build of this melodic anaphora, until at its peak Streisand's high note—insisting on those "things" now won and owned—blasts open this negated cascade. It does so with a prolonged, trumpet-like "nooouuwww"—opening on its own resounding terms the very space of elation in just such a vocally dilated "moment." It is a moment immediately laid claim to and "now" rounded out by the ringing ten-second last syllable of those ineffable things "about to be"—at last and after all—"miiiiiiiine." Riding in at the height of one passionately achieved desire, her yearning for a learned life, immediately in the next scene the ensuing optical comedown for Anshel the student, in the person of Yentl the woman, is to see all too well, given the image of Hadass in her own mirror now, what Avigdor sees in her. It is a recognition that propels the film into its decisive next stage.

What then follows—in the gradient of erotic frustration—is in fact another fluid and complex mirror scene that is ultimately precipitated by Avigdor's appearing up close and stark naked before Anshel at the nearby river's favored swimming spot. "You're really missing something," says Avigdor, just inches away from her seated gaze: meaning the cooling water. But comic dialogue finds again its opening. Peering with embarrassed secret eagerness over the edge of her book, beyond which everything imaginable seems laid bare, her answer offers up another of the script's equivocations-turned-questions in the form, this time, of an internalized triple entendre: "Am I?" The sensual pleasure of skinny dipping, of nakedness together; the forbidden glimpse in voyeuristic close-up, very much hers for the taking; the potential erotic consummation on at least one of their minds: all knitted together in Streisand's wry raised eyebrow. Another such slipped gear of dialogue follows. Refusing to strip, despite Avigdor's aggressive prodding—resisting what would amount to reciprocal sexual "exposure"—Anshel is next rescued, not by her own sly quip but by having words put mercifully in her mouth. When Avigdor, thinking to have outed her, says he's guessed why she won't join in the naked camaraderie, her momentary spasm of panic leaps at its relief in echoing his misfired guess: "That's right, I can't swim!"

And it is this ruse of double talk that leads next to that further double (mirror) image, more intricately intertwined with desire and its split purposes than ever before: the male dorm room turned self-confessional boudoir. In this sense it is quite fair to say that the motif of doubled but estranged presence in the chain of mirror images keeps reflecting back on itself with each new instance, especially when reframed by the shifting parameters of the film's crisscrossed melodic lines. In fact, with quiet dramatic tact, the one Top 40 hit from the soundtrack, the erotic ballad "The Way He Makes Me Feel"—its long *e*'s given even more phonetic play in Streisand's delivery than the smoothed-out alliterative impact of "*m*akes *m*eee"—arrives at the convergence of two leading streams in the text: the motifs of watercourse and mirror alike. The song is set loose, in private relief from the heroine's sexual nerves—the mix of excitement and feared unmasking at the river's swimming bank—when she's finally alone in her room. We learn from the DVD commentary that an unself-conscious Patinkin, as Avigdor, disconcerted the whole crew, Streisand in particular, by going for full frontal nudity after his swim, as the camera tilt-pans from his bare feet on the grassy bank up his hair-streaked wet legs to a sudden cut, just in time, at mid-thigh, to Yentl perturbed and nonplussed by an overplus of twitchy curiosity. Now, in her solitude, contemplating her own true undressed image in gendered release, that recent and carefully framed eroticism is reprised upon the luxurious *self*-recognition of her own body in the internal framing of another looking-glass.

But one is always listening, as well as watching. Begun in unsynchronized monologue when Anshel rushes from Avigdor's nude blandishments, "The Way He Makes Me Feel" has broken out into voiced song as Yentl moves free of the rowdy students into a dizzy cinematographic privacy. At its climax, the song's dramatic overlay of mirror and soliloquy positions these narrative features as figurative redefinitions of each other yet again—and does so, as in "Where Is It Written?," within the analogous functioning of the cinematic medium itself. In a dissociation of visual register from identification, the heroine stares into her own eyes so as to analyze, across the assonant linkages of the lyric itself, "feelings I hardly recogn*ize*," and again with a clinging hold on the I-rhyme ("eyes" virtually hidden within it), as "miiine." Yentl watching herself sing in a mirror doubles unmistakably for Streisand seeing—managing, executing—her own image dubbed, lip-synced. And this for a lyric imprisoned still in the third person of an absent and unapproachable "he." Allowed to animate the lips only in solitude, hers is a voicing of desire incapable of any intercourse.

In just this respect, that riverside camerawork leaves its own afterimage: an incomplete shift from the illicit look to the self-inquisitive. Alone in "their" room (inner plurality, not gender neutrality), Anshel, again Yentl, is confronted and accompanied only by her own image. Scrutinizing herself now in an undoing, a literal unwrapping, of her male disguise, still shaken by her riverbank desire, she breathlessly undresses, including the unstrapping of her gauze-flattened breasts—the first we've gathered, let alone seen, of this prosthetic negation. Its constraint is laid bare here like a bandage over gender's injury and its emotional bruising. Two low-keyed metaphoric turns in the Bergmans' lyric converge on this transition from waterside to mirror: the "river of surprise" (sustaining the film's long-standing motif) that is "flowing through my body" and the "bundle of confusion" literalized by the tight swathing of that body (fig. 26). With the horizontal panning frame shifting right so as to elide the last of these unwindings, Yentl next stands presumably naked as the camera moves up, replaying the vertical pan of Avigdor's nakedness, from her own bare feet and knees to mid-thigh—at which point her nightdress, rather than an edit, is the curtain lowered into place just in time. The two answering vertical shots are inflected by a second "framing," however, that folds this parallel genital tease into a more telling structural sequence. It isn't just narrative camerawork that draws the parallel between deflected crotch shots but in particular Yentl's own POV, since the naked image of her as the fabric drops—confirmed for us only after the fact—is again hers of herself, investigative rather than exhibitionist,

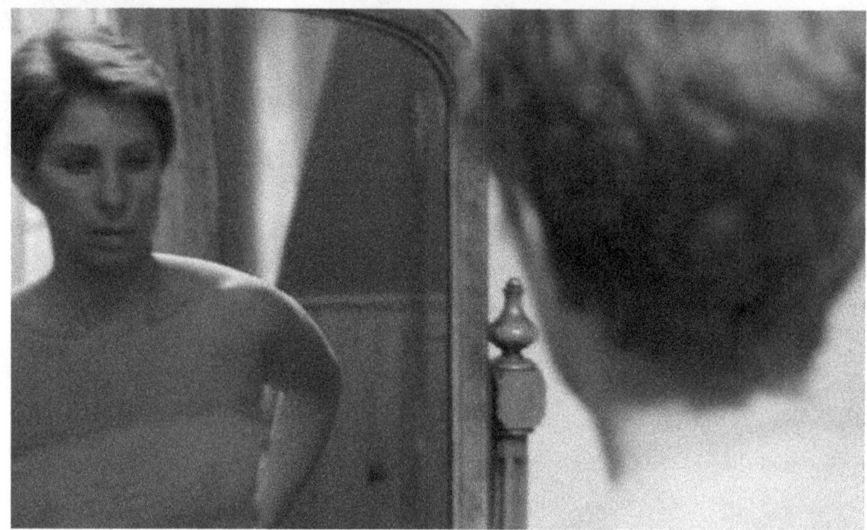

26. "A bundle of confusion" (*Yentl*: "The Way He Makes Me Feel")

caught this time too in that same full-length mirror, whose frame is now manifest in delayed reveal by a widening vantage of the camera.

But this redemption of voyeurism by autoerotic self-consciousness is only the second cinematographic ingenuity in this pivotal scene. What has preceded it is as tricky to describe as its gliding optical subterfuge is hard to parse, even on rescreening. Before that subsequent play between screen plane and the mirror's secondary field of optic in(tro)spection—and thus between levels of identification, with camera and star respectively—there has been an even more remarkable transition in the narrative field of vision. In an elusive dexterity of montage elision, this whole sequence has begun with the camera panning right from Anshel, fully clothed on "his" bed, to Yentl disrobing in front of the disclosed mirror just to the right. With no time elapsed for her physical shift in position, the temporal lag is fudged by the atmospheric blur—like a slur in the articulation of narrative itself—of a fast and barely detectable diaphanous dissolve on the intervening wall. Streisand is so wedded to the long take that it must at times be tricked into continuity through its antithesis in the cut. Even before we close in on the optic doubling of Yentl before the mirror of self-examination, here then—here; there—are literally two bodies in tension, as well as attempted transaction, with each other: both sharing the *same space* at what, by a finesse in the edit, has been rendered as virtually the *same time*. In Streisand's own terms elsewhere for the musical rhythm of montage, elapsed in this case is the film's smoothest "legato" as its own sublimated cut—its own blurred disjuncture—between alter egos. Difference squared: a single cramped film set containing two incarnations of the star, yet again cloned into self-division. To group together, as the film's sixth mirror scene, both this unexpected pan to one such looking-glass and the subsequent dollying back, all over again, to its revealed frame—is to recognize how the barely separate shots (disguised student on bed, stripped anatomy under inspection) blueprint the film's foundational duality: between embodiment and the longing it must *face up to*.

It is just this self-recognized desire in the almost visible "way he makes me feel" that now, ironically, precipitates the story's more extreme turning point: Anshel's willingness to play along with Avigdor's idea of marrying Hadass—as marked again by mirror fragmentation. Along with the mottled glass door noted in this book's Overture, by which misrecognition is so lucidly figured by partial occlusion ("People are *blind!*"), this narrative's whole corkscrew of erotic plotting makes it clear that the bridegroom's threefold full-length mirrorings in the tailor shop are designed to splinter and redistribute the character's image at this cusp of the crisis before the wedding. Erupting across this episode as well—this fitting of the misfit—are a dozen flash-forwards to the eponymous "Tomorrow Night," with Avigdor and Yentl staring ambiguously at each other in the wedding procession. These answer to a previous barrage of seven split-second flashbacks. Those spurts of resurgent memory, on the verge of Avigdor's flight from town in a crowded carriage, have brought to Yentl's mind's eye all that is about to be lost until, to forestall his departure, she changes her mind and agrees that "nothing's impossible" (the marriage he proposes for, rather than to, her). After that resulting tailor-shop's split of her image from itself, with Anshel being "groomed" for heterosexual consummation, the film's remaining mirror is the one in front of which she (still as Anshel) primps as the new couple awaits Avigdor's arrival for another dinner—and for an imagined celibate threesome that fails completely when he realizes that Hadass has actually fallen in love with Anshel. The idealized perverse menage can't succeed after all, and Avigdor storms from the house.

Until then, one excuse after another has had to be fabricated for Anshel not claiming his conjugal duty from his bride. But Hadass's own frustration has become too painful for Yentl to endure. As the unrequited wife falls asleep once more unfulfilled, Yentl begins actually to sing again in company (however oblivious her spouse)—as she did, in the film's first song, beyond her father's bedroom door. While others sleep, her unconscious wells up. Letting her voice out is the whole point, a desire unveiled this time from behind the bedroom curtains. Replacing a quieter ballad, "The Moon and I" (available, unfilmed, on the DVD), "No Matter What Happens" begins with an overlay of moon glow on Yentl's face that marks the fade from indoors to out: the strolling nocturnal lyric becoming a kind of (re)constitutional. "I wanted the shadows," she admits, but "I don't anymore"—as marked by the song's gaining pulse and volume in her moonlight walk. Bringing the mirror motif to a climax in lyric rather than image, or in other words in pure metaphor, her compulsion at last—in the new consonance of internal rhyme and lengthening vocal intonation—is "to see myself" and so "to free myself" and thus, bloomingly, to "beeeee myself at laaaast." And to do so, in tapping a "voice deep inside," by having this phrasal series dwell, at first, on the same alliterative pitch, while swelling only its volume, until reaching the suddenly and emphatically scaled-up last note of "at LAST," where vocal tone seems rising as if to its own relief. Leading up to this ladder-runged "*see, free, be*" crescendo—in the convergent vectors of recognition and release—is one of the best of the many crisp lyrics from the Bergmans. Yentl's avoidance of a "*sun*light" that would reveal too much has been put into cross-word rhyme with the moon as the "*one* light" that "I walked in," a fact we see presently—if now transitionally, vanishingly—enacted. But here grammatical rhyme takes over from sound rhyme, so that this moonlight is also what "I bathed in" and what, we next assume, "I held in"—until that sense of internalization is immediately switched instead by syntactic swivel (a kind of internal poetic volta) to the new grammar: "held in . . . my feelings."

At this turn of phrase and volume, we are treated to one of the surefire adrenalin rushes of the Streisand filmography: the reverse-tracking shot giving way to transitional determination as she charges straight toward the camera, a signal difference between stage act and cinematographic action. We've reviewed such moments briefly before, but they come to mind again here—almost as if intentionally—in this accentuated strutting of her vocal stuff. There is the railway station exit in "Don't Rain on My Parade," straight at the camera, and then in side view past the stroboscopic flash of railings that animate her momentum with a kind of filmic flicker effect. There is Dolly's hello again to life (after her previous charge toward the camera in both "Just Leave Everything to Me" and "Put on Your Sunday Clothes"), striking out finally after an address to the dead husband at the reverse-dolly launch of the "Before the Parade Passes By" number—with her revitalized forward progress technically "wiped," whipped away, to an actual street march. There is the title song of "On a Clear Day" in her sweep toward the camera across the campus rose garden. Later, the release at last from Nick's spell in *Funny Lady* in transit along the endless hotel hallway of "Let's Hear It for Me"—after her earlier bout of aggressive negation in the forward-stalking bitterness, from dressing room to empty stage-front, of "How Lucky Can You Get?"

Capitalizing on this backlog of forward motion at the "No Matter What Happens" pivot in *Yentl*—and before the closing scene's reprise of this full-stride power walk toward a now-shipboard (then helicoptered) camera—the dynamic is already unmistakable on this eve of revelation. When the "voice deep inside" is getting "stronger," it is also, by the blocking of an emblematic ground plan matched to the contoured terrains of the voice, visualized as getting closer—in one of those perfect scalar duets of camerawork and orchestrated vocal force. After a few yards and a few bars of advancing confidence in "No Matter What Happens," the lunar mood has moved through opalescent hues on the soundtrack along the shimmering climb of Streisand's high notes. Awaiting, as we probably guess, their brutal disenchantment in the next turn of plot. But for now, change is its own narrative as well as libidinal imperative. Indeed, in the full semantic arc implied by the new number's shortened title and rounded out in the lyric's actual last cadence— "No Matter What Happens (it won't be the same anymore)"—the song's open-ended erotic resolve may well allude to that "nothing, nothing, nothing is the same" of her early hit (and Glenn Gould favorite) "He Touched Me." As always when at full throttle, Streisand's voice takes its stand for difference embodied.

After this episode of lyrical determination, the musical texture of the narrative is suspended, longer than previously, for the sad denouement of her new hopes in the disclosure to Avigdor. It is only after hazardously casting off her disguise, and then losing her chance with him by retaining the spirit of her masquerade's aspiration, that she can find her voice again—where, after another reverse-tracking shot onboard ship, the reverse zoom of a technical rather than psychological *long shot* can take to the skies in open-ended closure. Before which, however, with the Streisand sound in abeyance, Streisand the director achieves some of her most exacting work with her own script.

"No Wonder"

No matter what happens, another river is now to be crossed—and, as might have been expected, a bridge too far. In the new commitment to her passion, and promising Avigdor the disclosure of a secret in coming excitedly to Lublin (doubled by Prague and the Charles Bridge in an extended crane shot), Yentl is ready at last to render her relation with him, in the words of the precipitating ballad, not "the same anymore"—in fact to explode the ruse of sameness by opening both her heart and her shirt (or should we say blouse?) to him in the confession of her long subterfuge. As if to stress her supposed beardless youth in the original Singer story, Avigdor's "eyes widened" when she vows to "get undressed" so as to prove her point. Boyhood on the line, it "occurred to him that Anshel might want to practice pederasty."[3] Panicked and enraged at first in the film (whatever his wide-eyed reaction might have implied in the story), he can warm to the idea of desiring her only once he cools off regarding the previous deception, about which his outrage is in itself a revelation. In Yentl's attempted "normalizing" of relations, the film thus enters upon its genuinely queerest nest of inference. Once his fury has subsided, relief is at one with new desire. At least he wasn't smitten all along with a real boy! So long confounded and deferred in the warring factions of Avigdor's mind, but now divided further by ethnic and cultural as well as gender entrenchments, the hetero/normative regime struggles to assert itself. Predictably enough, his desire for a woman so much like a beloved pal is bested by his expectations for a culturally valorized femininity. Hadass is bound to resurface again, a check on untoward desire: the renewed and standardized fallback option. Yentl is willing to run away with him—but not from her dream of institutional learning. This he refuses, and so she refuses him. But in the heat of disclosure and closed ranks, the turning point is at least as erotic as it is sociological.

All this takes the time to unfold that Streisand's direction is willing to give it. Until now, the ocular ricochets of the threesome have made for a splendid and heady comic dilemma, milked (and miked) to perfection by script and star alike in and out of the musical numbers. The plot's dizzying lines of affiliation in the cross-purposes of scripted desire have kept both our senses and our expectations on edge, even as the musical ligatures (especially in the rococo cross-cutting of the nervous "No Wonder" dinner theater) have worked to tighten the subjective focus, and channel the emotional voltage, of scene after scene. Threading these episodes of erotic relay and abnegation together, queer perspectives proliferate and refocus each other. With Hadass's subplot read through a lesbian lens, from her point of view there may well be something of the unglimpsed female that she thrills to in the person as well as temperament of her restrained boy groom. If only men could be as soft and sensible as women . . . but that's putting too mildly the nevertheless downplayed sexual hints at her end of the unconsummated scenario. Flipped to Avigdor's side of the unstable equation, the homoeroticism is more tangible and intense—though in its own way fairly easy for him to dismiss in the upshot: a passing phase (boys' school and all) on the long way round to sanctioned marriage. This erotic dimension of intellectual rapport is briefly defused by the initial comic scene of their shared hostel bed. Yet it is never forgotten by the plot in driving toward recognition. Implicated here are the many quick-cut glimpses of Avigdor's touch-buddy roistering with Anshel, his affectionate jabs and hugs, which have regularly served—beyond near-miss exposure in the disguise comedy—to cast a tentative sexual shadow, or glow, over their student bonding.

When sex with Hadass has been particularly on his mind, he's all the more likely to deflect the physicality of his desire (while still unconsciously to direct it) toward his innocent friend Anshel. Giddy over the prospect of the "wedding night" when still engaged, his roughhouse tousling forces a jealous complaint from Yentl: "Why are you always grabbing me?"—an objection whose premise he immediately denies. Instead of being defused in process, in a boys-will-be-boys mode, the queering of such insular Yeshiva norms goes far toward explaining, not what it is that finally prevents Avigdor, once the shock is over, from accepting Yentl as an insistently strong woman still seeking access to a man's world of learning—a conjugal dead end dictated by cultural stereotype—not that, but something else. We begin to understand, once his guard is down, what kindles his volcanic rage at the discovery of Yentl's identity in the first place. He immediately fulminates against her "demon"-like violation of the Talmud, not his personal betrayal by her con job. But the outrage is indeed personal, physical. The latter he comes to relax into, flattered by its motive: her admitted passionate love for him. Until then, however, there seems something filthy and fiendish in female desire outside of its passive place in sex—and by inference something fearful as well, no less, in a warm male response to its masculine disguise.

It may be easy on first viewing to write this stance off as orthodoxy in uptight recoil: the stance, but not its convulsive fury—which Patinkin understands so well he inclines to overdo it. In the rehearsal tape for this confrontation, from the DVD again, we see Streisand in the throes of double consciousness. She is playing her heroine's part under the painful lash of Avigdor's contempt while also, askew to their confrontation, redirecting with her left hand one of the two camera operators needed to compass the emotional vortex of this intrepid wheeling shot—even while urging Patinkin to tone down the volume of his outrage. Her complicated technical idea amounts to having the polarized couple circling each other—an emotional abyss yawning between and beneath them—rather than having them face off in anything like a straightforward intercut debate. Emotion is indeed spiraling out of control. Even the idiom of Avigdor's incensed rage and panic reverts to the protective vernacular of a bitter but still almost half-unconscious paradox, spluttered out in the midst of his screaming frenzy: "Why didn't you tell me that you weren't a man? C'mon, answer me like a man." Even with such an idiomatic cliché cruelly rearing its head, he seems trapped between nostalgia and bitter irony, still addressing the vanished Anshel. But when he begins to accept both her truth and her motives—Yentl's now, the transgressive woman's—his only language of recognition reverts to the celebration of pure sensual desire reprised from the much earlier "No Wonder" montage. It was there that Yentl was so readily able, if still ironically, to plug into Avigdor's facile acquiescence in Hadass's deferential modesty and manicured charms. This time it isn't a woman recognizing the obvious appeal of another woman but Avigdor himself recognizing what he should have seen through to in the eager camaraderie of his prolonged homosocial bonding. Twice repeated for emphasis, even in its ellipses, as the flip side of Hadass's realized charms: "No wonder.

Oh my god, no wonder. I wanted to look at you, to touch you." To vary the full earlier lyric: no wonder he loved him. "I thought there was something wrong with me." Yentl to the immediate rescue of homosexual shame: "No, it was me." Even in exonerating him, at this point she is still declaring herself, Yentl rather than Anshel, as the source of the blameful deceit—and in the process excusing his conservative self from erotic guilt, a charge reduced to a mere lapse of heterosexual perceptiveness.

From which lapse, he doesn't immediately recover. Bafflement persists—until her ultimate romantic (as well as gender) confession. Why did she continue the escalating complexities of the deception? Why preserve the masquerade amid the literally geometric complications of triangulated desire? Why not flee, rather than risk pain and exposure? Yentl's final wrenching declaration—"Because I loved you!"—only serves to disarm and "unman" each of them, in relief and exhaustion at once, as they collapse to their knees and into each other's shoulders, their faces for a long few seconds hidden from the overhead camera. What follows when they look back at each other, and upon the truth, is an exchange that Streisand carefully designed (we learn from the DVD about this cross-cutting) so as to flatter him with backlighting while training the stark "hot light"—riveting enough in a different way, of course—on herself. Eventually the camera shifts ninety degrees for a close-up two-shot on their faces moving in on a kiss: with lips touching, but not quite opening yet, for just as long as they did in Yentl's resisted kiss with Hadass in the preceding episode. With the camera building toward this *interruptus* of a tempting but arrested passion, as reciprocally approached from each side of the hypercharged two-shot, the orchestral score has been notably mounting as well—only to shut down on the instant with Avigdor's abrupt blurting out of the exorcizing name "Hadass." Marked there is the death of some fluidity of feeling that melody—passing in and out of song until now, and back and forth from monologue to emoted lyric—is meant to essentialize. After the two syllables of "Hadass," the silence is, in terms of drama and genre alike, ear-splitting.

And there's no discounting the homoerotic pressure on this seemingly legalistic second thought in a recall of the wronged woman. Voiced out loud, in that single female name, is not so much an alternate yearning, distancing him from an embrace of Yentl, as it is, so he is quick to explain, a concern over the former's own false marriage, for which he rightly feels responsible—and about which Yentl assures him a contrite explanatory note from her to the rabbis will easily annul. But the erotic spell is broken, and precisely by such social anxieties, such patriarchal legalisms, such conservative reins on desire. And, of course, by the tacit relief they can be expected to bring. Even a moment before, on the cusp of discovery and revision, we sense that the kiss would have been too much for him, this open erotic embrace of the boy who was(n't):

too backward-glancing, too much the indulgence of a nostalgic and deviant fantasy. Unequivocal hetero-doxa must intercede—as well as compulsory patrilineage in the choosing of the fitly subservient bride. In the hero's backing instinctively away from a marginally acknowledged queer desire, Hadass proves the perfect retreat.

Both before and after this blocked moment, this drop not just to their knees but into silence, so much thought has gone into this scene, so much preparation, that the camera seems to think it out for us. And again, as at the start of the film—with that excised "entrance" of Yentl excluded from synagogue participation—another deleted scene may appear to retain its dialectical impact even in the final cut. When Yentl has earlier offered to stitch up the funerary rip in Avigdor's lapel, enough time having elapsed in mourning for his own brother, his astonishment at a boy being able to sew is one more nail in the coffin of her disappointed wish that he would recognize her womanhood beneath the tactical trappings of masculinity. With a trace of frustration and annoyance, as his shadow falls over her seamstress features: "You're in my light." So, we realize, in the later revelation scene, would he always wish to steal it. In a similar but now strictly figurative way—when he is confounded by her continuing desire, if they were to elope together, to study still in public—a similar darkening blot falls over her face from his looming presence. It's not just that he's now, and would always be, in her light, blocking access. Even more pointedly this time, although unmentioned in either the script or the commentary, the shadow all but effaces her closed mouth—as if moving to stifle her voice altogether—when he promises "to do the thinking for us."

The subsequent camerawork in the tailing off of this scene, subtler yet, is no less emphatic. With Streisand explaining earlier on the DVD how being "from the theater" inclines her to as few edits as possible in a given scene, letting the actors bridge their own transitions, as it were, the most striking exception to this, after the shot/countershot of her bared womanhood, follows again now. In contrast to the orbiting camerawork of Avigdor's ensuing ferocity, now sex and gender are costars in the reversible impasse of this last shot exchange, biology and emotional teleology. After the circling frenzy of the sexual revelation, that is, the overlapping gender thematic of this climactic episode, peaked at its truncated kiss, subsides into the settled confrontation of opposing "views"—and cinematic viewpoints. This transpires, with all hope of compromise expiring with it, across no less than eight crosscuts as the camera progressively dollies in by turns on each of them, she in the window seat, he across the room, his back to the door. It is here, finally, that Yentl holds firm, with a little insistent shrug, on the "more" she unaccountably wants—with the camera then closing in on his sad but definitive shaking of his head in fade out. Departing from the single takes Streisand quite effectively favors, what she has devised in this case is a masterly capture of difference in the deliberately broken rhythm of montage. A two-shot no longer possible, the closer the camera comes to each of them separately, the farther apart they feel, isolated against each other.

Beyond "The Same Anymore"

So we're back where we started, if not quite, with the original nuptial expectations restored. And so, on Yentl's part, space is made again—a gap opened, a void awaiting infused promise—for yet another and final "solo." The castrating force of role reversal—the man nervously in love with a boy but not with the woman s/he would become, the woman more in love with learning than with a man who can't tolerate it—leaves only one way forward. And with a valedictory moment to confirm it: Yentl still bent on her own destiny beyond the sexual selections of orthodoxy, Avigdor literally taking the horse-cart reins of his return to Hadass. In their parting dialogue we get the film's last and most plangent same-sex gesture: "I'll miss you," a doe-eyed Avigdor says, more than convincingly, into the continuing face of her disguise. Miss not the woman he never had but the friend he doted on and cavorted with. In this final separation, that is, he rubs Yentl's cheek, wryly allowing how her "beard will probably never come in now." This lighthearted quip delivers a heavy dose of homoerotic irony. Here, vanishingly, for one last touch, is the smooth-cheeked boy he has loved, stroked in restraint while the woman's lips have been left unkissed, deflected to a hug instead. His "Goodbye, Anshel" is, for this reason among others, corrected at once: "Yentl," she gently admonishes. And he accedes. Goodbye to both, to male pal and to possible partner, freed as he has been to caress one last time not just the remarkable woman he's giving up but the intriguing young man of his lingering fantasy.

With a last chaste embrace, this detachment from Avigdor in the name of Yentl's own self-determination is now soliloquized, and in deliberate reversal of her congratulatory hug from him back at the Yeshiva, by the leading refrain from that "One of Those Moments" number. What she'll "remember" all her "life" is the parting of their ways and lives. This emphasis on affect already memorialized, just by saying (or singing) so, thrusts all romantic feeling into the bracketed, the always unactionable, past: a node of closure in going forward. Life must still be lived—must be made, if possible, further memorable. And here another melody will recur, for further impetus, in the film's final transitional moment. This reprise of the film's first lyric, asking as it did where the limit on desire is "written," is folded into the film's multistaged climactic aria. What ensues is a lyric of local severance and forward-looking self-asseveration that begins, in a detached voiceover, as if further back than we've ever been privy to. "It all began," we hear at the start of "A Piece of Sky"—initiating a kind of retrospective loop, catching up the psychogenesis of her disruptive desire even before we encountered her obstreperous energy in the early mirror scenes. It all began, that is, when she noticed that her domestic horizons were limited by a "window" vantage on only its one eponymous slice or sector of the outer world. And when she asked where it was forbidden her to look further for herself.

The dubiously written, the correctively read, the relinquished, now at last the released. Then, too, the trickles, runnels, creeks, streams, and rivers forded or bridged until now lend momentum to the ocean-borne finale in a musical epitome set loose, at a deliberate moment of overlapping dissolve, from a transitional density of text itself into the reboot of the original "Where Is It Written?" query. Just before, that is, and fading into, the arriving finale with "A Piece of Sky"—in its exuberant shipboard departure—the now contentedly married couple, Avigdor and Hadass, read a letter intercut with Yentl's writing of it, just her hands in frame moving across the reframed paper rectangle, wishing them well and hoping that Hadass will continue with her study. In the very process of its inscription, the eventual reading of this private epistolary text segues through a lap dissolve—music building behind it—to a heavy Talmudic volume in finger-tip scansion by a preteen girl under the watching eye of an older woman on the upper deck of a crowded steamer, freighted (from this image forward) with new promise. This image fades in over Yentl's closing of that well-wishing goodbye letter with a modest mention of herself: "As for me, I'm going to a new place, where I hear things are different. Anyway, we'll see." Hearsay splintered into "hear" and its potential "see." Visible, one may almost think, in this overlap—and quite beyond its muted wordplay—are the intervening hands of the star, as first-time screenwriter, drafting this very revision (with its American telos) of Singer's story.

Hearing and seeing, cultural rumor and lived confirmation, old and new worlds, pivot on these paired idioms of audiovisual conflation, weighted toward a future that, at the very least, can't be "the same anymore." And certainly isn't—in what now stretches before us in this complex and madly effective climax, building as it does toward the explicit hearing and seeing of Yentl herself in the coming song's last lyrics, where being able to "hear" and "see" and "feel" her father's spirit, she expects the same in reciprocation: his ability to "watch me" in her new world-historical venture of emigration. With the love plot molted and sloughed off behind her—its energies further sublimated, sublimed—this epilogue becomes a pure cultural prognosis, song unshackled as Yentl's final free-voiced liberation. All because she has found a way to resist the dictates of patriarchal script in moving from an opening number, in resistance to the always and already prescribed, to what the camera has figured finally as an image of the pen in her own hand.

After that dissolving inscription from private text to printed sacred volume in the younger girl's shipboard lap, the climactic sequence takes its own spirited time. There at first, on a wintry day under leaden skies, the camera seeks out, from behind, a single windswept figure. She is wrapped tight still, but now in female coat, cap, and muffler. She stands alone on the stern cargo deck of the freighter, taking her bearings by looking back, then steadying herself at one point on an auxiliary steering wheel—as if warily charting her own course at last. After reviewing her life ("It all began") in synchronized lyrics, open-mouthed, fully voiced but still uttered in solitude, Yentl soon moves to the crowded upper deck for the second phase of the finale. What follows is of course obliquely reminiscent of the tugboat staging for the Broadway showpiece "Don't Rain on My Parade" that closed the first half of her debut film. Surely this harking back to one of the most famous musical numbers in Streisand's career is a deliberate and considered attempt at what might be called corrective allusion. In *Funny Girl*, Fanny Brice leaves her stage career in dry-dock to chug after her man, trying to intercept him on an ocean liner bound for Europe. In passing the Statue of Liberty in New York harbor, as everyone remembers, she mimes it with a torch of wilted roses, comic emblem of her supposed liberation. In *Yentl* Streisand reverses the pattern. Reconsidered, an emotional turning point has become closure, satisfying in its very attitude of latency. This time out, Streisand as Yentl—leaving Europe behind, as well as the man to whom she could not capitulate—moves toward a mythic New World alone, a self in waiting but no longer in hiding. The other corrective allusion might well refer the film back to the tragic close of Garbo's famous "trouser role" in *Queen Christina* (1937), a movie that also brings the transvestite heroine and the hero together for the first time in a country inn, and that ends with the indelible fixed close-up of Garbo at the prow of a ship, her lover dead astern, her face blankly turned from him, looking forward but mostly away.

But no intertexts can erode the force of Streisand's finale, nor the way it entwines and escalates the film's own subtexts, even the mirror motif. Certainly the power of this "A Piece of Sky" number is by no means all there in the movie's recorded soundtrack. Its own true hearing needs seeing. This last song's first lyrics emerge distanced in voiceover by a cavernous faint reverb, more prominent than before, as if some expressive distance is already in the process being crossed—as Yentl lets out her story from the stern of the ship, looking back while moving on. It is just before this, as if interrogating the passengers massed on deck, or speaking for them of their own hopeful itineraries, these tired and poor immigrants huddled together in expectation, that we have heard in reprise that nagging question from the film's first song. It has grown even more rhetorical in breaking off with an underspecified rhyme on the reiterated adverb: "Where is it written, tell me where . . . ?" Namely, the bare-bones interdict ". . . that

I can't *dare*?" Unlike the first version of this melody, when the question was quickly rounded out in a descending cadence (the trope of knowledge in a prohibited instinct "to taste the fruit of every tree"), the "tell me" imperative remains more open-ended this time in its bridge to the new closing number. Why *can't* I "dare"? Dare whatever it is? Who's to say I shouldn't brave a dream? Gone is the explicitly biblical "fruit," with all resisted interdictions generalized in the moment of their refusal. Held open in the process: Streisand's voice sustaining that note(d) "dare" on the misted sea air until her own visible singing, now sourced on-screen, comes in over it with the deeper backstory of "It all began." Derived from that formative moment when she realized her housebound domestic access limited her to only a windowed "piece of sky," a mere sliver of possibility, the song recalls how she finally "stepped outside" and "looked around." As eventually phrased in the "No Matter What Happens" lyric, plot has been driven throughout by the urge that things should not "be the same anymore," should split from themselves in clarified renewal, freed from the "shadows." This is just the desire so often scrutinized in the many mirrors of difference that the film has framed, mounted, and angled in on, dodging their technical capture of the reflected camera whose projected screen image they at the same time emblemize.

From the moment it "all began," hers was an eagerness refigured at last, no shaded moonlight cover needed by this point, under an uninterrupted oceanic skyscape—but whose struggle seems optically replayed one more time as she makes her darkness-drenched way through the ship's stairwell in a transitional effacement before reaching the upper deck. No opportunity in the film has been passed up to pass the camera through one kind of black void or another in the transit between lit spaces, beginning with the tracking shot of a black-clad rabbi ascending the steps into the synagogue in the film's first village scene. Every threshold in this film has been a split-second rite of passage, a trial by interim erasure. This is more than Streisand's stated love for a painterly aesthetic of black, as schooled by studying the Rembrandts in Amsterdam with her cinematographer David Watkins. Especially in the ship's unlit stairwell as final instance, we are presented not just with a stylistic "look" but a kind of narrative blackout, a syncope in the seen, a channel of renewal, you name it. And even if such lighting effects had gone unnoted until this point, or been judged superfluous to the story, they would now find stunning justification in the blocking of this scene's seamless mobile camerawork, where the impulse to "step outside" in the lyric has become the star's own stepping fully forth in song. There is no over-reading the subtle staging—and chromatic stages—of this seaborne, and figuratively airborne ("Papa, watch me fly!"), apotheosis. The spatial expansiveness and vocal emancipation of this final number can only be read as a *transport* for the heroine in every sense. The lyric is heard pushing beyond a past whose former shadowy cover Yentl has ceased to seek—and from whose literal rehearsal by a narrow, darkened passage she here emerges.

Vocal Flight

As Yentl climbs between decks crammed with cargo and passengers alike, she lifts above this last of many intermediate effacements into something like public singing for the first time in the film. Come finally to light, Yentl is now found moving her lips as she moves along the peopled deck, at home on its "boards." Other passengers seem to notice this animated figure—as if talking to herself—at just about the point in the song where she exclaims, "Papa I've a voice now!" And in her moving among and past them she is also barreling toward us in the most crowded and complicated tracking shot yet in her film work, capstone moment for her career's frequent gravitation to this trope of telescoped audiovisual distance. What is achieved by fixed frame with that final seven minutes of cemented close-up in *A Star Is Born* is matched here by a gliding choreography of camerawork: together offering alternate figurations of vocal focus in action. In *Yentl,* moving to her own inner imperative, as if again putting the stride of assertion back in an always mellifluous stridency of desire, the heroine is redoubling the ship's momentum with her own—emotive rather than mechanical, though, and rearward in its valedictory orientation. For part of the push-pull complexity of this two-tiered "staging" is its subtle way of literalizing the proverbially definitive sweep *from stem to stern*—all caught up in another of those reverse tracking shots that seem to give marching orders to the incremental breadth and resonance of the Streisand sound.

And when Yentl announces her found "voice" to "Papa," for the first and last time in Streisand's film career, quintessentially, we can literally see that voice, that expressed breath, in the Atlantic chill: an aerated will to song in double condensation. Passing through the cold sea air, breathing it in, and in her freedom giving it back warmed as melody, Yentl permits her voice to be made visible at last as a hovering, vaporous presence on the screen. Yet the musical action of this number, it must be remembered, is not an act, a singing performance inside the drama: the film has not taken a generic turn into a standard musical finale. Threading her way through the crowd to keep up with the camera, Yentl is still only singing as she might be talking or humming to herself, full of her own thoughts, incautious as never before, as she couldn't afford to be, about their incidental overflow. *Yentl* the film has hereby opened itself to a social space without becoming diegetic spectacle, song transformed within the narrative to an expressive gesture of personality without becoming shipboard show. Part of a communal exodus to a new land, nevertheless the heroine does not provide through song the stabilizing social focus on which generic musicals tend to close. The effect is nearer to her later second thought, as we'll see, about the ending of *Nuts*: "I should have started singing." In genre terms, the communal space at the center of which such a ritual moment would be possible has not yet been achieved in Yentl's search for a new home. Filial structure, or rather a single paternal bond, is still the largest social unit consolidated by her lyrics. In a second and last call to her father only, the heroine asks no one else's attention—but is not afraid of it either.

The number has come round in the process to its title lyric with the last of Yentl's questions, at this point only rhetorical: "Why settle for just a piece of sky?" The affirmation that now resists this, as stepped off in vocal ascent across the planks of expatriation, is so rousingly paced that no critical attention can exhaust it. Filmed amid the steerage passengers at this point of self-confidence, Yentl is alone again on camera a second later, reframed in a medium shot from a lower angle that excludes the company of fellow-travelers. Framing thus provides a last moment of paradoxically private extroversion—and the final attenuated instance, perhaps, of the film's leading optical motif. With a focus on Streisand's mirror of difference as steadily emblemized in this one film, commentary can surely be forgiven for finding a diagrammatic mirror effect in its final single-shot composition. With Yentl looking screen right in sudden close-up—and thus giving us Streisand's "bad side" first, her supposedly less feminine profile—she then swivels screen left as a kind of reverse image, then straight ahead, all in the process of floating the tripled assonant continuum of "Papa I can h*ear* you . . . *see* you . . . *feel* you." The "mirroring" vowel of this sensory convergence is then taken up in the objective-case pronoun of "watch m*e*"—or not so much taken up as zeroed in upon by a sustained tight framing on that third and frontal close-up. Where the earlier elegiac song in *Yentl* wondered in the interrogative about her presence to him ("Papa, Can You Hear Me?"), the lyric is now reversed to the point where she is channeling the sound and sight of his ongoing supervision—and impetus—in her demand for recognition, pitched as testimony rather than question. And then the ultimate *command* performance: "Watch me"—in particular, by hearing me, and taking off right here and now—"fly."

If one does read the symmetrical flip of Yentl's gazing profiles as calling up a kind of serial cinematographic mirror, then one of the organizing motifs of the film here seems to look back at us—even as we on it. Those three panels of at first inverse, then stabilized frontal imaging—a kind of kinetic triptych—achieve their centering resolution as an interface with cinema's famous fourth wall, across the breach of which the "look" of elation (eyed directly by the camera) is ours to meet. Along this pulsing optic groove, it is by scaling to a high-flying rhyme with the "sky" of the song's title that voice alone has claimed not just a "piece" of it but its whole horizoning arc.

This happens when the interrogative ("why settle?") turns vocative, the questioning prayer to imperative, in Streisand's longest-held screen note. Achieved in its reach is a dissevered assertion of the "I" released from within the twenty-second last lift of "Papa, watch me flYYYY"—or, more to the piercing point of this final blast-off, and with that high note from *Funny Lady*'s "Great Day" in mind, what we hear is the sustained syllabic updraft of "flyyyHIYIGH." As could ordinarily be justified only by the stage-musical logic of a number like "The Woman in the Moon" from *A Star Is Born*, Streisand seems to look almost straight into the eyes of the film (rather than theater) audience at the start of this last note of appeal, her own giddy, ecstatic gaze narrowing in medium close-up toward some metanarrative vanishing point.

The film's teleology of sung monologues is complete in this unequivocal convergence of the heroine's impetuous "hIgh" with the star's pyrotechnics, sealed in a knowing glance of tacit cinematic recognition (fig. 27). Yentl's virtually meeting the gaze of Streisand's audience (by just the slightest of deflections) is not a flaw, a crack, in the fiction, through which credibility is inadvertently bled away. Rather, after all the heroine's suffered reflections in the various mirrors of a difference she couldn't acknowledge, she can now look past her own regendered image—out on a world invited to look back. "Are you watching me NOW?"—Esther asks, of her dead husband and the audience alike, at the end of *A Star Is Born*. It is the ultimate filmic question. Even with Streisand deciding this time to let the finale's last word and note ("fly") drift up and away, rather than lock on a freeze, it is held quite long enough to confirm its own

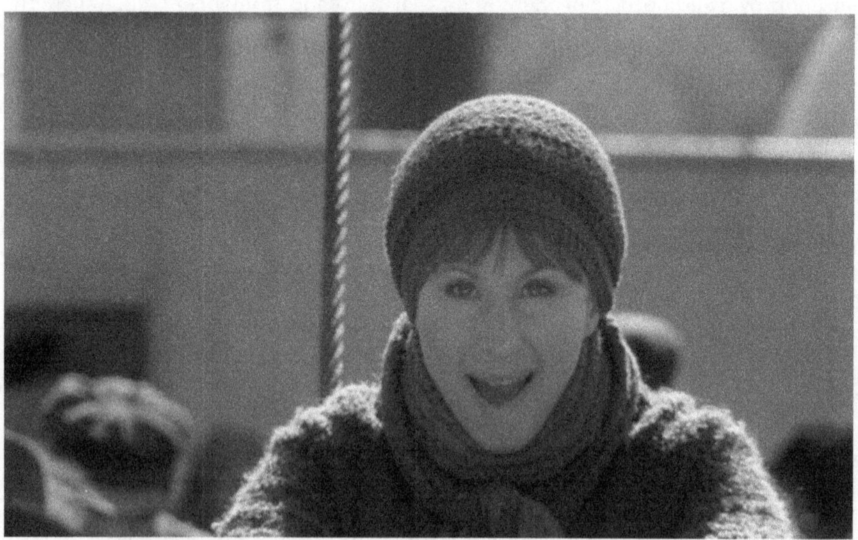

27. The unsutured gaze (*Yentl*: "A Piece of Sky")

wish yet again to be watched in delivery. In this wild (and wide-eyed) realization of the Streisand sound as narrative destination, the last note becomes a place unto itself, once again a terrain and a plateau—elevated by its own rhyme of "fly" with "sky"—where we do indeed, as with Yentl's rumors of America, "hear things" that "are" indeed expansively "different," incomparable.

With a sense of the heroine's previously untested possibilities suddenly achieved in the reach of this calling out, Streisand's self-directed camerawork, more than ever before, feels indelibly wed to her space-making vocals. After the "dynamics" of a final thrust both visually and aurally piercing—the hurling note, the lancing glance—the camera next deflects the angle of identification by about forty-five degrees in a cut to a medium long shot that begins the reverse-zoom trajectory of the final note. And of the ship with it. But yet again the Streisand sound, in its pervasive and all but haptic shiver of intent, reverberates undimmed despite the shrinking image. Moreover, there's an extra touch in this framed recession, rounding out the shot change: an effect so perfect that in her DVD remarks Streisand can't fail to mention it with some wry satisfaction. The orchestral score that succeeds her last high note comes to a final downbeat just where she had initially thought to cut off the image—and move to end-titles. But since she had more of the expensive low-angle helicopter shot in the wake of the ship, the camera hovering behind it as it plows its path forward and away, she decided to include that footage. As she explains with a little laugh in her voice, as if at a characteristic cost-consciousness, she just "let it roll." Film and ship together, convergent in their shared departure. Waste not, want not. The decision is perfect, with the narrative's emotional trajectory extending beyond and outlasting even its musical scheme. Yentl's new direction is freed fully by its own accumulated energy—and of course by that last stratospheric high note—to continue receding in frame, beyond the lapsed song score, for a few rippling "realist" seconds . . . until the up-tempo end-title medley sets in.

Able to look back while going forward, the heroine turns distance to volume, filling a void with voice: star's and character's at once, at one. With a screen persona so insistent in its difference, Streisand has never, as we know, managed to find a comfortable niche in a movie genre ordinarily centered upon the communal, the socially harmonized, has never claimed easily the generic legacy to which her talents as a singing comedienne were natively suited. The lack even of duets in her musicals is a recurrent symptom of this. *Yentl* has found one incomparable way around the impasse, not just by its seamless quilting together of song and interior monologue but by backdating the crisis to a point of historical precondition, indirectly alluding to that Jewish immigration at the turn of the century that helped shape the musical comedy tradition on the American stage. The film would thus be historically situated to precede—and thematically anticipate—even the Hollywood genre of which its particular narrative is a provisional rethinking. In these terms Streisand's masterwork can be thought to close by opening up(on) its own formal lineage. We do not have to imagine Yentl on her way to New York in 1904 to become a vaudevillian and eventual Ziegfeld star to feel the film driving toward, while stopping short of, a generic vision of integrated singing on-screen. This holding back, it should now be clear, is required even at the last by the film's whole logic. The pervasive motif of "finding a voice" in *Yentl* has sustained a sense of private expressiveness for which the complexities of the soundtrack have provided metaphor as much as transmission. Such a voice can preserve its figurative integrity through to the end only by anticipating, not yet accomplishing, its own literalization in and as straightforward "song," its registers still oscillating in shipboard passage between public and private release. Yet there is no missing the fact in this epochal transit—dredging the depths of Streisand's talent in catapulting it to new heights in this last unmoored heave of sound—no missing the fact that vocal delivery is, not just a transport, but its own mode of deliverance. To borrow a readily available refrain from the film itself: in the annals of unforgettable singing on-screen, this surely, among many Streisand benchmarks, is "one of those moments."

ONE VOICE TWICE OVER

5

In a mid-1980s political fundraiser for democratic senatorial candidates, militating both against Reagan-era Cold War armament and for a kind of green awakening after the Chernobyl disaster, Streisand left her long-time bastion in the recording studio to sing live for an outdoor (and then eventually broadcast) audience for the first time since *A Happening in Central Park* nearly two decades before. *One Voice* was the result. Performance anxiety was mitigated, she claimed from the private stage, by having only her Hollywood cronies ("You're all my friends!") in the invitational audience, and she seemed as much at home as she indeed was: there in her own tree-canopied backyard at her Malibu ranch. The performance, recorded on September 6, 1986, was, by any standard, a revelation and a knockout. On hold for so long, the technically unmassaged (and certainly not autotuned) voice was still all there—and then some. For a stand-alone recorded event, released just after Christmas on HBO and then on DVD the next spring, the supple beauties of Streisand's delivery, enhanced by the probing camerawork that captured it at often intensely close range, made not just for a lone voice, on behalf of others, raised in protest—but for direct audio access to the Voice of Voices showcased (and one might add enacted) at its peak.

Following Streisand's long-awaited reunion with the stage mic, just one month later she went into production, and back to the Hollywood sound stage, on a screen version, her first film since *Yentl*, of the Off-Broadway (and briefly on-) play *Nuts* by Tom Topor from 1979. This time she was leaving, nominally at least, the director's megaphone to Martin Ritt in order to concentrate (too weak a word) on her performance—as if there were anything much else to worry about in this story (for all the A-list supporting cast) than the furnace of the heroine's concerted fury. If only the play had been either more original or more gripping before Streisand, in every sense, went to work on it, this might have been one of her unquestioned career highs. Instead, even in its failures, it remains a fascinating transitional document in her foraging for expressive material. And more than that, the juxtaposition of *Nuts* with her *One Voice* outing represents—a decade after the watershed 1975/1976 transition from Fanny redux to Esther emergent—another mode of dramatic (both senses) cloning. The split difference occurs here across the theatrical acuity and close-up aesthetic shared equally by a song recital, on the one hand, and, on the other, a narrative gauntlet free of all sweet notes except in outlier passages of fabricated erotic come-on by the prostitute heroine. From love ballads to bald excoriations, musical serenades to raw tirades, we move within the electric circuit of a singular talent's diversified field, absorbing the alternate force of one voice twice over.

A certain level of fame tends to send talent into lockdown, with any veer toward innovation—as with the decade-long struggle to get *Yentl* made—coming up against dissuasion from every side. This kind of hurdle persists not just in the recording industry, of course, but all the more so in film production. Joni Mitchell, there in the audience for *One Voice*, had sung long before about "stoking the starmaker machinery" that always operates "behind the popular song." And that's nothing compared to fueling the maintenance apparatus of screen stardom, where the bankable is typically the tried and true. Yet Streisand, with *Nuts*, all her clout brought to bear, had somehow managed to go into production with an uncompromising straight dramatic role having neither music nor comedy to recommend it: an offbeat stage transplant whose only recognizable Streisand feature was its tacit feminist polemic. Was she nuts? Certainly her character Claudia isn't: that's both the script's given and its dramatic problem—so that a second look at the film is forced to diagnose *it* rather than her supposedly troubled character.

What, then, in the same creative cycle, might seem most immediately to link the magnetic intimacies of *One Voice* to the acrid outbursts of *Nuts*? Nothing but the different registers of intonation issuing from One Face. Take the concert's quietest example. In the variably extreme close-ups for Sondheim's "Send in the Clowns," Streisand's performance, its "text" lifted from *The Broadway Album* of the year before, is dramatized from within by added visual signaling. At "isn't it rich, isn't it queer?" her delivery of this interrogated arch irony is accompanied, for instance, not just by arched eyebrows but lids lowered resignedly, a dimension of Streisand's facial theatrics that had come wonderfully with age. The line targets an irony compounded at the vocal level when her rounding out of this self-critique—"losing my timing this late in my career," a musical trope for missed erotic chances—is contravened by the legato precision of delivery. For at this turn, as if for a full few seconds of song time, her voice hovers between "my" and a three-beat skid into the dramatized falling-off of "CAHHarreer": the neat treat, in short, of timing reclaimed in the teeth of its lamented loss. As the camera slides in and out within a tightly bracketed framing of this number, we may realize, looking back, how the full emotive register of such a poignantly micromanaged and exactingly paced close-up would have been right at home—its poignancy replaced with vitriol—in *Nuts*. And in fact a very near match for this camerawork does find a targeted home there, as only some close-up attention to the film's uneven dramatic logic can prepare us to estimate in its own tight optical range.

One Voice mostly rallies the fundraising troops with familiar hits, as expected. But retracing the lyric lifts and ridges of a "new song" can perhaps best serve to consolidate a sense of Streisand's vocal acting at this transitional point between a one-off return to the recital stage and, by immediate and drastic antithesis, the incited bursts of her dramatic alter ego in *Nuts*. Reminiscing midway through the concert about her fondness and admiration for Judy Garland, which might well have prevented her from encroaching on the former's most famous ballad, "Over the Rainbow," she admits that "what the hell, I decided to sing it anyway." And the hell out of it, at that. Including the seldom heard intro, not even recognized by the show-biz audience—where Streisand hunches up her shoulders in putting the winsome "high" of the shimmering syllable itself into "rainbow HIGHway to be found"—a note that is echoed a verse later with "beHIGHnd the sun." Here, again, is what we might call the aerial topography of her voice. In the slow piano transition to the song's famous title line, and followed by another "way up high" cue, the most distant crane shot of the evening takes over. Filming lifts away from the quickly diminished figure on stage, in a kind of rainbow vantage, until we cut back to a close-up just in time for the second bursting iteration—visually elated as well as ear-popping—of the "Somewhere over" refrain. With the song finally identified by audience applause as the famous tune from *The Wizard of Oz*, it is Streisand's own vocal witchcraft that can be felt to refilm it—but less on camera even than in the mind's eye of its vocal ascent. Streisand breaks unforgettably with the sweet diffidence of the Garland version as if to scale, then almost to ski, an invisible layered rainbow of her own. The result seems an answer to the concert's opening with the *Broadway Album*'s spine-tingling "Somewhere." Streisand achieves the concert's midpoint vocal feat with the exuberant onset of the same over-syllabified adverb in "Over the Rainbow," her notes this time buoyantly cresting the bold first slope of "suh*UHUH*mmWHehERE"—and then holding on the exploratory word, one may imagine almost prismatically, along a continuous arc of space-making vocal coloration.

By the starkest of contrasts, except for a shared vocal intensity, everything is constricted in the lyric-free phrasal contortions of *Nuts*, with its legalistic chokehold on the heroine's expressive freedom. Playing a private-line call girl accused of murdering a client, the arraigned jailbird refuses, as it were, to sing. Instead, she explodes in a series of verbal arias raunchy and raging by turns (or both at once)—and calibrated across each twitch and wince of expression as deliberately as if they had been a stage number in delivery. Yet in this dramatic context the one (self-exonerating) voice that matters is in danger of never being heard, gagged by legalistic protocols. Same year as the *One Voice* concert by that name, same frizzed hair length, the blond just gone more tawny, same unaged clarity of features, same frame ratio in the camera distance, same nuanced intensity—but all the galvanizing charm of her vocals replaced by an exercise in negative magnetism: a searing performance it is impossible to warm to. Within the rectangular aspect ratio of her close-ups, what Streisand brings off is remarkable, but it remains hard to square at times with the narrative premise, even when one quickly realizes that the eponymous epithet exists only in the scare quotes of false accusation. Or as an angry slang rejoinder to the very idea. Power structures, both familial and institutional, have every interest in putting this protagonist away before a criminal trial might air her side of things—before she can speak, let alone shout, her truth to their shaky power.

So it isn't hard to think of this turning point, from concert to drama, as another cloning of the star into two versions of her own intensity. In this sense *Nuts* offers an unflinching theatrical performance delivered to film through one close-up after another, their importunate claims coming across as the fiercely aggrieved inverse of the lustrous ingratiating camera technique for the fundraiser. What might have been an unconscious divided loyalty on the star's part between her singing career and this most extreme dramatic departure could then explain director Ritt's reported annoyance over her distracting work on the concert agenda during pre-production for the film. Streisand's career has often, as we've seen, been a matter of considered flip sides, divisions and reversals, mirror refractions that help tally the dominant facets of a multitasked persona calling up related aspects of her talent in each new move—and movie—of her career. But no one could have predicted *Nuts* after either *Yentl* or *One Voice*: a role in which her non-singing monologues, barely dialogues at all, are spat out in venomous critique of male power, often with no shred of modulation or harmony in earshot, let alone the trademark self-deprecating humor: no quarter given, no prisoners taken in the courtroom fray. On the heels of the aspirational concert video, the heroine of the conspiratorial plot in *Nuts* is not found bravely if secretly forging her way in a man's world of learning, as Yentl did. Rather, she is seen actively beating back the institutions of patriarchy, medical and juridical, in their open attempts to incarcerate and silence her under the name of supportive hospitalization. Streisand's Claudia Draper is so unleashed, if never quite unhinged, so savage if not nuts, that she ends up stealing scenes even from herself—by rubbing at times against the already questionable grain of characterization in the script. But no matter in the long run. *Nuts* is a film no Streisand fan, even left cold by it, could wish away, nor any serious film historian. Beyond the strain of its flawed storyline, it puts forth a side of Streisand's dramatic commitment, and gauges its commanding force, as never before.

If one grants the premise that the Streisand persona, as *odd one in*, has queered forever the even-featured symmetry of "8 Beautiful Girls 8" with a bracing imbalance in the very outline (as well as profile) of screen stardom, the result might well be called, in the current buzzword, a creative disruption. This understanding of her impact, in its continuing drive for new directions, would help in responding to what follows most immediately from the cross-dressed apogee of difference in *Yentl*. For there, with a delicacy and nuance previously undreamed, the powerhouse doyen of Hollywood musical comedy, what was left of it, had put both her vocal glories and her stardom's "recognition value" under on-camera wraps—in fact, the tight anatomical wrappings—of a sustained disguise as 1 Cute Boy 1. And this involves an ethnic recuperation in no way to be foreseen, either, by the fast-talking Jewish shtick that drew her to the earlier script of *Funny Lady*. For in *Yentl* she replays emblematically one aspect of the whole Jewish diaspora in an escape from stultifying religiosity at the film's open-ended finish. Whether or not her heroine there was vaudeville bound, where could Streisand herself go next? What ethnic identification was left to enact or rethink? What gender disruption? What other mode of role reversal might follow from her time as Anshel? Or at least follow it? What contemporary feminism to be rebooted from *A Star Is Born* in a new guise, with clothes no longer "from her closet"?

To such questions the answer may be neither easy nor satisfying. Under political impetus with *One Voice*, Streisand has finally returned to the center of her vocal stardom. When she suddenly appears—almost concurrently, for her next screen role—not in camouflage as a misperceived boy but in the slovenly garb (just as atypical) of a falsely diagnosed mental patient, the swerve can't help but interpret itself. With the star's maximized doubleness pitched now toward imputed schizophrenia within the plot of *Nuts*, the no-holds-barred obscene swagger of the resulting performance is not just a matter of star power squared by dramatic license. In its exaggerated casting against type, more even than with the endearing masquerade of *Yentl*, it marks a primal queering requeered: the fetching offbeat comedienne gone smutty and half demonic. *Nuts* was very much Streisand's project, her own calculated departure. The star's hands-on involvement as executive producer with the script's many rewrites—especially in their inserted flashback structure (first tried out in comparably jagged form in *Yentl*), as well as with the decision to break from the airless studio filming of the courtroom for the exterior shots of a revised conclusion—makes *Nuts* exactly the film she wanted to make. If it turned out to be a kind of dead end for the star's unshackled actorly ambition, it remains a notably transitional work, anticipating a return to her directorial ambitions at the start of the next decade. For it is through the swivel of antithesis, yet again, that she will next direct herself as a psychiatrist, rather than psychiatric patient, in *The Prince of Tides*.

From Malibu to Bellevue

The intentionally claustrophobic courtroom drama of *Nuts* offers Streisand a New York theater role for the first time in her career since *The Owl and the Pussycat*—playing, as it happens, another no-nonsense prostitute, but one under arrest this time in a crime drama. Yet with a sex-worker protagonist like Claudia elegant on the job rather than tacky (we see in flashbacks), cool and aloof rather than goofy like Doris, the role is wholly ungraced, however boisterous, by diverting comic turns. No clichéd whore-with-the-heart-of-gold, just a canny, self-employed business woman, attracting gold-star customers with a fixed price list of erotic services—until, after fighting back against a brutal client, she ends up facing a manslaughter charge. And facing the exculpating trial she wants and deserves only if she can convince the judge in an interim hearing, convened within the warren of the Bellevue mental hospital in Manhattan, that she is fit to stand for it. Everything in Streisand's full-bore impersonation would have worked in the theater as well: the vocal depth and lunge of that contralto growl, the pissy shuffle, the punctual flailings and flame-outs, the pitiless, mirthless desperation of a character, rather than the performer, furiously *acting out*. But there's a whole new and literal *dimension* to this version of the character when it reaches the screen from its Off-Broadway genesis: a measure markedly rectangular, close-up, almost unnervingly *in your face*.

On-screen instead of under the proscenium, as actress as well as singer, and in ways that have never been fully appreciated in critical scrutiny, the overnight Hollywood sensation of Streisand's feature-film advent brought before the camera a face that registers its character's every word, sung or otherwise enunciated, and its undertones as well. It was the unbeatable comic mugging of this face, its expressions "more" than those of the "Barrymores," that initially won screen audiences over in droves to this Broadway interloper with the giant voice: the humanizing moments in between the demanding grandeur and range of that voice's song styling. A counterpoint that is also, however, a continuum. When Streisand sings up close on-screen, when she acts up close, feeling is distributed organically, dispersed, reinvested in the corners of eyes and lips, generating almost a facial pulse—delegated to separate nerve centers rather than to any simple set of expressions. It is not a craft that can be learned. It is an emotive given that can be coaxed by art but not coached by technique: a facial projection that meets the camera's eye at least halfway—no matter how close the latter comes.

Streisand set out mid-career to *learn* direction as a skill. In contrast, her kinetic features together with her unmatched voice: an endowment, not a prowess.

All this we know, this bankable screen and microphone magnetism. But in *Nuts*, sheering the actor away from the visible song mic so recently reengaged, a legendary face as versatile as her singing voice must wrench its way to cogent expression—across a derisive mask that has its own thesaurus of inflections. Self-expression must struggle first, that is, from out of Claudia's defensive cocoon, taut with ridicule and disgust, then from an unwanted medical drugging, in order to vent its caged energy for the big two final soliloquies, one on the witness stand, the other off (holding forth in front of the bench). In both the struggle and the upshot, under the pressure of far greater narrative constraints than in any Streisand role before or since, we are transfixed—in Claudia's bursts of manic combustion—by the concentrated expressive spectrum of the star's *look* itself, rather than just the Hollywood innovation of her looks: this time a cold eye queering the very demeanor of the screen close-up. And certainly too, in a more particular sense, this is Streisand's most aberrant sexual characterization: not only because so male-wary and variously humiliating to the men of the law but because so abnormally, even in plot terms so destructively, uneager to please outside of the for-hire bedroom. Even in her own legal self-interest. Playing an entirely unwinning woman in a courtroom fight for her life, what also takes the stand in *Nuts* is Streisand's own ability—motivated here by feverish defiance—to stare the camera down, as well as light it up, in every shot exchange. Guilty as charged, or, say, supercharged.

For the first and last time in Streisand's career, the star (who by now, and long since, has become a category, so that script doctors are often called in to "make the dialogue more Barbra") must as actress disappear, her place usurped by an entirely contextualized person. But a regrettably unstable one, in script more than in psychology. With *Nuts*, what is attempted amounts not just to a character study but to a "character part" writ large: not just casting the lead "against type," and in a non-singing role, but suppressing, warping, or torquing all of the star's signature screen instincts, and touches, in the urgent motivation of such an unappealing role. Brash is certainly one component of the "Barbra" effect, but not brazen: feisty, even fiery, but not (except in the self-irony of a song number like *Funny Lady*'s "How Lucky Can You Get?") ferocious; sexy, but not lurid. The script has carried a star persona into uncharted waters, where the effort to crest one too many trendy contemporary currents at once—medical malfeasance, recovered memories of paternal child abuse, a feminist lashing out on the (grand)stand against the coercions of mansplaining—threatens to capsize it. With her aggravated angst, Claudia can herself seem rudderless in her rage. Streisand certainly brings to the onetime stage part an unrelenting stress on the role's own splintered impulses across a spectrum of rude intensities and crude sarcasms, all the while tasked to navigate a maelstrom of psychic damage and its management. Holding nothing back, she throws herself so completely into the part, so fearlessly, that she can appear to have thrown it out of narrative whack: becoming, contra the dramatic premise, a character so unharnessed that she may seem in fact coming unglued. The spectacle is as exhausting as it is, in its intermittent brilliance, exhilarating.

It would seem that her role as director manqué this time out (deferring in the credits, at least, to veteran Ritt, but with the authority of executive producer over the final cut) has ultimately worked at cross-purposes with her character's own role. Starting with script consultations, where she argued for an incremental flashback structure, Streisand presses for more dramatic pace and impetus, more *direction*, to the developing incest plot. In doing so, she may ultimately have set her instincts for montage and narrative momentum at odds with the guiding psychology of the character, muddying a hard-won personal autonomy with an overplus of embedded trauma, divulging not just the corrupted bulwarks of parental and psychiatric intervention but a certain undermining contradiction in the whole story's courtroom logic as well. You can't take your eyes off her performance, but you are not always sure what you're seeing. In the expanded gritty exchanges, so much more colorful than the play's, and even in the jagged flashback montage of violence and outrage, there is much movie-making craft on view, but it is never really *moving*. So that what should have been, and on its own terms is, a minor triumph of screen acting comes off like a strenuous exercise in search of a credible person—as if a star were taking self-direction in grappling with the elusive and in many ways unstable persona to which she has committed.

Nuts is certainly a hard movie to crack, in or outside of the Streisand filmography—as it seems to split itself in half within the shell of its own impacted conception. After killing an enraged client in self-defense, the prostitute Claudia has so discomfited and demeaned her prison psychiatrist that he strikes back with intimations of paranoid derangement. He is abetted in this by parents eager to protect themselves, as well as supposedly her, against public exposure in the manslaughter trial she insists on—gambling, as she does, on being able to prove her innocence rather than accept a virtual life sentence in a mental ward for the criminally insane. In the hospital's on-site courtroom, in a hearing called to "contravene" the psychiatric findings, all she needs to prove at this point is that she understands the charges against her. This she certainly does. Nor would she have any trouble "participating in her own defense" if going to trial. It's a no-brainer—turned rapidly confounding by her uncooperative behavior. After slugging her parents' chosen high-priced lawyer and stuck now with a state's attorney (Richard Dreyfuss, wonderfully nervous and convincing as Aaron Levinsky) whom she seems to distrust as much as she does the shrinks, Claudia acts as if her *willingness* to assist in her own case seems, improbably enough, less than obvious. On the stand, the chief hospital psychiatrist, Dr. Morrison (Eli Wallach), says she would be hampered in any self-defense by her paranoid delusions. "Define paranoia!" barks Claudia in interruption, against one of the judge's repeated admonitions to hold her tongue. Finishing his claim, the psychiatrist doubts that she would be able to distinguish "the difference between criminal charges and persecution." Heedless again: "Oh yes I can. This is persecution!" With the defendant all defensiveness, sharp as a tack, and as stabbing, only her rage threatens to incapacitate, not her, but her case for clearheadedness. One suspects that Streisand's typical "research" before a role, in this case studying the behavior and expressions of mental patients, gave her more material than the story could coherently take on board.

The plot couldn't be more transparent in its broad outlines, nor at the time more timely: with female blowback against coercive patriarchal structures spurred to a fury by a slowly revealed incestuous backstory, two touchstones of 1980s screenwriting joining wrung hands. But the law, civil rather than criminal, seems arrayed against the heroine not just unfairly but implausibly, given only a vindictive impatience on psychiatry's part in the film, with no authoritative diagnosis—in contrast to the play's more fully worked-up charge of psychosis. As a result, the focus wavers. No dramaturgic synthesis pulls this together—not even Streisand's multifaceted Method performance, drawing as never before on her early devotion to the Actor's Studio. The histrionic scores of the actor, one caustic taunt after another, don't finally add up at the plot level. We're not left nearly as befuddled, surely, as when Janet Maslin, in her unaccountable *New York Times* review, so bluntly missed the point in complaining that we don't believe in Streisand's performance at all, never think of her as "nuts," just "Crazy like a fox."[1] Of course: that's the point. The psychiatric (pre)script is the false note, the malicious cover story, and Claudia is adamant—as she climactically says twice, in borrowing directly from the play's chief metatheatrical punch line—about not being willing to "play that part." Never does. But it is the way she also avoids playing the legal game itself to her advantage, never keeping the lid on her bitterness and revulsion, that is always in danger of derailing credulity as well as her case.

To what extent it is Streisand's hand in the final script rewrites that compounds the problem with a greater emphasis on incestuous violation: even this is not easy to sort out in the crosscurrent—and frequent cross-purposes—of the heroine's defensive (but not defense-canny) affect. The traumatized and emotionally stunted victim is asked to inhabit the person of a functional survivor out to prove her own competence, her own responsible agency: two sides of a nearly unnegotiable coin. The two emphases contaminate rather than enable each other, so that, in a gathering knot of flashbacks, a slowly disclosed pubescent molestation of the heroine arrives as the potential explanation of a schizoid behavior that has already been ruled out, by the play's main legal animus, well before it might have needed explaining. One keeps worrying over this logical annoyance because it repeatedly gnaws away at our concentration on the undeniable excitement of Streisand's performance. The trouble with *Nuts* as a histrionic venture, then, is something like the inverse of the usual screen challenge for "Barbra." A persona with so many cultivated facets is hard to distill into a narrative person. *Yentl*'s girlboy fusion was an inspired synthesis—and solution. The problem with *Nuts* is an opposite one. So single-minded is the dramatic effort to countenance no restraints (or say to face them down in one close-up after another) that the heroine seems to be doing herself in even as the star outdoes herself.

Flashback Flare-ups

When Streisand, as executive producer, first came in on the script process, she immediately advocated for flashbacks to punctuate the hospital and court scenes with explanatory "clues for the audience," as she explains in the DVD commentary. But, given the simultaneity of their cognitive filtering, these inserts of course serve as opened wounds for the defendant as well—and, by association, for her complicit parents. The narrative force of this, as well as its perceptual orientation, cuts two ways at once, in some respects against the plot's own motivating grain. The "clues," to begin with, certainly draw on two separable if linked timelines. Though their trajectories are not easy to separate, they bear divergent juridical weight—and are given in reverse order: first, inset references to Claudia's recent life as a prostitute and the violence by which she found herself cornered; then, suggestively intertwined with these, to the childhood violations that have implicitly led to that endangered life. The former are only relevant to the criminal charge of manslaughter, however, not to the present hearing over her "mental competency" to stand trial on that charge. And the latter are technically immaterial, as well as functionally redundant, to the film's manifest evidence: evidence by now clear for the audience as jury, if not immediately for the judge, the latter without benefit of the behind-the-scenes consultations with her lawyer to which we've been privy. This is the unmistakable corroboration, in short, of Claudia's willful and shrewd capacity. No amount of backstory can wholly shore up this split purpose in the dramatic subtext of impinging recall—but only weigh it down with more contradictory baggage. In this way the narrative discrepancy is widened with each new wedge driven into Claudia's far and near past, the flashbacks operating now on the side of prolonged victimage under male cruelty, now on the side of psychic resilience and embattled self-determination.

And as this recursive structure of increasingly fragmentary insets complicates without consolidating the thematic divide, its pattern affords the most obvious way to track not just the plot's fissured emphasis but the means by which Streisand's performance must struggle to bridge it.

Before the first reversion in this twofold flashback structure, the film has staged its opening in crowded medias res. In a hubbub of over-voicing from a women's holding pen, the narrative's first disorienting image arrives after initial white-on-black titles, by fade in, as the camera pans along an apparent graffitied wall that turns out to be a ceiling, with more painting in process by one of the inmates on bed-top tiptoe—anticipating Claudia's own distracted drawing and caricaturing throughout the later trial episodes. As our protagonist now joins a lineup of female junkies and prostitutes in being transferred through the male cellblock, the first of the flashbacks arrives only about halfway through this distended credit sequence—partly because it is more a psychic figuration than a memory trace in a not yet consolidated plot. Its effect is more like that graffiti mural, albeit with live figures, than an actual scar of recall. What emerges from this cellblock, in fact, is a so-called montage cell: sex-starved men in prison intercut with a kind of epitomizing group portrait of the prostitute's typical upscale clientele, not in this case a memory so much as a metonymy. Edited into the prison footage, that is, we get a cross-sectional mock-up of her business model at point-of-sale. As the parade of female bodies is herded past the leering male inmates—tongues lolling out of their mouths, arms flailing beyond their barred cages, all catcalls and frustrated aggression—a kind of visual pun sets in. For we cut from this orgy of prison frustration to the phalanx of suited urban gentlemen implausibly crammed together at their own version of a swank *bar*-bound space, too close for comfort, all eyes on the traveling camera where we expect the answering shot of a female body. Not yet.

Unreeling a generalized tableau of the lecherous male gaze rather than the recall of some actual overcrowded watering hole, this tracking shot certainly implies a female POV even without delivering its anchoring reverse shot. The camera simply glides past the multiplied male stares among the squadron of gawkers, slowing briefly to single out only the one groomed Black man in answer to the impassive Black inmate in the previous camera take. For the logical reverse shot in this unmistakable schema—namely, the returned gaze of the woman—we must wait a good while—and for an actual flashback at that. It begins, after Claudia's first courtroom tantrum and subsequent drugging, with a match cut from her exiting a hospital cell, led by a sleazy psychologist who, aware of her previous behavior in court, has slimily advised her to save her passion for the bedroom. Now, his gesturing her forward, in mockery, toward

a meeting with her lawyer segues by slick graphic substitution to the suave maître d'
who, recognizing Claudia in her dressy glamour, escorts the welcomed "Mrs. Draper"
toward the corner table for a rendezvous with her latest (and now late, we soon realize) client, long dead by her own hands. This time she haughtily ignores, in passing, the less schematic clustering of three-piece suits at their cocktails. She too means
business. When she proceeds to tantalize her client with the fingertip, crimson-nailed
caress—and salacious sipping—of a phallic champagne flute, we may well register this
shot as a barely veiled allusion to the famous episode of décolleté-with-wine-glass in
the banquet-table seduction scene from *On a Clear Day You Can See Forever*. If so, we
might also recall that Cockney Melinda, in Daisy's own flashback, is only executing
a sleek impersonation of high-born abandon. Such recognition in *Nuts* would mark
this moment, too, as one circumscribed self-conscious performance within another,
Claudia's for her paying customer as Streisand's for us in the role of Claudia all told.

This look-over clearance "date" with her john is rounded out by the fatal assault
scene only later, in another and complementary flashback sparked by her lawyer's having "invaded" her space, the cordoned-off murder scene of her apartment. He has gone
looking for some respectable clothes she might wear in court—and has also encountered there a kind of further audio flashback to the now-dead client's first phone call of
approach on the answering machine. Claudia's rage at the lawyer's unauthorized trespass prompts an inset return to the earlier brutal scene in full visual exposition. We see
the client forcing his way into her bathroom and momentarily blinded by face powder
in the act of smashing her vanity mirror (shades of that comic powder-puff bout in
front of the dressing room mirror in *Funny Lady*), a shard from which is then her final
defense against his smashing her skull. Given the numerous career intertexts, it's hard
to resist thinking, in this extreme reprise of an emblematic prop (and trope), that the
mirror of difference has finally been weaponized. In any case, the unmoored flashback
replay of this assault scene turns suddenly to the retroactively marked form of a recurrent nightmare when Claudia wakes panting in her cell later that night. As often with
this mode of flashback, its tunneling into the past can also burrow forward toward a
subsequent moment in narrative time, taking its further psychic toll in transit.

More abruptly self-contained, by contrast, the first of the more deeply mined flashback retrievals erupts when Claudia first appears in court and, seated in a row with
more blatantly low-life women facing charges, peers out guardedly, disgustedly, from
among them at her unwanted parents on the other side of the legal bar. The interchanged glances of this triangulated family shot exchange, as if in the exposure of
implicit recognition, are then intercut with a younger actress playing teen Claudia in
the act of chopping off the last of her long hair in front of an open bathroom cabinet

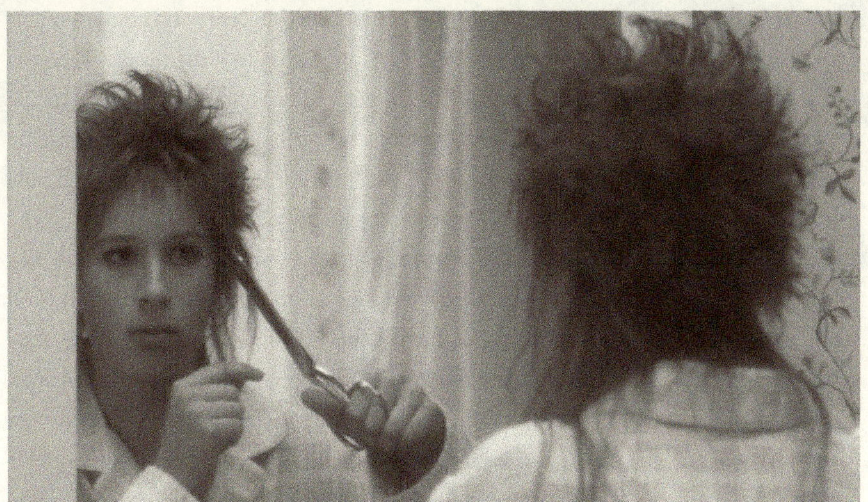

28. Gender violently repressed (*Nuts*)

mirror: protectively defeminizing herself, we later realize (fig. 28). The mirrored surface is a door going nowhere, a failed escape hatch, that, when immediately slammed shut, reflects her parents intruding in shock on that scene of the girl's self-mutilation. Sprung from this shifting surface of mutual recognition, we will soon move across subsequent flashbacks, further back yet, into separate private memories focused around the conscience of the two parents in intersection with Claudia's embittered recall, the mother's in denial, the stepfather's dredging up his repeated acts of predation. But in the desexing haircut, the intertextual seed from *Yentl* is also sown.

The earliest plot pivot of Streisand's previous film comes almost unavoidably—and indeed pertinently—to mind, though there it was the impersonation of a young girl, then a young boy, by a middle-aged Streisand herself. Inverted now—as if by a further kind of mirror reversal—is the brave homage to the heroine's father in *Yentl*: a determination to follow in his footsteps via the self-assumed privilege of male disguise, shorn locks included, as figured in a ritual of self-abnegation as well as self-empowerment before Yentl's beveled dresser-top mirror. Whether or not this allusion to the predecessor screen narrative is meant to be salient, the new movie has turned the previous heroism inside out. This involves more than the perverse hint of paternal modeling in *Nuts*: that of sexual barter. Implicit in Claudia's rather than Yentl's case already, but eventually confirmed in this same channel of pubescent flashbacks, is the way these memory traces come into linked interplay with the adult violence of her own immediate backstory of self-defense. Very different from Yentl's, Claudia's effort at the mirror is to de-eroticize herself in flight from her stepfather's desire and abuse—rather than in admiration of his gendered privilege—before taking to heart his other lessons and accepting money for sexual favors. This can well be thought to contribute to the entrenched queerness of Claudia's adult persona. Wearing the dress picked out by the lawyer to be respectable in court, her own manipulation of desire's Oedipal circuits comes through in batting down his compliment by identifying his chosen frock "as the dress I wear when they want to sit on Mommie's lap." In all her insistence on being "responsible" for her own sex work, there is no suggestion of that reciprocal pleasure asserted on stage, not that we believe it there either, in the heroine's rejecting altogether the prostitution tag for her livelihood: "Whoring is getting paid for work you don't want to do."[2] However we take the film's sudden mirror image of defaced teen femininity when it first breaks through, whatever depth of the repressed we assume it returns from, certainly Claudia's eventual manslaughter charge—with a slice of shattered mirror as weapon—marks one dead end for the long-standing motif in her films of reframed self-image on-screen.

We don't *necessarily* suspect the incest backstory with that first bathroom mirror shot, though we *might well*—given the ubiquity of such abuse in popular discourse at the time, and not least in Hollywood thematics, where child violation, including Oedipal rape, claimed in those years a decided market share in the economies of the melodramatic flashback on the mainstream screen. Indeed, well before the 1980s, in the traumatology of such violence, cinematic editing had become a metaphoric paradigm for the eruption of unwanted memory traces in the discourse of trauma theory and the vocabulary of its flashpoints. According to one scholar in the field of such trauma study, it is "hard to think of the contemporary psychology of trauma outside an imbrication with photography and cinema, with cultural metaphors of flashbulbs and flashbacks now literalized in scientific and cultural theory."[3] It had also become hard for Hollywood to think of trauma, and the flashbacks that accent it, the Holocaust excepted, without the specific burden of sexual abuse either incestuous or in loco parentis. Such associations were stoked in the latter case by the hysteria around the McMartin preschool trial in L.A. County (with its copycat accusations of predatory violence) still raging during the filming of *Nuts*. Such inferences, in Hollywood hands, were often made to seem especially damning when linked to image media—as when, as late as 2002, Robin Williams in *One Hour Photo*, as chain-store photo-processor, is revealed as the formerly abjected childhood subject of his father's porn snapshots. Certainly the general coincidence of cinematographic structure, including its photographic rudiments, and the meme of childhood sexual violence was all but unavoidable at the time that *Nuts* was adapted from the stage, even before the more recent exposé of clerical pederasty in the Catholic hierarchy. And it was not just topical but linked to a long tradition of backstories from the confession of incest in *Chinatown* (1974), without recovered images, to the flashback articulation of multiple personality disorder in *Sybil* (1976). So that Streisand herself is only turning the tables, for her next film after *Nuts*, with the flashback structure of boy rape that punctuates the revelation scene of *The Prince of Tides*. Although her supervisory *tact* in the deployment of those early flashbacks in *Nuts* is expert and discreet enough in visual terms, the questionable aesthetic *taste* of the script in overplaying its hand in this respect (so Topor, the original playwright, thought, given that the recall of less egregious child abuse was minor and marginal in the stage version) is not just dubious but narratively skewing.

In a shotgun wedding of this issue with the equally timely feminist emphasis on a woman claiming authority over her own actions, her own body, the troubled plot of *Nuts*, as well as its lead character, is in danger of being pulled apart at the seams. The flashback disclosures come piecemeal and abruptly, but without the power of real surprise—just more like filling in the blanks of Claudia's icy stares. We don't at first know, it is true, what is fully implied in the manslaughter scene—besides the fact that her client aggressively overstayed his billed time and his welcome—when, angering him by her refusal, she says matter-of-factly "I don't do baths." But we aren't made to wait long in finding out, in a sequence where what has gone on behind a locked bathroom door in the familial past is thrown open to view. This incriminating flashback sequence begins with the mother on the stand (Maureen Stapleton), testifying to how she found the change in her daughter at puberty inexplicable, her withdrawal from affection, her refusal of all care and support. Yet at this point, with Claudia looking down blankly during the testimony, what the flashback calls up—implicitly to both daughter and parent alike—is a brief scene where the mother, wandering down the hall with a hefty snifter of brandy, quietly closes the door on the pleading look of her weeping pre-teen child.

Soon enough, once the mother gives over the witness stand to her husband (Karl Malden)—the suspect (but supposedly by his wife unsuspected) stepfather, himself the prime mover in the effort to institutionalize Claudia—all stopgaps have been exhausted. What the introvert clench of the adult daughter seemed hoping to shut away, between bouts of more impersonal testiness, comes crashing through with the full weight of the inevitable. Suddenly the flashback engine goes into overdrive, each regurgitated episode from here out just a few seconds in length. First, when the father flatly denies that he hated Claudia's husband, we cut, after her obstreperous courtroom objection, thus serving to confirm the implied rivalry, to her hiding from the latter in a locked bathroom. Water is coursing into the tub that she sits dressed alongside—with the never-seen husband (pure abstract threat) pounding on the door in mounting frustration even as he promises not to hurt her. Cut again, by a second-tier regressive flashback, to shorn teenage Claudia in a previous domestic bathtub, water again running as if in part to drown out the noise at the locked door. And then the climactic match cut—back from the girl's hands over her ears to the adult Claudia covering her own in court, hoping to block out the father's increasingly panicked and defensive admission pried from him by Levinsky's hectoring cross-examination.

As the attorney asks for a second time "Did you make your stepdaughter your lover?" we see the young girl's hand unlock the door after a twenty-dollar bill has been slipped under it, and then the father, locking it again behind him, approaching the scared preteen kid, long hair still intact, with a towel spread wide to dry her after her bath—and perhaps, by association, to curtain his lust. The cumulative effect of these ambiguously "shared" memories between father and daughter is certainly more complicated—more emotionally charged in the reopened lesions of inflicted mental wounds—than the quick-cut memories of affectionate moments with Avigdor inserted into the crisis point of separation in *Yentl*. And less centered in a given character than the more prominent use of flashbacks in *The Prince of Tides*. As discussed in Streisand's Criterion Channel interview, they were deployed there, in *Tides*, expanding mere dialogue report, to take the cinematic image itself "back to traumatic events" in present reenactment. They do this in *Nuts*, too, of course, reciprocally for victim and perpetrator in the same quasi-telepathic interchange. In sync with the last of these recovered familial memories, when asked a second time if he funded his daughter as his lover, the father in a frenzy breaks from the witness stand, screaming "it isn't true," swearing his love and begging her to exonerate him. And as she falls to the floor in dodging his lunge at her, each of them quickly restrained by court guards, the last brief flashback in the midst of this—reverting to the attempted murder scene by her client—sums up all her threats in one embodied male assailant. All by contrast, including that prolonged and aggravated paternal rape of her innocence, with the downplayed sexual violence in the play itself. On stage, all the stepfather has ever done is bathe her well past any decent timeline for pubescent privacy—and, villain of the piece though he clearly is, he gets an ameliorative kiss from Claudia at trial's end. Unthinkable in Streisand's version.

The screenplay's pattern is clear, even in its deliberate jumbling and ricochet of flashbacks—the pattern and the point: there are memories of male aggression that no faucet or freshet, no cleansing bathtub stream, can rinse away, memories that will flood the present when released under enough hammering pressure. This is what Streisand must have sensed would alone animate the character as more than a bureaucratic victim, alone motivate Claudia's ill-considered tantrums in a competency hearing.

But the cinematographic rhetoric backfires. Given the witness-stand testimony to which the flashbacks further testify, who could blame this abused and emotionally abandoned child for being half nuts, suffering from paranoia about betrayed trust at every level, medical and judicial included? Who would find absurd the implied stirring of schizoid personality disorders in the careening mood swings of Streisand's own keyed-up and hyperkinetic performance? Yet these are all the wrong questions, of the sort prejudged by the shrinks. This isn't the way the plot, let alone its pivotal performance, is meant finally to come off. To whatever degree traumatized in this case, at least in this legal case of competency per se, Claudia is only maddened, not mad, so that for all their added narrative vitality, the burden carried (forward) by the flashbacks is in danger of sabotaging the script's structural contempt for the protective snap judgments of psychiatry.

The stakes, as noted, are much more sharply, and thus infuriatingly, drawn, in the play. There, a totally coherent, street-smart, divorced young woman, party-planner turned hooker, is explicitly and falsely diagnosed as mentally incompetent on the frailest of evidence—and in blatant revenge for her being unresponsive to psychiatry's leading questions and its dignity. The outrage of this is the play's main target, the brunt of its single-minded dramatic vector. What Claudia's stage lawyer tells her point-blank about the plot's bottom line goes unspoken, as such, in the film, yet it is capped with a specific dialogue line—call it a wardrobe warning—transferred to a passing remark of Streisand's instead. This is the risk of living her life out in prison garb: "I don't want to lose this," badgers the play's Levinsky, just "because you won't play the game. You'll play, and you'll play our way, or"—here the voiced fear of Streisand's Claudia herself—she'll be "wearing that bathrobe till . . . collecting Social Security." No matter how much the Dreyfuss character tries to restrain Claudia on-screen, however, an unsparing derision remains unabated at the core of her performance: a rebarbative smutty Barbra, a Claudia emotionally lawless, all claws out, who fortifies herself with incautious blasts of snarky noncooperation. In contrast, the original stage Claudia does play along, tacitly passing the lawyer offstage clues to the father's behavior in leading up to the explosive interrogation scene. Streisand's Claudia wants, at all costs, to keep this bottled up, buried, its disclosure not just too painful and shaming for all parties but even likely, she may think, though we never really know what she's thinking, to undermine her sanity claims with the damage it might well have caused. But which diagnosis of mental trouble her own uncontrolled "contempt of court" only exacerbates.

Acting on Trial

Whether Claudia fully realizes even this, we never know. Everywhere in the screen version, motivation takes second seat to emotion, cause to affect, the heroine to the actor.

Maybe there's a hint that Claudia's extreme recoil from the shrinks is not solely the result of their cruel boorish stupidity, let alone their vendetta. Easily believed is that it is because, as spat out in an early rant to Levinsky, she doesn't want them "crawling around in my head asking about my toilet training"—as if by association with those other bathroom issues of developmental psychology that she wants more pointedly to repress. In any event, once seated before the judge in court, for a woman so quick, so rational, there remains no excuse, on the score of self-defense, for her belligerent and unhidden scorn. On stage, Claudia was falsely claimed to be psychotic, whereas here the pallid worst that the shifty Dr. Morrison can come up with is "impossible to talk to." On stage, too, a full battery of knee-jerk cultural assumptions was amassed against the middle-class girl turned whore: "A broken home, a broken marriage, dis-illusion, despair, terror, homicidal rage—we're talking about breakdown. Breakdown. Where there's a breakdown, it's our job to put the pieces back together." No such full-scale litany of diagnoses, however clinically suspect, surfaces in the film version, where Claudia collaborates with the shrinks in being her own worst enemy in the matter of an aggressive derangement, even while she knows better. In her own late words on the witness stand: "Okay, so I had a lousy childhood. . . . That has nothing to do with what we're here for." Too true. Which can only mean that the flashbacks were overplayed, a subplot exploded into the main dramatic trajectory to which it lends morbid color rather than pertinent narrative weight. Vague psychomedical aspersions of uncooperative behavior, "hostile" and with an "inappropriate sense of humor"—a far cry from the "personality profile" of our renowned screen comedienne—are all the establishment can muster against Claudia in the film version. This is a far cry from the supposedly authoritative finding of "paranoid schizophrenia" in the play, equally ludicrous but harder to disprove in the face of sworn psychiatric testimony. Put simply: an angry and recalcitrant attitude in court, and a foul-mouthed grudge in preceding consultations, is hardly enough, given the professional assessment on-screen, to spark any real suspense in the legal drama, but only to ignite the star's blazing performance. And on fire it is, from first to last. It is something to see, to marvel at—as well as, in the wrong sense, to wonder at: its plausibilities worn ragged at times by conflicted signals.

To the detriment of courtroom tension, then, the only signs of instability about Claudia in her unrelenting struggle for control—control not so much of herself as of the situation—are the continuous undulations of the star's face, always warily at-tentive and on edge. Claudia's share of the script isn't at all bad in its scabrous dia-logue, but these other (facial) lines of Streisand, timed to it, are the best in the film: lines, delineated emphases, in the very working of her look—and her looks—in close-up, sustained for nearly two hours of full-frame collaboration with the camera.

Not so much her harried or disheveled looks in the superficial sense, but the *look* itself. This includes the squints of frustration or bafflement, the readily arched snarl of the nostrils, the tightening of the jawline under sudden duress, the creased brow like a strung bow waiting for the next tactical zinger. Most of all we see, whether in close-up or not, the sly curl of the spitfire lips in snide reaction shots, caught in the rictus of a sarcastic smirk—or their tightening into withdrawal as if she were almost swallowing rather than biting her own tongue. And then, in the climactic monologue about her prostitute's services and their manipulative allure, we get the verbal equivalent of her "flashing" Levinsky in their first consultation—accompanied by a gorgon-like stare of mock-erotic seduction when apostrophizing the prosecutor as "darling." Her eyes in this monologue are like retinal lasers answering back to the pinpoint lighting of Andrzej Bartkowiak's camera, as if one lens could penetrate the optical other in a gaze of such intensity.

Shot on the stand over the shoulder of the prosecutor, who is cast as a kind of white-haired middle-aged double of the dead assailant (Robert Webber for Leslie Nielson), Claudia's retailed price-list litany of pointedly serviced lusts (cleaned up, but not all that much, from the play's rimmings and enemas) can still chill the veins it is also inflaming. Having been cajoled into spelling out her career as hooker, she drops into what feels like a rhetorical flashback, coming on overtly to the prosecutor as a proxy for some former client: "Do you want the best? . . . Do you get what I'm telling you, darling?" This lubricious soliloquy is capped shortly by a further harangue from the courtroom floor, with unlikely permission from the judge to finally speak her mind outside of the witness box of cross examination. It is there that she rails against their expectations, refusing "to play the part" they want, refusing "to play nuts." The screen part Streisand has hereby just played in this *refusal*, together with her pornographic checklist on the stand, is like none other in her career. This isn't just a star's opening her whole bag of tics or tricks at once; it is a deeper dredge into her emotive range—and with an extra narrative dividend. Quite removed from all the typical mercurial bursts of Streisand's seasoned comic timing and its dramatic equivalents, until now Claudia's erratic swoops of mood can seem to have undermined her cause. But they have jelled here at the end into two strategic performance pieces, salacious and polemical by turns, shaped by the lunges and crescendos of sheer female force in recoil: equal and opposite, if only in raw audacity, to the power structures that assault it.

This is all part of the play's inherited and inherent metatheater, but brought forward to new and riveting prominence in Streisand's close-ups. True, in a dubious mood, a viewer might tend to suspect that nothing quite links the lithe, suave, and preternaturally glamorous hooker to the vixen harpy of the hospital consultation rooms. Except, of course, that each persona on display is an act of *self-presentation*, whether in cool control or not, each a kind of command performance—if, in the latter case, involving a histrionic rebuff of the institutional scenario she's been handed. Over each part, hooker and hellcat, the character, as well as the actress, has immediate performative control—except when violence erupts, sexual or juridical. Whenever the shots, as they repeatedly tend to be, are held tight in an objective correlative of the spot she's in, never has a performance by Streisand—in the relay-race of affect criss-crossing her features—been more blisteringly deliberate, as if steeled to resist the frame-up of the camera's own framings. And to emphasize any such "directorial control," however mismanaged on Claudia's own tactical behalf, there is a scene in which the film's executive

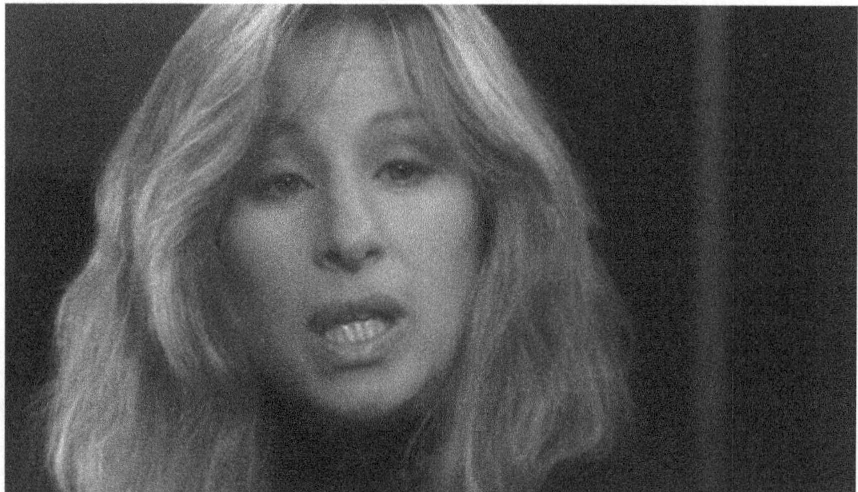

29. Send up the clowns (*Nuts*)

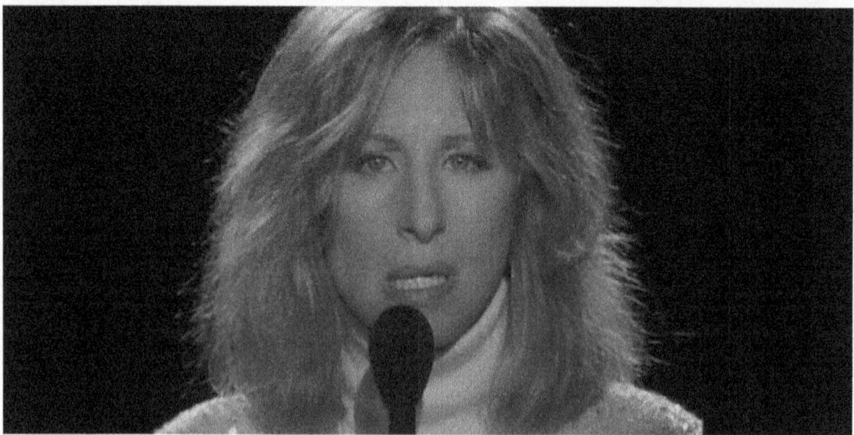

30. "Send in the Clowns" (*One Voice*)

producer actually cues the actors—as characters—in the delivery of their own canned dialogue. "We love you," from the mother, is met by Claudia's "What?" Puzzled, and soon more so, the mother tries offering further assurance, as much to herself as to the daughter: "Do you know that, darling? We love you." For her part mockingly quizzical, Claudia just repeats "We love you," and then: "One more time. We—Come on, we—." The singing star as vocal coach (fig. 29).

And this time she has cajoled the father, too, previously spoken for in the plural, into repeating the rote phrase. It is as if Claudia were taking charge of the film's own script and gutting its false sentimentality by an evacuating iteration. Dutifully they repeat after her, each word in detached enunciation, until finally, as the third shoe falls, she says, stonily, "Outstanding": ambiguously for both their coerced recitation and its emptily declared affection. On-screen rather than in the theater, up close, in tight, face on, the symmetrical counterpoint with *One Voice* is never clearer. Claudia's markedly different inflection of each sappy monosyllable, on an ascending scale of absurd brightening tonalities, reads to the camera like a conductor ventriloquizing for her pupils their own hollow protestation. Mute the soundtrack on your home video and the first "We" (from whose aped plural Claudia's irony entirely excludes herself) has the look, though of course mic-free, of some ironic escalation to a hard-won high note in a filmed song number, as here in an ironic turn from the previous year's "Send in the Clowns" (fig. 30).

And there is another curious hook between *One Voice* and *Nuts*, again oblique: one that emerges in Streisand's voiceover commentary seventeen years later for the DVD reissue. Concerning the film's closure, she lingers over a rejected idea for the last shot—and a regretted missed chance within what she had filmed instead. On the former score, she explains that, once Claudia is cleared for pending trial by the sanity hearing (and a voluble *hearing* it has been), the script's original idea—as if suspending Claudia's subsequent criminal rather than civil fate in liberated midair—was to end with a freeze-frame. It was to be followed, then, by the end-title scroll that foresees the real Claudia's acquittal—and that surprises many a viewer, no doubt, with this film's proximity to docudrama as a fictionalized "true story." In a sense the freeze, despite the shadow of cliché, might have worked: a tacit rhetoric of "enough already," enough of legal accusation and courtroom oversight. But Streisand had her second thoughts in time to act on them. She remarks on the DVD that, in the last stages of production, she happened one day to see a man walking down a crowded street, singing loudly and unself-consciously to himself: the kind of unguarded emotive gesture one is quick to assume as the result of a loosened screw. She wanted to put Claudia, now released "on her own recognizance," in a similar position, and inserted that equally unguarded (in every sense) male figure onto the pavement along with her, amid the crowd, in the film's closing wide-angle shot. In this revised ending, we therefore have the scene of her release (bail- but not scot-free yet) onto the Manhattan pavement to await her later felony trial—in the meantime stealing a fetching red accent scarf from a wheeled garment rack crossing her path. Streisand wanted to suggest that Claudia, too, would be thought crazy to be wending her way through the urban crush in nightdress, robe, and flimsy slippers—another aimless nutcase, "even though we just made a whole movie proving she wasn't."

For Streisand this is the last mark of what she calls the "illusion and reality" issue in the film. Sure, the stop-action arrest (almost as a negative visual pun) might also have worked, serving this idea from another angle. To anyone in the court who will let down the guard of protocol long enough to listen, Claudia keeps refusing in her last monologue to be the "picture" of her "you have in your heads." To cap that refusal, the freeze might have marked an escape from picturing altogether by stop-action: a last trace, a last fixed image, peeled from the object of scrutiny in leaving her otherwise be. This while the subject escapes (as if out from under the arrested image) in real time: slipped away to something other than whatever snapshot evidence the medico-juridical apparatus is after in working to pigeonhole her as a psychotic ward of the state. But after all the Method intensity of Claudia's embodiment by Streisand, the freeze-frame reduction to mere image, even as a coded escape of the woman from behind the imposed "picture," would stop short of full *release*, affective as well as juridical. The way out of the story should instead be *out*. That's what her rewrite gives us.

But there is something more in play, as well, beyond any visually punning contrast—there amid the avenue throng—between freed woman and the other sense of street-walker. We glimpse this extra dimension of the wide-angle last shot thanks to Streisand's own, not Claudia's, testimony on the DVD. With the narrative camera having avoided all previous establishing shots of the hospital site, the heroine is set loose for the first time into the film's, as well as her own, exterior field of view. There, in the screen's crowded panoramic frame—with a lighter shrug of irony than any in the film so far, when faced with that sidewalk male songbird—Claudia's footloose last move would appear meant, just as it comes off, to hover between a throwaway "And they call me crazy!" and a passing nod of solidarity. Reviewing this long-held shot for the reissue commentary, with the presumed loony passing Claudia on the street in the midst of his inaudible solo, Streisand now says, more than half seriously: "I should have started singing too." Not as Barbra, of course, but as Claudia. Streisand certainly didn't mean a real number, soundtrack worthy: some private-in-public ode to liberation. But the merest hint of such euphoric force, already hovering there by association over the slightly unrealistic ensemble framing of the busy street, would have gone a long way to free Claudia one notch further into Barbra's trademark comic spontaneity. Set up like a musical crowd scene, it could have been Streisand's first grand finale without a high note.

The mid-career diptych I've been suggesting, then, between the Bellevue melodrama and the Malibu recital, is not in any sense intended as a rescue action of this sometimes flat and in many ways self-deflating film. It is, rather, a response to its camera aesthetic in light of the breakthrough concert—and of what's coming in her directorial projects, both on and off the live stage. Fans may come back to *Nuts*, or may well not, but it's a movie hard to recommend, despite the quite extraordinary performance. And there is something worse at stake here than just an underappreciated and seldom revisited mastery in Streisand's embodiment of Claudia. For this unstinting effort bears with it, as perhaps its chief regret, the fact that, given its lukewarm response, Streisand has apparently never been tempted again, either as actor or director, to venture so far from the sentimental as her surefire turf. But beyond two major self-directed screen roles remaining in the 1990s, along with three minor comedies in a next and very different century (the two *Focker* films and *The Guilt Trip*), there is a more sanguine way to put this, given the landmark live concerts coming. Registering *One Voice* and *Nuts* as a two-sided coin in the cinematographic concentration of each performance mode, overlapped as they are in the fall and winter of 1986/1987, marks a productive and un-expected career transition. From here out, for another decade, and despite committed film efforts, singing wins the toss—with screen camerawork a steadily acknowledged, and constantly ramified, part of its delivery medium in her recorded tours.

Claudia Faith Draper may have taken once-aspiring actress Barbra Joan Streisand as far as she could ever have hoped to go in one direction—and, working that out of her aesthetic system, cleared the pipeline for more of what the preceding concert, *One Voice*, seemed to foresee as a new performance horizon in store. After all the angst her character had enacted, "I should have started singing too." As the star had in fact done in public just months before, and would continue to do in the com-ing decade of revived performance ambition. But even that way of putting it needs qualification—or amplification. For there is a broader recognition as well that discus-sion has wanted to highlight. Streisand's voice is a fine-tuned instrument even when she is not singing—and even when anything but mellifluous. It has always known the music of fury as well as of melody. That's what this chapter's point of juxtaposition between live song concert and courtroom drama, recital and the vehement recita-tion of soliloquizing dialogue, has meant to keep in touch with. Whether Streisand is singing or not we are inclined, from here out, as never before—after all those years during which she held back from live performance—to audit the implicit generative interchange in her talent between concert stage and narrative screen, lyric reading and line reading. Even mounted alternately in this mid-1980s contrast, by turns rather than by genre fusion, such is the incomparable work, to repeat this chapter's entitling claim, of *one voice twice over*.

INTERMISSION (2)

Genre Detours

As charted in our first Intermission concerning the immediate wake of Streisand's musical-comedy trifecta (*Funny Girl, Hello, Dolly!*, and *On a Clear Day You Can See Forever*)—closing out her ascendant stardom in the late 1960s—the five films discussed between *On a Clear Day* and *Funny Lady* were also lapped by five albums. In contrast to Streisand's later norm, the pace was breakneck. *Stoney End* and *Barbra Joan Streisand* (both 1971) showcased her rapidly mastered contemporary panache, followed by the more traditional fare of *The Way We Were* (1973, a separate collection from the soundtrack release). The experimental arrangements of classic American ballads on *Barbra Streisand and Other Musical Instruments* (1973) were answered by her return to straight pop with the catchall and ramshackle *ButterFly* (1974). When successful, variety was the very spice of the voice. In her album work, the sampling of different genres on separate tracks didn't produce the cognitive dissonance to which the lesser screen comedies were prone. And with a catchy tune, in its typical exquisite delivery, one didn't miss a plausible story the way, in a feeble film, one missed the singing. In the emphasis of this book, there's been no intent to question Streisand's decided gifts as an actor, in comedy and drama alike: estimable on both fronts. But it is the absolute preeminence of her stardom when combining these with her vocal mastery that has demanded tracking, in and out of its consolidating moments and its forced separations.

Even that restless fetching after movie material in the non-singing parts of the early 1970s may best be understood alongside her graduation in those same years from the Great American Songbook to a post-Beatles contemporary sound, folk as well as rock influences included. This involved covers of everyone from Joni Mitchell to Stevie Wonder, where record sales certainly paid off—even well before the triple-platinum *Guilty* album ushering in the 1980s. Her embrace of a mainstream pop register over the post-*Star Is Born* decade, and its evolution into disco, was increasingly highlighted by going-for-broke original singles, produced by the likes of reliable hit-makers like Quincy Jones and David Foster, in albums from *Superman* (1977) through *Till I Loved*

You (1988). Ever since *A Star Is Born* in 1976, the voice was expanding, if not exactly growing (how could it?), the vocal tonality loosening and stretching in the confident reach for the pounding big notes of pop arias, while doing no harm to the sweet shimmer of her quieter numbers (hear the self-descriptive "Clear Sailing" from 1984's *Emotion*, a performance of almost seraphic levitation). But all this did involve what seems to me an unwelcome detour in her "screen work." In every way but the caliber of her inherent dramatic focus in lyric delivery, the singer/actress so exciting to watch in song must have seemed an inevitable candidate for music video, however unnaturally she came to its established protocols in unactorly lip-syncing. But with the result that this second "intermission" in her career, between her most ambitious film work and her magisterial return to live singing, entails a new kind of genre crisis in the showcasing of her mature and pop-enhanced vocal reach. Intermission (1) examined the rather desperate "triaging" of ailing or inapt genre options for Streisand's talent in the early 1970s: their "sorting out" or in some cases forced "revival"—after the decline of big-budget musicals, not to mention of screwball comedies. The genre miscalculations two decades later were at least shorter-lived. The detour was only just that. After no more than a few serious missteps, instinct prevailed over the pop zeitgeist—and Streisand left MTV behind for music-on-TV (in her broadcast concerts) as never before seen.

From Screen Musical to Musical Screen

Everything that was meretricious about MTV as an autonomous aesthetic form (to the extent that it was sometimes imagined as such) worked against the mode's assimilation of Streisand, or she it. All was antithetical, rubbing her vocal and actorly gifts the wrong way. The half-hearted imposition of humorless narrative shape onto lovelorn ballads and dance tunes alike; the manic shifts in editing, often from singing artist to unidentified projected avatars seeming in some disconnected way to approximate the lyric emotion: these had no performance integrity. Amid such whiplash switches from one scenography to another without the segments cohering as a scene, the occasional insert of an arena performance to reconsolidate the rock-star power squandered by inert narrative gestures, most of them deadly serious in their witless sexiness; everything juiced up and watered down by the editing techniques familiar from TV advertising: all that made this video mode especially wrong for Streisand. Musical drama on-screen is her defining medium. Music video is something else entirely. It's fine, in 1981, to see her working out the drama of the music in the recording booth for Andrew Lloyd Webber's "Memory," so good, in fact, that every undermotivated cutaway—to black-and-white photos and dated urban footage—at first distracts and then gradually subtracts from our concentration on that of her performance.

It had been even worse. She herself can't help making fun of the fog machine that accompanies 1977's "My Heart Belongs to Me," whose clouds she tries waving away in the musical bridge before jokingly accepting the applause of half a dozen recording technicians at the song's close: a direct mockery of the kind of audience reaction that can generate energy in an actual live performance. All this sabotages the interest of her otherwise noteworthy vocals in that song. In the new roll if not rock of her singing—and sometimes its earthy, almost Country twang, often elevating above a distant chorus of backup singers—the Streisand sound finds in that lyric a (syllabic) opening for one of her characteristic mimetic effects. The opening syntax of "My Heart Belongs to Me," with the independent-woman emphasis it shares with the eponymous and high-flying title song of this *Superman* album, entails a phrasing that skates halfway between one clause and two: "I got the feelin' [that] the feelin's gone." The repeated noun is shifted from the language of suspicion to the euphemistic code name for a waning passion. Feeling fades away in the very grammar—as further evacuated in the climactic refrain when the vanishing "fe-e-E-e-e-lin" is dilated across its several very long *e*'s of emphatic and then thinned-out desire. Any attention to this vocalized rise-and-fall is dissipated faster than the feeling itself in the hokey video treatment, and certainly faster than the fake fog, a treatment so sloppy it seems like a rejected cut—and is certainly in the other sense an "outtake" from any real trajectory of the star's career.

Guilty was such an instant success three years later that it needed no videos for promotion. Besides its three hit singles (the #1 "Woman in Love," and two duets with Barry Gibb, the irresistible title song and "What Kind of Fool"), the album included a further string of inventive gems. A fiercely stirring delivery on another track inverted the plangent sweetness of the famous opening "memmm'ries" of "The Way We Were" to the slamming wail, and dragged-out wake, of "Make It Like a Mmmmmemoreee," a self-attenuated "dreaeaeam unreeeal." As usual with Streisand's most urgent vocal production, one can, in a song like this, picture the whole force field of sound across the vanishing terrain of the mind's ear, no video translation required. Same, on that nonpareil album, with the title line of "The Love Inside"—internalization pried wide by "insihihihed"—or with the completed thought of "Run Wild": namely "out on the edge" of an almost spatially distended "tiiiiiime." Four years later, by contrast, the dance-oriented title song from her last full-bore pop outing at album length, *Emotion* (1984), though flanked by some richer if not catchier material (including that crystalline "Clear Sailing"), became an overblown six-minute video. This ersatz extravaganza entailed dozens of costume changes, a supposed dramatic cast (including Roger Daltrey and Mikhail Baryshnikov, as the sluggish husband and Himself respectively), and a predictable series of comic double takes at the aggressive leering of imagined male gawkers. The skeletal melodrama is all meant to play out as the heroine's fantasy of a more intense *affect*, the titular "emotion" distilled undiluted—like a return to the illusory screen-genre alternatives for the trapped housewife in *Up the Sandbox*—but with no real acting, and even less character, to moor its silly gimmicks. Indeed it is all a dream within a dream, as it turns out, to be awakened from by a frowzy, unromantic avatar of the sex-starved main persona.

The intertextual roots of this "Emotion" video go so far, though scarcely deep, as to begin the number, after some "flash-forwards," with a long-standing Streisand trope. The opening lyric finds an elegant-enough housewife self at yet another dressing-table mirror—where, expressed with a puff-cheeked mugging resignation, the song sets out by lamenting that "the face in the mirror," framed by its then-familiar mid-career curls, always "looks the same." Moreover, as if to exaggerate the production's departure from anything one typically associates with a Streisand film or taped concert, and not least given its barrage of jagged montage for this partisan of the actorly long take, this frenetic and uninvolving video was the dubious beneficiary of an anomalous distribution scheme. Thinly packaged as a brief documentary about its own making, it enjoyed an unprecedented release mode: playing in actual movie theaters as a "trailer" to the main feature. Arrayed here was the big-screen diminishment of the fabled star in one long over-choreographed false step. All the synthesizer-enhanced "motion" that her own voice pumped into the reiterated four or five syllables of "emotion," until it amounted to a kind of audial wordplay in its own right, did nothing to put the three-times repeated, incrementally insistent closing lyric—"Can you hear me?"—into any useful resonance with the metafilmic variants of the question in *Yentl*. As signaled by the earlier dressing-table shot, what we suffer instead is the Streisand mirror of difference in joyless submission to the new video norms: the kind of woeful (re)capitulation that brings with it none of the enhanced self-allusion of true style. The same lack of dramatic focus, even when stripped of all comedy, hobbles another video ("Left in the Dark Again") accompanying this *Emotion* album, "co-starring" (the scare quotes say it all) Kris Kristofferson in a barroom erotic triangle of no conceivable interest. So continued the leeching away of the star's honest emotional uniqueness—as actor and singer alike—by MTV protocols, a process grandly staunched only two years later by the genuine vocal performance of *One Voice*.

In the meantime, far more successful as TV-geared work, in their lower-keyed directness, were the 1985 videos from *The Broadway Album*, especially the studio "documentary" based on a recording session run-through of the "Putting It Together" that opens the record. The other, more ambitious video from the career fulcrum point of that album, directed by veteran filmmaker William Friedkin, begins by isolating Streisand on an empty stage, with New Age synthesizers accompanying her version of "Somewhere" from *West Side Story*. Her soaring delivery is alternated with footage of arriving immigrants to Ellis Island, whose ethnic mix is then projected into the italicized demographics of the in-theater audience—with, no surprise, a heavy European Jewish inflection. With both performance and audience rendered somewhat abstract and artificial in the intercut MTV mode, though slowed here to follow not a dance beat but the swooping chord changes of the Bernstein/Sondheim theater song, this video becomes, in effect, the coda to *Yentl* from two years before: the immigrant dream come true.

That's looking back. Looking forward, her clarion delivery of that operatic "show tune" is a harbinger both of *One Voice*, which opens with it, and of the first two of her live concerts, each closing with it. More broadly, too, as a shove forward rather than a revisited stage nostalgia, *The Broadway Album*—together with its equally best-selling sequel in 1993, *Back to Broadway*—has opened up Streisand's repertoire in ways that would make a return to concertizing more richly promising. Unlike much of the background-heavy pop material, these were songs that, on the live stage, really sang. In the meantime, while Streisand was considering this return to live performance, the on-screen career of the actor-director scored a major popular success with *The Prince of Tides* (1991). This was a film smoothly watchable, for all its bursts of improbable melodrama, but so much less original or compelling than *Yentl*, her previous directorial success, and so much more (suitably) muted than *Nuts* in its star performance, that it falls into this intermission between her more compelling late projects. Just as, by the same token, her next directorial effort, *The Mirror Has Two Faces*, given its own musical closure, seems best estimated in its place between her two more engrossing concerts. In fact, the second of these folds *The Mirror*'s hit song (cowritten and performed with Bryan Adams) into its own duet segment—as well as, quite separately, staging again a segment of mirror imaging and its metaphors (with a prop literal and figurative alike in the "You'll Never Know" number) in connection with the casting of her own younger self as a duet partner.

The Transparent Mirror

The lone episode of "mirroring" in *The Prince of Tides*, entirely tangential to the plot's impending traumatic backstory of gang rape, can't help but seem deliberately woven into the fabric of this ongoing motif in Streisand's career, especially as it inverts *Funny Girl*'s opening "Hello, gorgeous" from self-irony to onlooker appreciation. Yet certainly by contrast with a subsequent film about conflicted self-image brandishing *The*

Mirror in its title, this one actual moment of image reflection in *The Prince of Tides* might even appear dramatically out of place in context. At that turn in this earlier plot, Streisand in her professional role as wealthy psychiatrist Susan Lowenstein—looking as svelte and stylish as she will in *The Mirror*'s transformation from dowdily layered-look English professor to buffed glamour-puss—is seen by the plot to need an emotional boost, out of the blue, from her troubled leading man's convincing her that she's a pleasure to the eye. The little bit of narrative context necessary to set the scene for this is enough to expose its digressive effect. The reframed optic duplication it involves has little directly to do with the movie's later deliberate return both to a film-within-the-film episode and to a traumatic flashback structure (combining salient dramatic moments from *The Way We Were* and *Nuts*)—and still less with the genuinely anxious mirror theme that punctuated *Yentl*. Put otherwise, the nexus of self-imaging and replication in the Streisand screen canon is so definitive and recursive that it can easily seem misjudged or flubbed in a given underworked repurposing.

Once victim of male psychiatrists in *Nuts*, Streisand turns the tables, from Claudia Draper to Dr. Lowenstein, and draws out the brother of her patient, the poet Savannah Wingo (Melinda Dillon), until his own traumas (Nick Nolte's as Tom Wingo, in suspected relation to those of his suicidal twin sister) can be manifested and purged. The sister, writing under the pseudonym Renata Halpern, has established her poetic persona as a Holocaust survivor, and the Jewish psychiatrist wants to penetrate this manufactured cover story: to see what the family has *actually* had to survive. Here is where that "mirror scene" of internal reciprocity seems not just tangential but implausible, however metaphoric in its ultimate therapeutic intent: Tom's grateful payback in convincing the stylish but humorless shrink, burdened by a loveless marriage, that she is nonetheless an appealing woman. In fact Lowenstein is so smoothed out, controlled, and put-together, so effortlessly glamorous—despite the strain of an almost preposterously grotesque marriage and a tediously snarky son (Streisand's own son Jason Gould cast in the part)—that she hardly needs help in the physical self-esteem department. But the psychological idea of *facing up to yourself,* if only in a makeshift storefront vanity mirror of reflective glass, must have had its own intriguing cinematographic resonance for the star-director, both as recessed optic framing and as a career double image: the last mirror scene in her film work before *The Mirror Has Two Faces.*

The episode unfolds as follows on unlikely location in a totally deserted street off otherwise 24/7 Washington Square. First, the high school football coach from the deep South with a crumbling marriage, who is also a well-read English teacher, connoisseur of gourmet food, and classical music lover (par for the course in this overripe novelistic plot), spots a window display for legendary violinist Herbert Woodruff's latest recording. The aficionado at this point assumes the famed musician is a client of Lowenstein's, since he's seen the virtuoso in her office. Even as Tom discovers that he's her husband instead (a man ludicrously vain and hateful, we discover in later scenes), a failing marriage is also implied by her tone. In this disclosure scene, filmed from behind the advertised husband's cut-out cardboard image, the wife is half effaced by the bulking public silhouette of the famous spouse. The effect is answered by what could be called a thematic reverse shot. This happens when Tom stops her in front of another storefront, half a block away, with a painting on display. He wants Susan to study appreciatively her own reflection, to see what a figure she cuts (fig. 31)—yep, in a dressy white suit with heavy gold accessories that was wildly out of place at the casual gay party in the Village, thrown by a common friend, where they happened to bump into each other. At first she thinks he's pointing out the painting in the window, but he just wants to convince her, by way of the glass's convenient reflection, "how beautiful you look in that suit," and how her "great smile" should be used more. Wriggling away from the embarrassing (at more than one level) testimonial, she admits "you've convinced me." The audience was way ahead of her. Well-intentioned enough as a turn of character study in some other narrative context, in this star vehicle the scene is indeed "all too transparent" in its self-appreciation.

But soon the image-within-the-image shifts back to the patient, not the therapist, in the transferential interchange of this plot. After a session of Tom's coaching Susan's belligerent son at football in Central Park, where she's been gratuitously insulted by the departing boy, Tom suggests that he and she "go to the movies." Her surprise—"to the *movies*?"—cuts to his narration of "rare footage from the Savannah Wingo archives,"

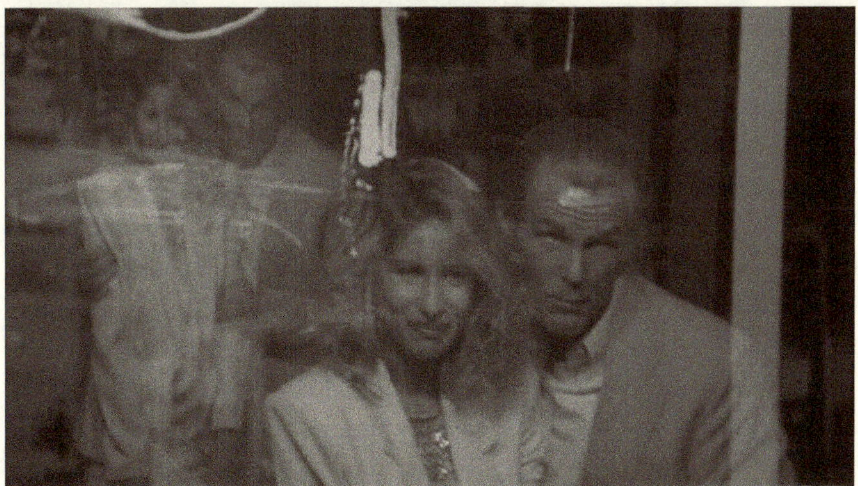

31. Planes of self-reflection (*The Prince of Tides*)

which he's found when snooping around in his twin's apartment. Cue the video lab for artificial antiquing. But there is more at play at this turn than some historically apt update of the black-and-white home-movie reminiscence in *The Way We Were*. The faded 8-mm color images of this amateur footage offer something like a material(ized) flashback in their own right. And they won't stay put in the screen past. When we cut from the images of the Wingo children and their mother back to Tom narrating the grievous family story from a quasi-psychiatric "couch" beside Susan, he's illuminated in an uneven light reflected from the screen—before eventually standing in front of it to speak about his beloved older brother Luke, killed in a protest after returning from Vietnam. His standing up at this point to occlude the image is as unlikely as it is symbolic. The screen image is now casting a silhouette of Tom over the dead brother on the projected celluloid spool—a superimposition (diegetic rather than editorial) that leaves the living body still bearing, in flickering and only dim "resolution," the vanished phantom of his loss. In this scene's impacted visual recess, the shot does appear at least loosely linked, after all, to the paired storefront optics earlier, where, inverting the patient/psychiatrist dynamic, Tom tries to bring Lowenstein's own self-image into focus. From her perspective now, it's clearer than before that what haunts Tom is another double besides his twin sister: the lost brother who, refiguring the obstructed home movie optic, in fact *shadows him*.

After Lowenstein's previous self-acknowledgment in a makeshift mirror, her joining Tom at "the movies" unfolds in this way as the documentary version of the otherwise subjective cutaways that have returned us earlier in the plot, via flash inserts, to his North Carolina backstory. These include at one point a two-stage regress burrowing back through his own cooking for his wife and kids to memories of a violent family meal during his own childhood with a brutal father. All these movies-within-the-movie, so to speak, build toward the gruesome "big reveal"—as with the equivalent sexual predation pieced out over the course of *Nuts*—in which mother, sister, and Tom himself were all raped by three escaped prisoners who are, in the process, shot and killed by Luke. It is here that the film's whole structure finds a metaphoric authorization from a typically ornate line in the Pat Conroy novel: "Rape is a crime against sleep and memory; its afterimage imprints itself like an irreversible negative from the camera obscura of dreams."[1] Indeed, in the annals of academic trauma theory as well as its therapeutic practice, as noted in considering the temporal underlay of *Nuts*, the filmic rather than photographic analogy is a matter of established vocabulary: the "flashes" and "flashbacks" of recovered memory. As if to align this shared sibling trauma, gender-leveled, with the child abuse subplot of *Nuts*, Streisand's adaptation backdates to age thirteen the rapes that happen in the novel, to twins Tom and Savannah, at age eighteen. So that in the screen version, he "didn't even know such a thing was possible." Nor should the knowledge be allowed to last, according to their shamed mother, not even in order to be understood and worked through; for both Tom and his twin, that is, the trauma has only been compounded—and driven into the unconscious—by this denial. Attempting to cleanse the degradation after burying the bodies—a cliché of repression made literal—the mother refuses to let any of the children ever speak of it. Only psychiatry can finally license the unearthing.

Has a more unabashed melodramatic plot ever been more openly crossbred with a romantic scenario—as the doctor and her patient-once-removed, his marriage continuing to disintegrate long-distance, strike up a passionate and giddy affair? But honor calls—via the wife on the phone—and, in the film's structural irony, it's the help Lowenstein has afforded him, in facing up to his troubled inner life, that has strengthened him for a renewed commitment to his family. Even in transgressing her profession's ethical limits in "fraternizing" with a patient's fraternal twin, the psychiatrist has worked a painful cure. The ill-advised romance has been convincing enough. All intelligent charm, Oscar-nominated Nick Nolte battles gamely and likeably, if succeeding only unevenly, with the heavy southern accent and heavier purple prose of the big Conroy speeches, especially laborious in voiceover. Opposite him at every turn, as sedate foil, it's *almost* interesting to see Streisand reduced to a mere sounding board for the emotional turmoil of another character. Almost, until we're reminded finally of the star wattage that we've been missing. Until, that is, after all the velvety poise and modest self-deprecation of her professional demeanor, she finally takes pained wing in their penultimate scene together, recognizing from across the street at her office building door, from the mere look on his face—with Tom appearing there unexpectedly to meet her—that his estranged wife must have called. And that he'll be returning to his family after all. In the parting couple's remaining scene together, he explains how he doesn't love his wife "more," just "longer."

But that would have been less than cold comfort at the previous moment of foreseen separation. Filmed from Tom's POV, and from across the street, yet in alternating long shots and close-ups, Lowenstein's cool professional manner wilts, withers, even as she tries inwardly to brace herself. In one of her classy tailored suits as usual, beige this time, and producing an overall monochromatic hue verging on skin tone, the look of recognition makes her seem suddenly washed out even before cried out. Nolte plays the scene perfectly in the attempted tamping down of his squirming sheepish pain. And outdoing even the muted sentimental acceptance that closes *The Way We Were*, Streisand is at her most affecting. Fighting for self-control as she approaches him on the opposite sidewalk, professional manila folder in hand, she can't stifle the cascade of expressions playing across her face in varieties of desolation and self-incriminating "I told you so's." Her crossing to meet him—no longer really halfway—brings them together in controlled but agonized recognition until, face to face, we get the ultimate tear-jerking catch in her throat: "We knew this day would come, but"—with her hands gesturing suddenly in a spasm between them—"you're never quite prepared for it." What vulnerable eye—certainly not Nolte's—could remain dry for the staggered gulp of her delivery at this point? The moment seems almost archetypally to embody the idea of jerking tears, first of course from the character herself. Followed, as she fights for composure, by her own sardonic comeback: "I've gotta find myself a nice Jewish boy. You guys"—and we can't help but hear "goys" as well—"are killing me," as if Streisand rather than Susan (forget the gargoyle husband) is looking back through Kristofferson to Redford (who had originally considered the Nolte part). Out of nowhere, all screen allusions aside, it is a perfectly judged moment: the Streisand persona rising to the aid of her character with a modicum of comic relief. The whole scene is an outrageously effective two minutes of cinematic blocking, lighting, and screen acting on both their parts, hers especially, and makes the unlikely last dance in the deserted Rainbow Room to follow feel like a mere afterthought.

All told, the movie veers uneasily between rom-com charm and Southern Gothic extravagance. Laud it or loathe it (I know people in both camps), return to it or forget it, one function of its transitional place in this second Intermission has to do in part with an intriguing facet of its legacy: its return by video clip in her 1994 concert tour. On the oversized arena screen, spliced together with snippets of therapy featuring Daisy from *On a Clear Day* and Claudia from *Nuts*, Lowenstein quotes her steep hourly fee in the montage. This is all part of the lead-in to a song segment framed as a psychoanalytic session—as if it were in part such therapy (an unmentioned but implicit suggestion) that had helped bring Streisand back to live audiences again in her famous overcoming of stage fright. In any case, directing and starring, without singing, has been part of Streisand's deliberate screen experimentation in the preceding post-*Yentl* decade, along with those separate forays into MTV video. It would seem that these two forks of this second major "detour," in their exhausting of at least certain alternatives, gets the star just where she needs to be going after all: directing her own musical staging on an actual *tour*.

As a momentarily aborted promise of just that commitment to performed voice, there is a further notable aesthetic (if not dramatic) misstep in the release print of *The Prince of Tides*, evidence of which is highlighted by one of Streisand's more tasteful and effective promotional videos. It was, no doubt, an utter narrative integrity that saw her bucking both the enthusiasm of preview audiences for the theme song in a rough cut of the film and the urging of the studio to retain "Places That Belong to You" in its scheduled upsurge over the second half of the end credits (deleted version on the Criterion DVD). This was a commercial pressure resisted by Streisand because the movie, as flagged by her taking second billing to Nick Nolte, should end, in her view, with his version of Pat Conroy's words, rather than Dr. Lowenstein in sudden song. It is a decision as impeccable as it is lamentable. Despite Streisand's loving and expert adaptation of the novel, nothing in the resulting material deserves this purity. The supple resignation of that ballad would have lent an anchor—and payoff— to the film's lush scoring by James Newton Howard. And certainly Conroy's decorative closing prose is no competition for a vocal catharsis that, in its climactic lyric about memories that "ebb and flow," would have bestowed upon the last word of the film's title, now singularized in a simile, eight mimetic seconds' worth of rippling vocal backwash in the brimming diminuendo of "like the tiiihihihiiiiid." Just before the song's final reflexive move, in the internal rhyme of "traces of a song" that "belawwhng . . . to you," Streisand's typically inspired tremolo has thus drifted off into that last syllabic hint ("tihide") of just such a sheltered *hide*-away for unsurrendered memories. Though she is hugging herself in front of the microphone for the video treatment of the song, as if in a cross-armed cradling of the same harbored dream, the voice alone would have accomplished that mellow protectiveness on the closing screen track. Indeed, if I may press one more time my sense of the cinematics inherent in the Streisand soundscape, it would have done so—in a kind of audiovisual tracking shot all its own—by following out the mimed withdrawal of that very long-*i*-ed noun. The cliché is all but unsayable in regard to Streisand, but she seems with this excision of the theme song—the actor-director trumping the singer—to have cut off her nose to spite her face. Whether a matter of ultimate commercial regret or not from the studio's point of view, or her own, Streisand's decision stands as another cleaving of, rather than to, the differential power of her talent. After a triumphal singing tour, it is a mistake she won't make again, as evidenced by the deliberate musical coda to her next self-directed film, *The Mirror Has Two Faces*.

Synesthesia: The Lens of the Voice

A further note on the spatialization of high notes and their hidden inner terrain, this time (alas) with no visual evidence to shore it up. *The Broadway Album*, then *Back to Broadway*, then back in the same year to the stage: the momentum was palpable. And expectations were especially keyed up by the latest CD material. Capitalizing on the breakthrough—or break-back—success of the first Broadway anthology in its return to Streisand's stage roots, for its sequel album (the first pressing sold out nationwide before its release) she was able to secure Andrew Lloyd Webber's permission, before his show had even opened in London, for two songs from *Sunset Boulevard*. The first, "As If We Never Said Goodbye," has become, from 1993 on, a thematically apt staple for the opening number of her serial "comeback" concerts, down through paired Hyde Park and Madison Square Garden appearances in 2018. The second Lloyd Webber number from that Hollywood film's theatrical remake, the more flamboyant "With One Look"—never sung live, alas, by Streisand—nevertheless captures, rapturously, in volume and vibrato alike, the electric charge of a live camera close-up. What her delivery achieves is the eerie sheen of silent-screen aura manifested—across an entire technological and sensory transfer—in the pyrotechnics of voice alone.

It isn't the chance of *one more look* at the returning silent star that is celebrated in this number. Stressed instead is Norma Desmond's own wordless looking, rather than her photogenic looks. Extolled, in the very tolling of its own vocal elegy, is the dramatically couched gaze of silent stardom per se: its being met, at whatever angle, by the camera eye from within the dramatic scene and its role—and through the camera's, that of the audience. Call it, in both senses, projection. It is this, according to the lyric, that, by the sheer play of light, "sets the screen ablaze," where the script-exceeding power of a single "frown" can't, in rhyme, be written "down," and where it's the star's own tearful "eye," in its hold over an audience, that can "make the whole world cry." But here, in this stage musical, unlike glistening silent clips in the Billy Wilder film, singing must compensate for the absent screening: its own form of technical intimacy, its own aurally prismatic lens. Even front-row seats in the theater can't bridge the distance that the shimmer of voice alone is meant, all by itself, to close. Yet it is the implicit audiovisual resonance of this number that takes us all the way back to the mixed metaphors of "a tingle . . . a sparkle, a glow" when capturing in part the haptic tremble of felt voice in Central Park's "He Touched Me"—desire fired this time, though, in "With One Look," by a more explicit figure of emotive conflagration (a "screen ablaze").

Streisand's incandescent chiming vocals on the expansive rises of this showstopper go to new lengths—and heights—to transfigure the poignancy of Norma's silent-screen ambition. In the on-stage lyric, but never with quite the vibrant impact of Streisand's track, voice embodies and crystallizes the gaze itself, singling out, in ear-piercing mimesis, the former star's searing look—as if it were burning a hole in the silver nitrate of her "glory days." The smoldering impact is certainly felt in the famous stage versions by both Patti LuPone and Glenn Close—but never so ringingly clear as in Streisand's stratospheric rendering, which becomes to my mind, my ear that is, a front-running candidate for her epitomizing theater song: the thrill of the look always incarnate in the voice itself. Or think of it this way, in a further gloss on the previous chapter. Given this treatment of "With One Look"—as if rounding back to the "With One More Look" / "Are You Watching Me Now?" medley from *A Star Is Born*—one might hear as well, beyond the camera-tethering "watch me" stare at the end of *Yentl*, a more recent fusion of the scorching close-ups from *Nuts* with the intimate flair of song delivery from *One Voice*. In any case, with the incendiary tones of "With One Look," as retrieved in narrative context from the lost glimmer of its own extinguished silent medium, we sense on the very pulse of audition how that singular *Sunset* power, in Streisand's treatment, is simultaneously revived and mourned in the voice's sustained firestorm of song.

And there's a further and final glissade in the Lloyd Webber number, as well, that may have intrigued Streisand's own ear as much as her eventual listener's. This is the ecstatic latch in the two pealing *e*'s of the swelling monosyllabic climax when, if allowed again that "one look" before the camera, once more "I'll *be me*." Certainly the attentive follower of the Streisand songbook, always happy to be riding or sliding along as one word in her liquid enunciation crests over into the next, may pick up—in this salvo of voice—an external as well as internal echo. Attentive, retentive: what other kind of listening does the Streisand sound elicit? Hold then on the shivering prolongation of the final "beee meee": silent stardom's very predication in the thrown *beam* of light. And so it is that we keep coming back, here by an inbuilt career echo, to a primal scene and song, "I'm the Greatest Star": that prophetic opening number in Streisand's first starring role on stage, then screen. Optimizing Jule Styne's typical lyric wordplay with her crisp enunciation, a fired-up Fanny, in dismissing those with no stage promise, "not a lump," brings to bear her comic feel for guttural consonants in asserting herself as a "big c/lump" of such "talent." Strange as it may sound to say, it's often such little things that make a good part of the giant Streisand difference. And so we keep ears peeled. Next, in "Greatest Star," the insistence on telling us "one more time" of her latent destiny is thickly, as if inevitably, rhymed with the tongue-clicking assurance that we could bet our "las/t dime" on just this. Her resulting promise to "flare up" in a way that requires the world to "stare up" follows a sideswipe at patronizing skeptics who, if "looking down," will never "see me"—and is followed in turn by advice to "try the sky," starhood's true medium, "cause that'll be me."

It is as if two very different lyricists, Styne and Lloyd Webber—yet each assiduous rhymesters, not to mention masters of assonance—have converged in the charged space between ordinary words in their transfusion, by lyric syntax, of two into one. The composers have, that is, given it to their very different heroines to say—now in debut, now in delusional comeback, yet in screen apogee either way in Streisand's channeling—that the cinematic heights will, via an inherent luminosity alone, "be (a)m me": will not just incarnate but, for the waiting audience, *project* me into aesthetic presence. Our hearing an echo of this slant syllabic merger, as leveraged by an even more immediate narrative relevance, when Yentl later rejects the penumbral half-light of "the shadows" in order to "*be my*self at last" in the breakout "No Matter What Happens" lyric—her face set transitionally aglow by the "moon" as no longer the "one light" of her determination's new day—would only richly complete this sequence of teasing phonetic segues. Distilled in all this is a typical thrill of the Streisand throat in action, her wording always so *pronouncedly* articulate—yet where music can still hold across notes in holding out for a further sense, or sensation, of meaning: an aural afterglow. As with the asserted conflation of persona and projection in a compressed phonetic trajectory like "be(a)me," listening becomes all the more immediately material and somatic in impact when it's left up to us to phrase any such vocal overlay: not just in the mind's ear but through the body's own resonant nerved circuit of attention. So much space can be opened within a given notation that the word thus contoured may readily trespass upon the next, a matter not of intended pun but of phonetic retention per se. Letting the melody meld two words into one in audition may seem in this way like the *bridge* of a song realized in minimal, fractal form.

Synesthesia: a final subset of discussion in this chapter, but more like a cross-sectional index of the Streisand difference over the entire course of her career. By received definition: the access to one sense through another, as captured idiomatically in speaking of a costume's *muted* tint or a song's *bright* first note. In practice, when in audial receipt of the Streisand sound: timbre turned to image. The visualized contours of acoustic terrain are made manifest as an inner cinema of association, whose vistas, whose virtualized spaces, are conjured and traversed solely by the listening imagination. All this as signalized, for instance, in that glowing pinnacle of the star's piercing high notes in summoning the blaze of *Sunset Boulevard*'s "one look." But there is another mode of trans-sensory perception as well, just sampled, that characterizes such vocal attention—common to all listening but enhanced, in its marginal departures, by the baseline of taut articulation in Streisand's typical delivery. Such is the sensory transfer—operating on a narrower syllabic wavelength—not from sonics to virtual optics but from syllabic sensation to alternate sense: from audible pattern to its auditory off-echo. This is where a phrase like "muted tint" could, amid a certain melodic flow, retone itself in strictly audible terms as a "muted hint," whether or not this extra lyric intonation were functional in context or not. Think what happens, because hearing it first, as the smitten clause "I felt a tingle" (when "he touched me") detaches its subsequent optical rather than tactile synonyms, "a sparkle, a glow," so that the noun seems to have spawned adjectives instead (*atingle, aglow*) in their own giddy vibration. Or, harder to incorporate grammatically, but no less persuasive for that, hear again the reflexive vocal "endeavor" in the terraced crescendo of *On a Clear Day*'s "forever and ever and ever more." Many such examples have been logged as evidence in our audial inventory of the Streisand voice—dependent for their sensory mix of melody and meaning on her regularly clean-edged diction. More await, perhaps even more stirring, with the live audition of her concert tours in the coming final chapter on her volumetric sound. If synesthesia realizes itself in what this transitional subsection figures as the "lens" of her voice, it may be that the realizing ear can best be understood as in its own right bifocal.

More than once I've singled out Streisand's sung enunciation as not just the hallmark or trademark but the felt *earmark* of her vocal power. Any singing, of course, allows for something like the auditory double-tracking under consideration. Streisand's is (just?) a limit case: inducing a mode of reflex action clarified and maximized by the purity of her "styling." For Streisand, as we know, every song is a kind of theater song. Always in embodied character, hers is an unmuffled dramatic wording received somatically in turn, where it opens to the secondary performance of interpretation in uptake. Echo neurons again: we silently sing along, and in so doing think along, sometimes inclined toward a fractional rehearing that plays the lyric line just a little differently on our inner tympanum. Such a retexturing of sense is, therefore, less a motivated effect than an affect of emotive response. Not solely evident in Streisand's vocals, to be sure, just more so. Regarding the labial *m* and its ambiguities recently noted in that roster of stardom's irradiation—with hinted glints of an audial aura lending that extra nimbus of gleam (or "beam") to "me"—once again music exceeds scripted meaning from within diction's own precision. Any such nuance needn't be thought deliberate in the least on the singer's part, or even on the lyricist's, but rather inherent and flexional: a re-sounding at play in a natural muscular production transferred—in reverb—to our listening lips. Once more we recognize the Streisand voice as its own kind of malleable body language, fully articulated only in transmission. The phrasal feedback loops of the resulting soundscape entail at times a certain rich aural interference in its heard wording. Interference—a buoyant noise in the system, a surprising overtone—that carries its own surplus inference. Before the ear can autotune itself to a given script, sung words may have clung differently to each other on the melodic run—and dramatic run-up—across a spread of notes that, in delivering those words, vary and enliven their span of meaning.

And along with the performed "text" of the voice itself behind any lyric sense (Barthes)—its legible grain, including sometimes (as above) its contrapuntal pun-like subtexts—there are, by this time in Streisand's career, always the notable intertexts as well. Compounding any translucent halo effect serving to blur one word into the next, we sense an allusion in *Yentl's* extralunar "beam myself at last" to "The Woman in the Moon" number from *A Star Is Born*—a satellite space within whose orb that avatar of female need can't, in fact, in the climactic flip of the lyric, ultimately be held. Though the inflamed silent-screen nostalgia of *Sunset Boulevard's* "With One Look" is never performed live by Streisand, the self-fulfilling prophecy of its irradiated high notes, as if further inflected with vocal lens flares, allows the metafilmic force of the lyrics to summarize the luster of those many songs—some curated few of them delivered live in her return to touring—that over the years have so often transfixed the mind's eye as well as bodily ear. And never with more (almost telescopic) power than when, through the piercing synesthesia of the Streisand earscape, the tiny performer on the arena stage, beginning on the last day of 1993, reaches to the upper balcony with the beamed drama of her gaze—doing so through the figured immediacy of closed-circuit video images in their mobile close-ups on the embodied source of voice. No screens ever less silent, no popular dramatic sound ever more ablaze.

Act III

COMING BACK LIVE

CENTER STAGE

Home at Last

1976–1983//1993–2000. After her early musical extravaganzas down through *Funny Lady* in 1975, such date spans mark the definitive later chapters of a progress (a "work in progress," as Streisand calls herself as well as her career) whose first phase we've charted in detail from the "musical concepts" of the 1976 *A Star Is Born* through the *concept musical* of *Yentl* in its salient 1983 renovations of the genre as a "Film with Music." For the non-singing parts in which Streisand directs herself after *Yentl*, the renowned actress-who-sings becomes the director who orchestrates. Her classic cinematographic sense of camerawork as dominant, editing secondary, in the scoring of screen narrative by musical analogy—with the mobile frame of a scene guiding its quasi-lyric tempi between and across transitions—derives in part, as she often says, from an actor's instinct for theatrical rather than technical virtuosity: clocked, as she puts it, by a style now "staccato," now "legato." When the aesthetic really clicks, and the script is up to speed, or in other words up to the variable pace of the filming in its measured pulse, her direction can for a moment *sing*.

But there's nothing to compare, in either *The Prince of Tides* or *The Mirror Has Two Faces*, with the self-directed plot arcs, emotive as well as autobiographical, in those concert tours of the same decade (1993/1994; 1999/2000): staged events where she herself actually does the singing in a continuous performance mode, recorded live and redoubled from within by ingenious closed-circuit video inserts. In their potent originality, these live performances serve to redefine the career they at the same time epitomize. In one sense, nothing could be farther from the cult rhetoric around a pop figure like Madonna, bringing up the rear in diva clout in the previous decade: the openly fabricated "material girl" who kept "remaking herself" in an instinct for trending styles of music and sexual display. As we've seen from the start, Streisand's differentiations were intrinsic if not inbred—and she had to reinvent whole genres for their fullest materialization. Like *Yentl* before it, *Streisand—In Concert* is a maximal accomplishment in this vein.

The shadow of misnomer might seem falling over the last two Acts of this book's Set List—if, that is, the sense of Streisand's directorial control were limited to Act II's

"Calling the Shots." Instead, her control of mise-en-scène and its filming vies with and then outlasts her big-screen Hollywood productions. When she comes back whole-heartedly to live performance—tested in the mid-1980s with *One Voice*, and then brought to full commitment a decade later in her two Emmy-winning ventures—she is again under her own dramatic as well as video direction, literally calling the shots of the broadcast footage, framing the staging as well as helping craft the scripts. Not just a homecoming to live performance, these stage spectacles offer an incomparable homing in on her unremitting and undiminished gift. More than the two serviceable feature films interleaved with them, these recorded shows are the paired moments from the 1990s—in the histrionic (as well as historic) arcs of their in-person exhilaration—that feature the true Streisand difference as performer. With apologies to the pompous and blowsy German diva she impersonated in *The Belle of 14th Street*, they are, arguably, her *Gesamtkunstwerk*.

How so, exactly? What could, what did, Streisand bring back with her to the live stage? The answer is her whole career, in film and song alike: alike and together, fused inseparably now—as they always were at their best—through two retrospective hours of audiovisual counterplay. One concert focused mostly on her personal life through song analogies, the second, though hardly rigidly segregated, on her early musical career down through *Yentl*: together answering any lingering doubt about the deep meld between actress and song "stylist." Style: that notorious double-edged sword. Even at the cutting edge of undoubted originality, whenever "style" seems stiffening into brand, the term can appear merely to label rather than appreciate. When an artist is faced with this, a certain measure of insistence is often necessary to hold one's ground. Defending his formal artistry against charges of the formulaic, stressing instead the building strength of repetition, Alfred Hitchcock once famously insisted (in an *Observer* interview, August 8, 1976) that "self-plagiarism is style." For *auteur* Streisand in her work as performer rather than director, the issue has of course always been more tightly bound up with personality, knottier as a result, even in creative periods when the actress-who-sings is bent on something new and intensely specific each time out. In the self-theft of fresh invention, the trap to be avoided, needless to say, is that of mannerism—together with the worse fate of self-parody. Streisand's century's-end stage return can be recognized to triumph over any such dangers in the doubly perilous gesture of live life story—beset, that is, by all the obvious performance risks of self-scrutiny's own unembarrassed script when enacted, stage fright held at bay, before a real-time audience.

With the recording artist forgoing her studio comfort zone, the contingencies of live performance are continually matched in these concerts with the audiovisual montage of retrospect, where borrowed and reinvested triumphs drive this new and tightly crafted mode of concert autobiography. In no phase of Streisand's career, certainly, was charisma ever in short supply. Yet she tended, in the nervous early years, to be aloof on the nightclub stage. Now bolstered by teleprompters and backed by a wide spectrum of memorable screen personae (often literally rising in clips behind her), she can summon unholy doses of rapport with the crowd. Absent is any threat of the predictable, the merely recycled, in the live risk of these mostly—as if oxymoronically—solo variety shows. In the wider field of music and media culture, of course, the whole idea of the *performing self* had taken quite other forms over the years of Streisand's own uniquely imprinted stardom. In contrast to her increasing directness, the chameleon morphs of the pop circuit put air quotes around the shifting inauthenticities of "self-invention" with no pretense of a signature artistry. In Streisand's case, by contrast, the inevitable plagiarist raids of personal citation and stylistic ramification come full circle in these late concerts, where an inimitable gift reviews itself under the ongoing sign, within the given, of its instinctive stylistic *differentiation*.

Genre Regenerated: Toward the Narrative Concert

Tentative steps forward can look, in retrospect, like teasers. This is certainly the case with Streisand's return to in-person singing after twenty-seven years of stage fright—since forgetting her words in front of a mere 135,000 listeners in her free Central Park concert. In occasional invitation-only fundraisers, the songs had been fewer and never free again. Close watchers of the career had every reason to fear that hearing her in her own backyard sing to five hundred Hollywood liberals in 1986 (*One Voice*) would be the closest one would get to a full live concert again—and no doubt it was enough to live on if necessary, given the elating DVD. But then came her blazing appearance in front of a particularly unique arena crowd, one standing ovation after another, for three songs at Bill Clinton's first Inaugural Gala in 1993. She sweeps down the aisle to the stage, accepting rapid handshakes along the way, after Warren Beatty has mentioned that, having been at a lot of fundraisers in Hollywood with various celebrities lately, "including a singer, a composer, a writer, a director, and a producer," he decided just to introduce them all at once: "Ladies and Gentlemen, Barbra Streisand." Even then fans couldn't have guessed that the three-piece pin-striped Beltway business suit, with the deep-cut and shirtless vest, would reappear in sequined white the next year. Where it would take the second-act stage for her breakthrough two nights in Las Vegas—and then, week by week, on the tour it heralded as tryout: a tour in which there were five million calls for a fraction of that number of available tickets, all venues selling out in the first fifteen minutes.

The pressure-cooker of expectation had built predictably across the continuous out-put of albums. There was a strong sense, if again only in hindsight, that the return to stage material with *The Broadway Album* (1985) gave a certain impetus to Streisand's potential repertoire in coming before a live audience again. Not to mention her success as director. In her elaborately staged and carefully written two-hour performance piece (there is no better word for it) at the 1993 MGM Grand launch of *Streisand—In Concert* (as well as of its sequel six years later, at the turn of the millennium)—each conceived and directed by the "singer" herself—there is no doubt of the Hollywood influence. Her feature-length work as director, by 2000 including *The Mirror Has Two Faces* (1996) as well, had lent further expert fluency to the strongly dramatic—and deftly cinematographic—drive apparent in both concerts. And not just as song sequences, but as instances, beyond *Yentl*, of a whole new genre of musical performance in "recital" mode: call it the *narrative concert*. Beyond the constructed through-line of a plotted vocal recital, here was a new kind of self-starring screen biography. The first volume (*In Concert*), as noted above, charts in song mostly the star's emotional growth, while the second (the new-millennium *Timeless: Live in Concert*) steps off quite explicitly the stages of her singing career by replaying her rise to fame in clubs little, then big, then stage, then films. This division of narrative labor, too, comes clearer in retrospect. At the time, the *In Concert* tour boasted simply, overwhelmingly, the long-awaited excitement of the star's return to live performance—and the burnished miracle of a voice that, perhaps by avoiding arenas for all those years, had kept itself wholly intact for more than studio efforts. Since the exhilaration of *One Voice* and its almost unnerving live close-ups, the star had aged some, but not the voice yet, nor even six years later for *Timeless*, by which time she was pushing sixty—yet even then without need to push the high notes. Still, six years earlier, the "comeback" *Concert* had the *frisson* derived of pent-up anticipation, impossible to match, whereas *Timeless* could seem less miraculously intimate, somewhat overproduced, at times a tad grandiose rather than just grand. Yet again: the problematics of surprise when trying to redouble itself, of innovation self-plagiarized. But a potent diptych narrative had still been told by the divided focus of the two concerts. The smaller-scale tours since—with the orchestra gradually pared back, the voice showing some wear, though never tear—are merely concerts on the road, whatever intermittent retrospects they might attempt. This is the case even in 2017 with "Barbra: The Music, the Mem'ries, the Magic," structured by a sampling of her #1 albums in each of the last six decades (a yet-unmatched record). It was still only a themed anthology concert, however, not a filmed narrative performance of the career itself. In those two epic programs from the 1990s, however, with unearthly nuance and punch, Streisand had filmed preemptively (who else could play her?) the otherwise impossible: her own biopic, a life in music and pictures, recessed screen after screen. At this writing, she still hasn't quite finished her long-awaited memoir. But we already have its digest in those two concert triumphs.

In Concert on Tour

The last night of 1993 first. Initially in Vegas, then everywhere from Chicago to London, it was once again, as in her first TV specials, all Barbra, all the time—but with an airtight script and a continuous dramatic build that turned the show, as with the next concert (*Timeless*) as well, to serial stories in song from our most storied voice. Alongside her many teamings with Stephen Sondheim in revising his lyrics, as she did with "Send in the Clowns" for *The Broadway Album*, and as she does early in the *Concert*, no such intervention is more fitting than the added lines to Andrew Lloyd Webber's "As If We Never Said Goodbye," from *Sunset Boulevard*, with which, as noted, she opened the 1993 event. Emphasis is shifted from silent-screen presence to the renewed commitment of a self-exiled performing artist. As sung by Streisand about her own shying away from live exposure, "I've been in the wings too long," but that's "in the past." Now, standing "center stage," and with a high-note rhyme to confirm, she is "come home at laAAAst." And of course absence makes the ear as well as heart grow fonder, rewarded with the art of a voice not run ragged by interim touring over the decades.

Then, too, the whole apparatus of cinematic stardom is on call in this concert revival, with a use of video footage both tactical, as entr'acte, and strategic in its overarching sense of consolidated audiovisual powers. Scripted by Streisand and her close collaborators, the Bergmans, each concert does have its own distinct scenario. The first amounts to a kind of Bildungsroman plot sprung from the insecurity of first infatuations in her growth as a woman, as recovered within the artifice of on-stage therapy with a voiceover psychiatrist. With emphasis on the early momentum of her stage and film career rather than her erotic tribulations, the parallel story in 2000, for *Timeless*, tracks her move from the lower West to the upper East Side in her Manhattan club dates. Recalling "musical concepts by" in the end-titles of *A Star Is Born*, these celebrated returns to the stage are credited as "Conceived and Directed by Barbra Streisand." But unlike a movie musical, signed, sealed, and delivered, the original audiovisual document of the *Concert* stands in retrospect as the dress rehearsal for a revised conception, part of its own particular work in progress. There is the Las Vegas "preview" on New Year's Eve, 1993, released late the next year as *Barbra Streisand: Live in Concert at the MGM Grand*, complete with a riotous guest appearance by Mike Meyers as Linda Richmond, Streisand's obsessive fan from *Saturday Night Live* (again available on YouTube). This record of the event appeared as a single DVD only after the release of the two-disc DVD version recorded for HBO at Madison Square Garden, and titled *Barbra: The Concert*, as well as the laserdisc of California's Arrowhead Pond appearance at the end of her twenty-six-city tour.[1] This array of "variants" offers the equivalent of a textual scholar's field day in imprint history, what with its chance for the collation of rethought song sequences and cut lyrics. Closely comparable in this line of revision, both the Arrowhead and Madison Square Garden versions—in their rethinking of the Las Vegas launch—record adjusted song sequences and added showstoppers in each act that had helped give a more dynamic pace to the tour format.

And in particular to its narrative arc—beginning with the numerous cuts made in the early autobiographical lyric of "I'm Still Here," twice as long in the MGM version. Sondheim now, rather than Lloyd Webber, is again rewritten for this second number, and then drastically trimmed after opening night. Such rhyming lines as "she'd be gone in a year, never fear" are pruned away, including almost forgotten jibes about nasal wailing in regard to her now universally lionized voice: "Talent she's got, but those scree-EE-eeches," as if her "throat's in a sling." This was a recalled complaint succeeded by the still persisting gripes about her politics: "Talent's she got," but forget those "speeches": why can't she just "shut up and sing"? Perhaps most revealing among the eventually cut-back lyrics arrives in close proximity to the finely gauged "either they cheer or they jeer" rhyme with "still here" in the Sondheim original. In this further verse newly drafted for Streisand: "Then comes the curse of exposés" in rhyme with "overpraise," each logged in as equally distracting. It is against the dangers of the latter, we would have been invited to think with this lyric, that her perfectionism came to the rescue, never allowing her to rest on her laurels. In the shortened tour version of this song, emphasis falls, instead, on her career shift from acting to directing in segue to the next Sondheim song in the medley, "Everybody Says Don't." These are lyrics that then sequence in turn—across a monosyllabic chiasm of negation in the ubiquitous imperative "Don't"—to her classic "Don't Rain on My Parade." On the way into this fabled manifesto of resistance we hear at the end of the preceding number—tucked into the continuing thematic refrain of the survivor defying her naysayers in the "I'm Still Here" lyric—the repetition of "Songwriting, acting, producing," first with "what makes her think that she can?" And then, in snarly rhyme: "Or better yet," as amended by repetition of that professional triad on the spot: "What does she think, she's a man?" Worse yet, it's "once you announce you're directing" that the *don'ts* pile on.

All told, those previous minor deletions in the lyrics of an early number are nothing compared to the major surgery that the later DVD and laserdisc release of the tour versions reveal in their definitive enhancements. A retained innovative session with a voiceover Germanic psychiatrist licenses the retrieval of certain early album numbers that Streisand grew famous with, thus serving to anchor the dramatics of her legendary performance history in a coterminous backlog of intense psychological identification. ("With all the transference and counter-transference, sometimes I don't know whether I'm the patient or the doctor," she says over intercut videos of Dr. Lowenstein along with Claudia Draper and then Daisy Gamble "under analysis.") The concert's therapy sequence is paced to recover the nervous excitement of young love from the tremors (and exacting tremolos) of a blind date ("Will He Like Me?") to a blissful rendering of that Glenn Gould favorite "He Touched Me." By moving the mandatory ballad "Evergreen" (from *A Star Is Born*) up to this segment, as testament to a more mature love rather than a screen triumph, and removing the video footage, space was freed to make the second half of the concert more continuously about Streisand's film career, beginning with the entr'acte footage from *Funny Girl* and peaking at the segue into *The Way We Were*. From there to the first of two inspired highlights new to the tour. It is hard to believe, once seen, that they hadn't been part of the plan from the beginning: first a *Yentl* medley and then a "big finish," after the plangently sung and valedictory "For All We Know" ("we may never meet again"), with her *Broadway Album* finale—and *One Voice* opener—"Somewhere."

But also introduced into the mise-en-scène of the tour's first act, when "Evergreen" is followed with the psychiatric optimism of "On a Clear Day You Can See Forever," is a passing allusion to the recessional title graphics of that latter song's film version—as her own voice's adverbial telescoping of "for ever and ever and evvverrrrrmohooore" triggers a multiple regress of Streisand's rear-projected miked image just before the lights cut off. What was merely a reverse zoom from a balcony camera placement on New Year's Eve now spends the rest of the new year, on tour, wowing crowds with this cinematic flourish of an infinite recessional "forever" timed to the visualized distended hold of her high note. Synesthesia yet again, in technological form. But vocally and optically, no added number is more successful than, in the second act, the "metanarrative" episode begun when a fifty-two-year-old Streisand is heard (and seen) over-voicing her forty-two-year-old's rendition of a young girl's aspirational steerage to freer air in the shipboard finale of *Yentl*'s "A Piece of Sky." (No hyperbole when filmed applause cuts to Jane Fonda, down front in the good seats, mouthing to the singer on stage her ecstatic "Unbelievable!") Surely this number can be said to rank with the greatest of career duets, Streisand's voice lifted to preternatural harmonies in an encapsulating self-difference. As cross-wired between yearning immigrant heroine and confident superstar, the double image is projected (both senses) as the American destiny in musical theater of a European Jewish heritage. In its resplendence, and its guaranteed standing ovation, this idea was too good to forgo, but only to attempt improving upon, six years later—with not just one screen-within-the-screen but three, as we'll see—in the *Timeless* version. And ageless it is in the multiplied self-plagiarism of its impact.

Notable also in the 1993 Vegas *Concert*, lodged among the mandatory roster of early tracks and later hits, was the terrific contemporary verve of "Ordinary Miracles," written by her Tony- and Pulitzer-winning conductor Marvin Hamlisch, with lyrics by the Bergmans, and tailored both to Streisand's grassroots political sentiments and to every ripple of her voice's dramatic build. Arrived at the closing celebration of the little miracles that happen (and transform) "every blessed dayayayy," once again her voice seems bursting the seams of a temporal designator (almost "timeless" in its delivery of that confident quotidian wonderment). Such is the thrill of pure prolongation, internal iteration—another of her "forevermore" moments. Or call it another adventure of the temporal modifier in song, like the adverbial force that actually brackets the entire concert, from a committed here and now to a queried when and where. The show opens first with her tentative descent of the staircase set, the singer baffled (in "As If We Never Said Goodbye") at why she's nervous "here" of all places (before an audience, on stage, home at last). A full anthology of hits later, the closing number has her backing up the same staircase on the way to a "Somewhere" (the idealized eponymous adverb from this *West Side Story* finale) that remains vividly unspecified—reaching beyond even the song itself, yet whose last syllables seem searching it out. Yet again, a "terrain" of contoured surfaces, plateaus, and all but unreachable peaks. And here the unresolved "where," that latent waiting "place for us" otherwise (utopian dream of the stage play's suffering ethnic outcasts), is dedicated in Streisand's spoken preamble to a world where "people are different" rather than "the same"—including, not just the politically and racially divergent, but "gay" as well as "straight." Her latest signature anthem is a song aimed not at some normative quorum but at a generously queered and unruly full house.

After the *Concert*'s filmed workout in song, most any return to bankable Hollywood material was bound to feel less urgent and purposeful—or to put it more succinctly, less thrilling. But as *The Prince of Tides* contributed in its way to the *Concert*, so did Streisand's next and last self-directed film serve to open a certain new conceptual space for *Timeless*. That save-the-last-dance-for-me trope in *Tides* saw the soon-parting couple taking the improbably empty floor at the Rainbow Room. It is an idea that—in a refurbished genre frame, and swathed by a more wholehearted orchestration, as if bolstered by her concert triumph in the meantime—will return half a decade later, if at street level (rather than the top of the RCA Building), for the musical-comedy-style finale of *The Mirror Has Two Faces*.

Mirror Reversal

The Mirror, in contrast to *Tides*, is a romantic comedy that has both its romantic and its comic moments, rather than a psychological melodrama that often feels emotionally threadbare and not sufficiently dramatic—except when overblown. But in the later film, mirroring is too close to home for comfort in its star vehicle. It plays as if its matrix were the scene of storefront reflection in the predecessor film (when the "beautiful" Lowenstein is made to admit as much) stretched to plot length. In this "sequel," however, the heroine must be seen to work hard, as Streisand of course does, for the same look. And labor so that—in words from *Yentl*, though there in a spirit more movingly extricated from sheer cosmetic self-consciousness—the heroine's goal is to "see myself" and thus "be myself at laAAast." Part of the mainstream success of *The Prince of Tides* no doubt derived from Streisand holding herself back in the role, drawing the man out instead, both in character as shrink and as director in a different kind of emotive transference. In *The Mirror*, however, plot requires that she break out spectacularly from her own alter ego, straining by over-explicitness the very differentials of her star persona. Rose Morgan is the down-to-earth and supposedly frumpy English professor heroine (why wear makeup, she wonders, since she'd only "look like myself, but in color") whose hunk mathematician husband Geoffrey (Jeff Bridges) has married her only because she doesn't excite and distract him sexually. So the plot has her working to normalize the winning difference of her inner Barbra, with its eccentric comic charm, by strenuously unleashing Streisand's studied glamour. As George Segal (returning here in a minor but strategic role) would earlier have been quick to note, in that celebrated differential from *The Owl and the Pussycat*: "two completely different girls!"

In her role as director in the pre-production process, in order that she might study in turn the presumed antithesis of feminine glamour in the trappings of a real-life college English teacher, Streisand did her usual fieldwork, as she had in visiting mental asylums (no comparison) for *Nuts*. A former student of mine—by then a widely published scholar tenured at Columbia, and in fact notably stylish herself—was assigned to show Streisand around, and the ropes: including what a professor's office would look like, whether there'd be a nameplate on the desk, that sort of thing. These details had to do with a scene either unshot or cut—and leaving us to wish that the director had asked for a few tips instead on what a credible Ivy League lecture might sound like, given the brief squirmer we're submitted to. The pedagogy is absurd, but the real discomfort is the glam transformation to come, with its inevitable reflex of self-congratulations. By an irony that can't quite redeem it, the result of this casual-rags-to-black-sheath trajectory backfires within the plot by intimidating the self-distancing husband, who now misses his no-nonsense academic bride. In order to achieve closure as what Stanley Cavell calls a "remarriage comedy,"[2] the now toned, blonded, and chicly coiffed Rose needs to be humbled a notch in the mystique of her new dieted and polished look. This happens when, in the closing scene, she is interrupted in her sleep, disheveled as she races to the street to stop Gregory's braying for her, and promising on the spot an inevitable reversion (she's "aging here," she insists, as he fumbles for words, things "falling" as we speak). But, in the spirit of Cavell's paradigm, the reversion is not just to sag and flab but to the sibling-like fun they used to have, ignited this time by sex but without the confusions of glamour. Here the second-honeymoon effect will involve the deferred consummation of the original marriage, according to a plot so improbable that Segal has in fact been brought back from *The Owl and the Pussycat* as gadfly. Long ago weaned away from bookish celibacy by Barbra's Doris, his only role here as womanizing professor is, right from the first, to tell Gregory he's crazy in his dream of separating the complications of sex from love and domestic harmony—just because this math nerd and undergrad heartthrob is so flustered by lust and so often dumped afterward that he wants to opt out. The corrective plot closely resembles Cavell's model, where the return to passion is triggered by the disruptive enlivening of a friendly marital routine that had grown too much like sheer familial comfort—or even sibling rivalry. As usual, though, marital recovery takes its own plot-long good time.

Rose is dismayed on their original wedding night that Gregory is eager to watch a movie, a long one, *Lawrence of Arabia*—one in fact (though unmentioned) with no women in it. "Just stick it in," he says (to her ironic grimace) when she kneels before the VCR, and he's long asleep when we cut to the last end-title strains of the score. Some time later, after her mounting sexual frustration, finally claiming her marital due in a way that Hadass never quite did in *Yentl*, Rose is miserably rebuffed when Gregory curtails his own obvious desire for her. Understandably enough, she immediately mistakes his restraint as indifference: "I don't want to do this, Rose." Beyond dramatic irony, his nervous fear of an overmastering lust has a curious undercurrent, oblique but intriguing. A similar trepidation attends the monologist hero of the later Off-Broadway play *Buyer and Cellar* (by Jonathan Tolins), about a gay steward hired to superintend the mall-like expanse of closet space in the fitted-out basement of Streisand's Malibu estate. This modest minion fears that her requests to come upstairs when her husband's not around may mean a pass rather than, as it turns out (spoiler alert), just a chance for her to test the brown of his hair against couch fabric to help her decide on pillows. Seeing the film's marital turning point in this later light brings to mind a certain unspoken aspect—or, rather, resonance—of Gregory's selective celibacy, quite incidental to the script. As far as possible from Jeff Bridges's persona or performance, it remains the case that, with Gregory queering the heteronormative course of marital congress, and reducing it to mere good conversation, this recluse from lust has a way of standing in for Streisand's huge *noli me tangere* gay following, smitten without actionable desire, fascinated from a happily enforced external distance. Where, for this queer audience, the brandished *difference* alone of her charisma is the mirroring recognition in play.

Rose, however, has actual mirrors to contend with. Several. And they don't quite add up. The full-length restaurant mirror in which she sees the windblown hairpiece (taxi had a broken window) that her mother had foisted on her for her first date with Gregory—comic marker of a cosmetic pretense her instincts once advised against—shows to her, in life-size reflection, the absurdity of such aspiration. This is the Rose who, as we've already been shown, would rather stare at the TV screen watching baseball in her bedroom than into the adjacent mirror when applying face cream before an earlier perfunctory date. But she never stops looking insecurely into the mirror when she must. And after her later marriage seems to crumble over what is to be found missing in such looking-glasses, naturally we then see, amid the jogging and training machines of the resulting exercise-regimen montage, a salon makeup artist studying Rose's image in a mirror, the cosmetician hard at work on the heroine's eyeliner. It is not Rose's vanity that is directly at stake, we're to think, but what can be done, objectively, with the face that she meets the world with. Earlier, when Rose first returns home to her mother's apartment after the failed nuptial consummation, she has studied her cruelly disappointed image in the family mirror (fig. 32). It is a shot that Streisand reruns over her later Criterion interview when explaining how the film was about self-esteem and its entirely subjective nature, suggesting in her own metaphor that "the world mirrors how we feel about ourselves."

Permission enough, she must have felt, for another "Hello, gorgeous" story in the making. But there's an extra autobiographical nod at this point in the film as well, beyond career retrospect—linked in turn with a further cinematic intertext. In the scene just before, on exit from her sexual humiliation, she has retrieved a portrait of her father and mother from the short-lived marital bookshelf in Gregory's former solo apartment. It is a black-and-white studio portrait in which Mr. Morgan, with his pencil thin moustache, looks strikingly like Streisand's own father—as often seen in biopic segments over the years, even concert montage. This is the father who (the screen father, that is) is later learned to have doted on Rose as the favorite child, rather than the nominally prettier sister: beautiful not just in his eyes but as confirmed in an early photo discovered and shared by the mother (the unaffectionate onetime beauty

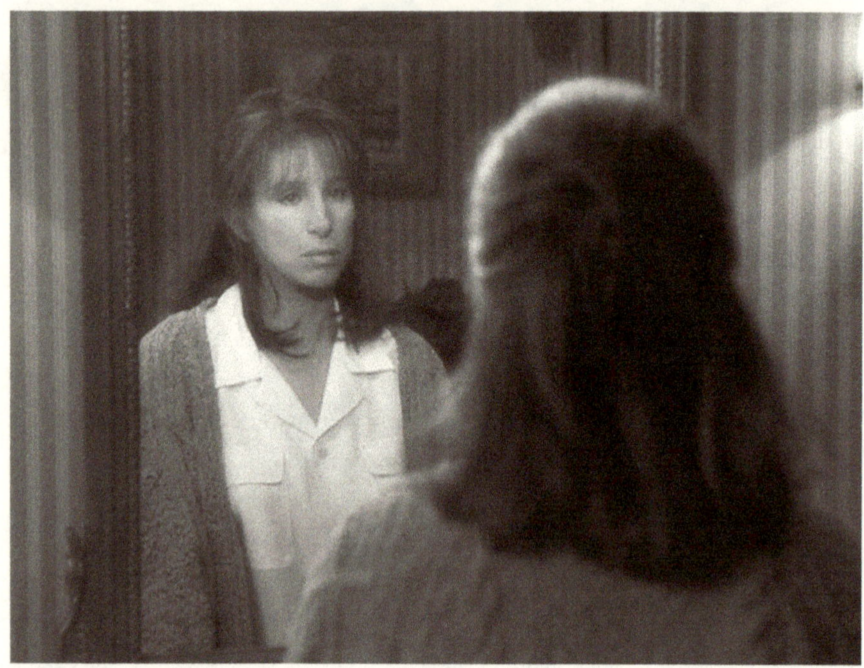

32. The mirror of rejection (*The Mirror Has Two Faces*)

played by a sardonic Lauren Bacall). But this absent father isn't the only link to the biographically freighted "Papa, can you see me?" motif of *Yentl*. Nor is his belated validation sufficient unto the day in securing this connection. More pointedly yet, with Rose weeping in the bathroom after her bottled-up passion has been repelled by Gregory in defensive recoil from his own desire, she reverses an early turning-point scene in *Yentl*. Instead of unshrouding a mourning mirror before which Yentl is soon to scissor away her visible femininity, here, in tearful elegy for her own gendered marital hopes, Rose throws a terrycloth towel over the bathroom mirror in bitter disgust. But the irony gets out ahead of any intended allusion. In contrast to the historical fantasy, and proto-feminist seedbed, of defied cultural norms in Yentl's yearning for a learned life, in *The Mirror* the Columbia professor, fully credentialed, is soon to launch a militant campaign of self-improvement in order to embody the modern-day version of comparable female stereotypes.

This can't in itself be allowed to succeed, to win the man back. The glamour must be humbled by self-deprecation, as noted, in a quintessential Streisand double play. In the last scene, wrapping her bathrobe around her on the deserted, predawn street, make-up off for the night, hair mussed, she jokes her husband free from the panic of allure—in another riveting over-the-shoulder shot (fig. 33) echoing the separation

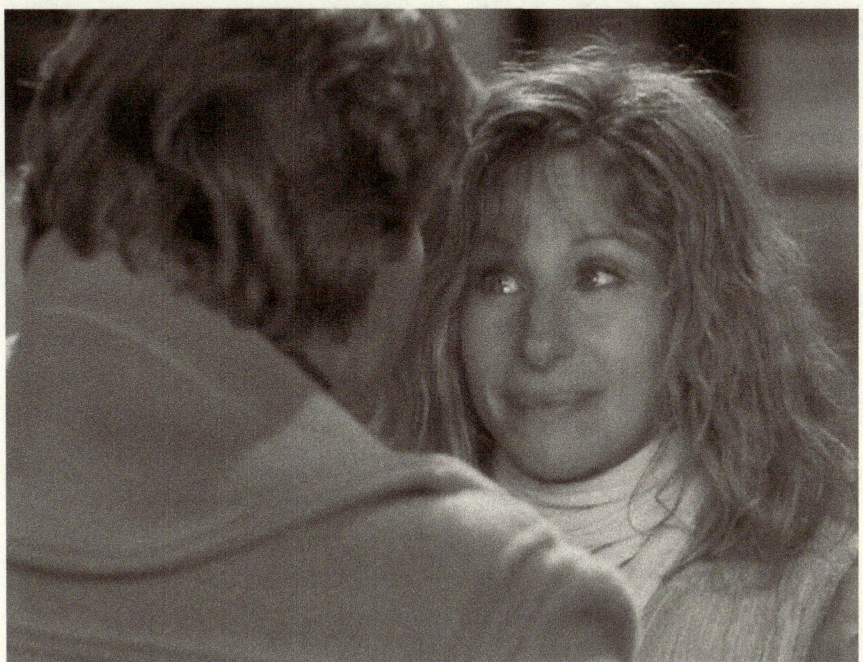

33. "I Finally Found Someone" (*The Mirror Has Two Faces*)

from Nolte in *The Prince of Tides*—but with, this time, tears of joy instead. Greg finds it "comforting" that all the body-toning will wither away into droop. But the double-bind of this rom-com plot needs one more move of celebratory rescue from the corner into which it would otherwise have painted its heroine, eyeliner and all—a genre shift quite possibly inspired by Streisand's return to vestiges of the musical form in her recent concert tour. What follows is every bit as unrealistic as its one-sided celibate buildup. But when riding in on Streisand's usual uncanny gamut of expressions, from impatience to sudden joy, it is nonetheless a contagious pleasure to watch. And a prolonged one. Its deferred bliss continues behind the credits—with a sudden freeform editing, by dolly and crane, capturing the reunited couple quite literally dancing in the street, in the twirls and dips of a new relaxed pleasure in each other.

As if evoking the song-and-dance duet no musical comedy actually made space for in her career, this impromptu pop ballet may be narratively unearned, or at least exaggerated, but it has been paid forward. It harks back an earlier moment of professorial comic relief in what we hear of Rose's sappy and implausible Columbia lecture on romance literature. There our Professor Morgan, when Gregory is first spying on her from the balcony, has suggested that the clichés about romance, or call it the music of love, are so powerful that if we don't hear the New York Philharmonic in our head on a first kiss, we "dump the guy." Gregory leaves after hearing this heartening cynicism about romanticized sex and its Hollywood illusions, missing out on the ludicrous student ovation she shortly receives for her corrective rhapsodic peroration (and latent tautology) on how "fucking great" love does in fact feel when it strikes. We are expected to remember that previous jokey turn of the lecture at the end when, with the couple embracing on the street in their new sexual rapport, they are stunned in mid-kiss by Pavarotti's "Nessun Dorma" filling the cavern of the avenue from (we see in cutaway to an upper window) a lone sleepless guy's combination of amorous approval and karaoke indulgence.

It might as well be the Philharmonic, but this returning irony doesn't exhaust the point, even as the diegetically scored scene closes on a freeze-frame, as in *A Star Is Born*, behind the first credit line: "A Film by Barbra Streisand." For suddenly this film, accompanied by other than a classical orchestra, becomes a music video, her best and most uninhibited. It is as if the "Puccini-like" triumph Glenn Gould heard in Streisand's "He Touched Me," detached and maximized here in the real thing, clears the way for her evolved pop vocals. Unlike the original plan for *Nuts*, in other words, or the hyper-"watchable" last "now" of *A Star Is Born*, the fixed image here isn't final. As if to confirm and amplify the film's authorship, rising now behind the end-titles is the winning percussive beat of "I Finally Found Someone," her cowritten duet with Bryan Adams.[3] To recover some vestige of genre charge in its larger Hollywood frame, the contemporary couple, suddenly caught up in a "musical" of their own making, needs to bond over a Streisand song—indeed a song and dance. So the two of them whirl away across the still mostly deserted street. Even with traffic coming slowly to life, the couple remains uncurbed in their fun, all to the accompaniment now of Barbra and Bryan in audible overlap with the hugs and dips of Rose and Gregory. The taxi that eventually whisks them back to his apartment is the same one, she's stunned to find, window still broken open, that had once disheveled her preparation for that first date with him. All such silly vanity, we're implicitly asked to think, is behind her now, absorbed into a less than superficial self-worth.

In the Criterion interview, Streisand explains that she wanted to make at least one movie where she gets, rather than must give up, her man. Matthau aside in *Hello, Dolly!*, in their joyless mismatch, or Montand on hold by way of clairvoyance in *On a Clear Day* till a predicted marriage in the next century, the others—Sharif, Redford, Caan Kristofferson, Patinkin, Nolte—all got away. All of course to the glory of the star in her splendid, soap-opera-transcending parting scenes. She might also have suggested, in such an interview, that she wanted to direct at least one more musical finale in which she wasn't consigned to solo resignation. In any case, some deep instinct must have told her that the more formulaic happy ending she had for once in mind could best be achieved by some measure of return to the genre that screen history's commercial determinations had forced her to leave behind. So in getting her man she also gets to sing with one, though not the same one she's dancing with. In a song once again coauthored by Streisand for the "musical concepts" of a Hollywood feature, like "Evergreen," and in fact becoming her last hit single, "I Finally Found Someone" tips over into biographical rather than just film intertext in its fine coincidence with the new relationship to James Brolin, her eventual husband, begun in time for him to attend the film's premiere with her. "Did I keep you waiting?" is one of Adams's lines in the bridge patter of the song's recurrent dialogue format, answered soon by his partner's swelling vocal revision in the very sense of the verb: "I can't *wait*," now that love has struck, "for the rest of my li-i-IFE." Unfreezing the closed-down story line in quick-cut to a melodic coda, this exit scene's narrative motivation may well seem flimsy, including all these giddy improvised spins in the street, but, with the poetic license of a momentarily recovered genre, it's close to irresistible. And no surprise that the ballad will soon be slotted in, by video insert, as part of a duet montage for her next concert, embedded there within the immediacy of live song.

Time Tunneling

With its unhedged risk of self-applause in the title, nonetheless *Timeless* (as in part a Y2K countertrope) is organized around bringing past moments of a career not so much to renewed appreciation as back to life as drama. What the *Concert* did by superimposing a cutout of Barbra's teenage self, when she first fell for Marlon Brando at the movies, over an image of him singing "along with her" (her image pasted over Jean Simmons) in "I'll Know" from *Guys and Dolls*, is matched—and technically exceeded—in *Timeless*. This happens by the digital special effect of scaling down her own live image into a rear-projected black-and-white duet partner for Frank Sinatra in his prime—in a now optically reciprocal "I've Got a Crush on You." But the real duet logic of the whole millennial concert (and subsequent brief North American and Australian tours)—a final stratum of self-mirroring in Streisand's career—is organized more in extrapolation from her self-harmonizing with her own *Yentl* persona in the *Concert* than from her duet with Brando: more nostalgic biography than collaborative fantasy. Borrowing, in effect, a favored mode, if not technical mechanism, from her narrative films, the turn-of-the-millennium extravaganza begins in an autobiographical "flashback" that springs a duet this time with her enacted teen self (played by Lauren Frost). In a fully theatrical prologue at Brooklyn's Nola studios in 1955, the thirteen-year-old Barbra has just cut her first record, "You'll Never Know," infuriating the session pianist when she refuses to stop varying the notes as written. As no one could miss, the historical stage is set for deviation, difference, as a potential affront. It is only then, ten minutes into this already manifest "narrative concert," as I've been calling it, that Streisand herself emerges from under the glimmering cloak of a tap-ticking Brother Time (choreographer and Broadway dance wiz Savion Glover). His figure serves from there out, like a neo-Dickensian ghost of milestones past, in usher-ing in subsequent returns to crucial moments in Streisand's career. It is as if the trau-matic if seriocomic flashbacks deployed via reincarnation in *On a Clear Day You Can See Forever*, and then structuring the traumatic climax of both *Nuts* and *The Prince of Tides* (as well as, more sparingly, punctuating a turning point in *Yentl*), have returned expansively here to the more relaxed mode of *Funny Girl*—and the reprise of its fram-ing idea in *Funny Lady*. They are structured once again, that is, as one long endeavor of career hindsight interspersed with the recovery of, rather than regression to, her "early little-girl self," the larval superstar.

The difference in set design from the *Concert* is one immediate measure of the shift in scope from emotional reminiscence to career retrospective. In its variation, and attempted upgrade, of the *Concert* set, that former residential (if rather manorial) interior—with its Jeffersonian-influenced whitewashed classicism—is more dramat-ically replaced, in a further temporal (historical) backcast for *Timeless*, by an abstract exterior pyramid behind the on-stage orchestra: the pyramid as icon and relic at once. This presumed ageless monument to endurance is mostly just a looming backlit peak until it reveals at last, along its front face, a staircase to be climbed. This happens when the first number, from *West Side Story*, the proleptic "Something's Comin'," has come round to the ever-receding destiny (again) of "Somewhere." With her "mini me," that still-embryonic possibility of Streisand, having by then rejoined her adult avatar on stage, this early incarnation of Barbra, midway through the lyric, now disappears up the steps, leaving her own achieved destiny behind—perched halfway on the as-cent, the rest to be climbed by the final high notes of the star's big finish. Two hours before, when "something" big was still only "comin'," Streisand urges the younger version of her vocal drive to keep plugging: "Kid, I like what you sang . . . Keep lis-tening to that voice." As we have been listening by concert's end, for many rewarded minutes, and for years before of course—and to more than the metaphoric sense of "voice" as inner call. Even the mode of ambivalent dialogue segue that once, in Strei-sand's coauthored script for *Yentl*, linked inner monologue to necessary human contact is recruited here again, in the opening number, when the star's younger self is yanked back—from the assurance that "something good, something great" is in store—to the stage mother's shouting out annoyed to the daydreaming "Barbara." The girl responds to that impatience, and the broken spell of the future summons, with the emotional comedown of a harried "coming, coming" in sound match with Streisand's song line. Though launched in the gap between mundane urgencies and the timeline of aspiration, *Timeless* is of course already its own self-fulfilling prophecy.

Frost's double for the young Barb(a)ra returns late in this first act in front of a hollowed-out full-length mirror frame (fig. 34), brushing her Yentl-length hair when singing the first strains, again, of "You'll Never Know" ("how much I love you")—in counterpoint with Streisand in the spotlight for "Papa, Can You Hear Me?" The star's teen avatar is staring straight through the empty mirror, in fact, at the camera and the audience behind it. Her lyric is matched, in this sense, to those same brief words of Streisand's own explicit love song to her audience—the "you'll never know" of boundless gratitude—at the Grammys a decade earlier, as recalled in the Overture: part of that acceptance speech we heard coyly presaging her stage return. And at just this point in *Timeless*, some expert video work kicks in to enhance the vocal overlap. At first still on stage next to each other, the two Barbras are soon conjoined—songs and personae both—in a split-screen superimposition. The young ingenue and aspirant looks forward into the future; the star, out at the audience and into the past of her concert-long

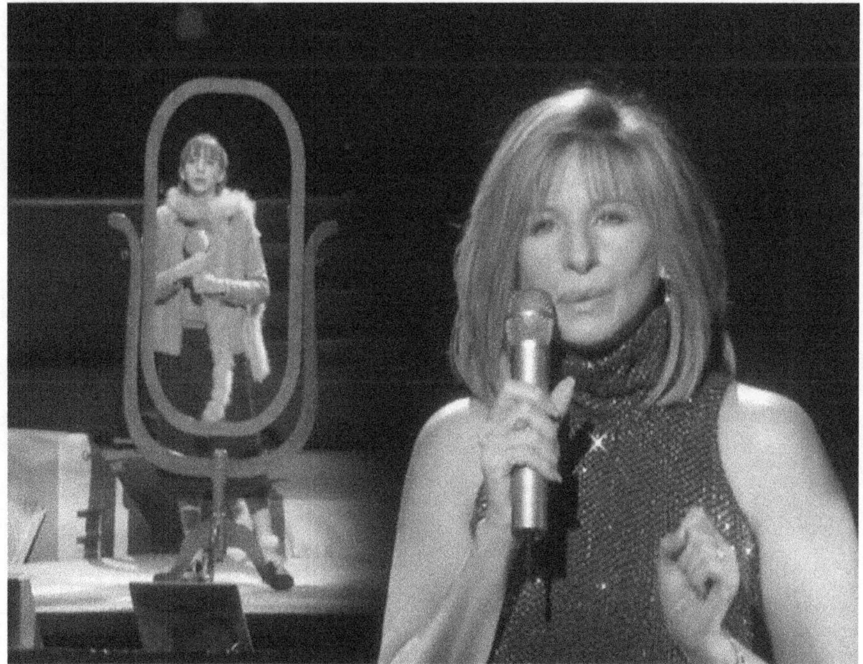

34. Through the looking-glass (*Timeless*: "You'll Never Know")

self-chronicle. With Streisand in the foreground in this split-screen shot, she takes the lead from the younger's self's melody—recalling the rapturous manufactured duet with her own early vinyl recording on *Just for the Record*—and narratively redirects the lyrics to "*Papa*, you'll never know." Among the other retroactive strands of audiovisual palimpsest in this concert's video treatment, even that late mirror in Streisand's career, as transparent stage prop, has its way of summing the actual revealing surfaces of the many other real ones before it in her films (from *Funny Girl* and *Funny Lady* through *Yentl* to *Nuts* and *The Mirror Has Two Faces*). As if figured here by the cleared-out mere frame, such are the reflective planes that often, when other than bitter and ironic, allow at their most "open" a glimpse beyond image into possibility. This self-redoubled number has begun after an intervening anecdote about Streisand's own real father, dead too soon for his love to register directly as a fostering support, that again blends psychobiography and career trajectory. At which point the camera dollies in until, rounding out the "You'll Never Know" number against a jet-black background, Streisand reaches the radiantly widened opulence of the emphatic capping phrase "if you don't know nOW-ow-ow-ow." A "now" that yet again seems like it could go on forever in its insistent present.

One does indeed never know what weight a lyric may be asked to bear in Streisand's treatment, let alone in subsequent iterations of a complex idea like the self-duet of younger and older vocal personae dialed up from a jaw-dropping audio track to on-stage video enactment. Nor does a viewer or listener always make full use, in response, of what one only half knows—by way of fleeting echoes and suggestions. So, with her mourned father in mind, a recursive moment here: for both the star's development and this book about it. In the second chapter—when referring not to Streisand's first recording session but, nearly a decade later, to her first film line, "Hello, gorgeous"—I promised that this closing discussion would watch Streisand's fuller career "elicit yet more pressure on the cross-gender identification entailed in the amorous 'gorgeous' of this otherwise unapologetic debut address." After already having recovered a number of easily overlooked appearances of that adjective "gorgeous" in the plot-long retrospect of *Funny Girl*—with its story only gradually catching up to the mirror shot of its framing discourse—I was alluding in particular there, for tabled attention, to a couple of dropped stitches in my citations and their extra hints. It is true that these comic fillips of dialogue may in any one viewing flash past in a flow of vernacular ethnic shtick more or less thematically uninflected. But even in reverse order, they build.

In tracking the flashback sequence of *Funny Girl*, we had noted how looker Nick had caught the eye even of Fanny's mother in just those famous terms: the third repetition of "gorgeous" (after Fanny to the mirror and first of all, irrepressibly, to Nick). And more, too, as we may now remember. For Mrs. Brice admits to the awed Mrs. Strakosh, after the latter's "Frankly, that's a good-looking man," that she's putting it mildly. The mother's gloss on the praise is as immediate as it is dubious: "Gorgeous—reminds me of Fanny's papa, my ex—also gorgeous!" A point hardly mitigated by the inverted Jewish lilt of good riddance: "Wherever he is, he should only stay there." And then there's Fanny's later line to Nick himself, as father, about the daughter he hasn't stopped to see when he's released from prison for his final scene with Fanny: "She's gorgeous—getting to look just like you." We've only seen her doted upon in the cradle, and, with no clear timeline in this part of the film, she may well be not much older than Streisand herself was when, as only a toddler, she was emotionally orphaned by her father's early death. What *Funny Girl* stages, in short, is a second-generation feminine presence gradually embodying—as if in the course of maturation itself—the special beauty, the enduring lure, of paternal magnetism. If this is still no more than one wrinkle of an intermittent dialogue motif in the first of Streisand's films, it will of course have become—with the prototype of beauty subsumed to nurturance—the dominant strain of her self-scripted *Yentl*.

And when that film's definitive moments of empowering father-love are subsequently recapitulated in the lyric retreads—and rethreadings—of the autobiographical *Timeless*, the psychological deep structure is clearer than ever: a father not just gone in the plot of her first film but famously long lost in Streisand's own life. Whose story's most salient through-line, stressed in many an interview over the years, emerges from the inner lack induced, for the subsequently unappreciated young girl, by just this parental loss. Even on-screen, of course, the result of any such emotional fixation is in no way overtly Oedipal. Nor just ethnic or cultural in its patriarchal resonance. It locates, rather, a matter of affective projection and reembodiment, of lived transmission through the generations—and a narrative archetype, in the process, for any auteurist reading of the Streisand masterplot. While only a latent ironic subtext in *Funny Girl*, this tacit thematic has become openly validated and inescapable in *Yentl*—from the Talmudic teacher-patriarch's death forward. Deserted again by a man at the end—by a transitional and slightly older mentor figure in the person of Avigdor (after his having passed through the inverted looking-glass of repressed gay desire)—the heroine will need to go it alone. Or almost. Not, it is true, without some measure of fantasized audiovisual reciprocation from the still-licensing realm of paternal absence. In the recuperative follow-up scene, as we know, Yentl is indeed heard calling on—and for—the eyes and ears of the dead father in the liberationist manifesto "A Piece of Sky." Years later, just before her revisiting that screen finale in *Timeless*, we note with some surprise how the emotional anchor of "Papa" in the film's closing appeal to "watch me fly!" has encroached beyond the climactic focal point of sanctioned impulse in *Yentl*, invading instead the second-person appeal of a more traditional love song. By run-up to this moment in the concert overlap of *Timeless*, the paternal address has been transitionally latched to a love lyric just before: this in the posthumous twist of "if you don't know now" for the revised second person of "Papa, you'll never know." He's certainly had time to learn—or at least Streisand's audiences have in his stead.

It is a point commentary need not belabor in the way the star herself has done in personal reminiscence. But if those first spoken words from *Funny Girl* operate as a distilled gender matrix whose inferences are only unfolded in flashback, they certainly have their own patrimony going forward. Granting that the handsome absent father and the handsome absconding husband of that first film intersect upon the site of the heroine's incorporated loss, we find this logic strenuously fleshed out not only in *Yentl* but then again in *The Mirror Has Two Faces*. And then worked through yet again in its familiar sublimation—dare we say purged?—in *Timeless*. Operating alongside the see-through concert prop of young Barbra's mirror, evoking a primal reflection of *engendered* difference, there is that passing hook of an interpolated "Papa" in the multifaceted serial medley. Spanning in this way from Streisand's first recorded love song to her directorial triumph in *Yentl*, this is perhaps the most telling move of all. Its yearning can be heard, felt, to close a career-long affective gap: between the gorgeousness yearned for and the gorgeousness both internalized and, in art, made sharable. And another dimension of this emotional armature is crucial. The fact that the father has in effect always been absent for her—not long-adored and then torn away by death but only a missing and idealized validation from the start—is what can most forcefully authorize Streisand's own ongoing appeal to an unseen audience ("Watch me fly!") as a disembodied abstraction.

In flipping back to and through instances of that signal epithet in *Funny Girl*—the "gorgeous" attached equally to absent father, divorcing husband, and, in lieu of each, Fanny herself—we can also be led to understand the film's ending anew: the star's arms held wide in embrace of an erotic emptiness, yet in a gesture not just valiant but defiant. All told, it is not out of keeping with the recurrent turns of the script we've been revisiting to imagine Streisand's most famous torch song coming to its end (after the opening "Oh my man . . . he'll never know") with a more drastic overcoming of the backstage loss. As set, lit, and performed at this closural moment, the lyric doesn't seem settling for the straightforward feel of its "whatever my man is" / "I am his" rhyme. It comes across more like the implosion of difference with Cathy's "I am Heathcliff" in *Wuthering Heights*, so that Fanny's stage solo, as linked with her opening salvo in the mirror, may appear to enact in mounting "self-control" the queered emotional equivalent of "For whatever my man may be, I am he . . . for evermore." Be that as she may, hers is a dramatic move to introject, via asserted power, the latest derivation from that most irremediable of gendered clefts: between absent father ("reminds me of Fanny's papa") and emotionally abandoned girl, funny or not, as well as eventually deserted wife.

"What does she think, she's a man?" goes the barked aside about directorial ambition in the *Concert's* redo of Sondheim's "I'm Still Here." Hardly, but being still there in 1993, after all those years, has involved, in Streisand's own mind, a career-long symbolic barter with male deprivation. *Funny Girl* can't help anticipating those gender negotiations in its seemingly tossed-off repetitions of "gorgeous" as a single smitten adjective-turned-noun. Long before defying Hollywood norms and asserting her right to the megaphone as well as the microphone, Streisand first went before the Hollywood camera in a way we can now more fully apprehend. For in the light of hindsight, within the film's flashback dialogue and within Streisand's career at large, tears may ultimately be welling up in these first-seen eyes not just because of the impending marital separation—and the "hello"-again and final goodbye to male glamour it will involve. Those eyes can seem responding to the wry formulation itself of "Hello, gorgeous" in its impinging gender irony: Fanny being, by erotic default, the only one left to bear that epithet—if she can bear up under it. For reasons more than obvious or canonical, then, as clustering around Fanny's renowned opening line, that scene's mirror reflection has always been this book's defining title scene. For here, we realize only after two hours of backstory, is an otherwise bereft incorporation of sexual disparity: a male loss colonized in despair as self-image in the mirror of imposed deficit—and of the embraced difference that remains.

Even Streisand's most diehard followers would be likely to admit that generalized anecdotes about the revered scholar-father who was lost to her by heart attack when she was only fifteen months old, before she even really knew him, grow a little thin in their bare-bones iteration. It is a self-mythologized storyline that has become a bit tedious over the years in talk-show talking points. But the plausible core of the story—almost inadvertently teased out in *Funny Girl*—goes some distance in helping us understand Streisand's vocation as performer. Something incalculably gorgeous needs always to be reclaimed. And the vocation, the calling, is not just for—but out to. "Watch me . . . ," "Watch closely now": every child's primal need to be seen is taken—and sustained—to the nth degree, where attention-getting gets reinvested again and again as creative quest. One thing is indisputable about this private history and its massaged traumatic loss. As an autobiographical storyline Streisand has repeated to herself over the years, it can only be called monumentally empowering. The surprise, in rescreening, is that its scaffold was all there in her first film—though trussed with irony at every turn. As initially played out in the form of desertion and cross-gender internalization for her character, rather than sheer rebound, Streisand's own continuing force of artistic will is a drive that has, for decades, shaped ambition into a recuperative mission, a force compensatory as well as lucrative, rerouting familial trauma into vocal and theatrical drama, redeeming narcissism as catharsis.

And never more fully staged than when the star comes "home at last" in the consummate live amalgamation of her hyphenated dramatic gifts as singer-actor-writer-director, scripting her own story in an on-stage syncopation of lyrics and video image. The heralded but unadorned title *The Concert* has its way of saying it all: signaling, in the event, a concerted meld of performative talents in what emerges as a sustained vocalized autofiction. An embellished story to which *Timeless* then arrives, at century's end, as companion volume—this time interleaving the early song career with the better-known biographical arc. Including yet again the offstage, the always missing, father. From the surprise insert of "Papa" in the romantic lyric "You'll Never Know," camerawork moves seamlessly to the first act's closing reprise of the *Yentl* self-medley from *The Concert* six years before, with video footage again from the climax of "A Piece of Sky"—a song that yanks up all anchors in its great last shove and rush of sound.[4]

Previously, in rear projection and finally closed-circuit double exposure in the 1994 *Concert* version (as with the Sinatra duet in *Timeless*), this sky piece had offered its own further slice of expansiveness per se, figured by image overlay and spatial recess. But this time, in *Timeless*, there are two creative manifestations of inventive difference and improvisatory gusto, early and late, flanking the screen image from *Yentl*—including their sync with those paired sideways glances of the heroine, operating as they already in themselves do by the kind of schematic mirror reversal explored in chapter 4. The bracketing flipped images of this serial shipboard triptych are thus matched (because co-sourced) below on the *Timeless* stage, even as enlarged in projection, by the parallel gestures—and assertive high notes—of Frost and Streisand, young and later self together, declaring their unbroken (vowel-chimed) contact with origin ("Papa, I can hear . . . see . . . feel you!"). Looking first left, then right, then center, the autobiographical duo on stage is ultimately welded above by the triangulated "average" in Yentl's own upward appeal (fig. 35), caught here just before that famous straightforward close-up in its final call to the father to "watch me fly!" The three panels of this array enfold the essential phases—and faces—of the gendered Streisand story: aspirant, protagonist, performer. And after the countless inner soundscapes of Streisand's vocal tracks over the years, what we hear and see replayed at this (high) point—in a kind of triple exposure that recalls the "Happy Days Are Here Again" split finish of her first special (fig. 3)—is a pullback to nothing less than the soaring voice's own expansive skyscape. Boostered by those left, right, and center stares into the fathering and sanctioning distance, the song reaches escape velocity in alignment with the camera's own rapid reverse zoom: the three figures of desire being watched fly together in their harmonized vocal trio as the first-act curtain sweeps closed.

All that can compete with this at the end of the concert's second act is that stair-stepped ascent of the background pyramid: emblem not just of career pinnacles but, no doubt, of the star's continual effort to surmount her own landmarks—as well as, perhaps, though certainly without embalming it, to secure the video perpetuity of her work. Early in the number, Frost's eager rush back to the stage is timed to the "hold my hand" line from "Somewhere," a hand taken by Streisand in acknowledgment that they're "halfway there" in an always uphill ascent. The achieved burst of lift-off in the anticipated ballooning syllable of "SuhuhuhmWHERERERERE" brings down the house, as always, and closes the curtain again, on this high theater of commemoration for a life in song. But we should linger at least as long as her final high note does, indeed a bit longer. For its competition with the first act's closure isn't just in the inordinately rich sonority of her ascendant vocals, resonant even without the choric playback of triptych delivery. The answering power of these closing notes resides as

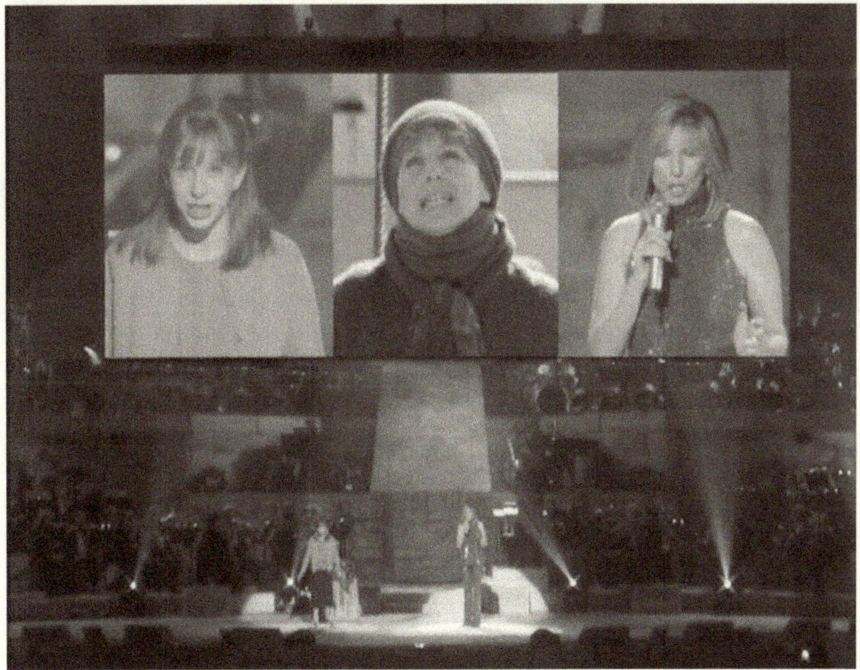

35. "Watch me flyyhiiigh" (*Timeless*: "A Piece of Sky")

well, true to form, in the inner shape of phonetic phrasing, its spreads and repetitions. We've several times noted its like in the big-screen musicals—and have been caught up by it most recently in the final three words of "Ordinary Miracles" from the *Concert*, the Hamlisch/Bergman number to which we briefly lent an ear above.

That number deserves another listen on the way to what Streisand's voice accomplishes with the "Somewhere" finale. Early in the "Ordinary Miracles" lyric we're asked to "see" the "way a miracle multiplies." And implicitly hear it too—in the kind of mimetic burgeoning that stretches, to four syllables each, the paired adjectives in the song's final phrasing "every blessed day" ("e-eh-veh-ry ble-eh-eh-sed")—only then for that dailiness itself to sprout, by a similar internal iteration, into a blessedly distended and brassily confident "dayayayhaaaay." If we hear overtones, beyond pure plurality, of a euphoric "yay" as well, that only typifies the way Streisand's upper register, even when seeming to evanesce into pure sound, remains dramatically expressive as well as colloquial. And a further curiosity. It is even symptomatic here that a tin-eared transcription of these lyrics on numerous websites mishears the rhyming buildup to that almost endless "day" ("Love in its extraordinary way-ay-ay-ay") as "Lovin' is extraordinary, Why?" Or if not tin-eared, entirely mechanical: voice-recognition software at work perhaps, stumped by the least phonorobotic of living sounds. In fact, there's not a hint of Cockney enunciation in Streisand's prolonged long *a*—no slide into long *i* at all for the note's hard-won height. But the greater natural ease of releasing the more relaxed, already "higher" vowel *i*—as contrasted with a tighter and more phonetically emphatic long *a*—may have mislead the faulty ear of even a human scribe in this case. Any such confusion would only be enhanced by the deep breath taken before "way"—as if perhaps, though mistakenly, about to shift the lyric syntax away from "extraordinary" as the modifier of a pending noun. The result, in any case, has been to drastically misconstrue the bravura lift at this turn. It is the reductio ad absurdum, via machine reading, of a typical lyric hearing of Streisand's talkable vocables as word forms. Another such phonetic problem might have beset the rhyming syllabic juncture, a line later, of "way" with "blesse*d d*ay"—except that, in Streisand's taut enunciation, the adjacent dental sounds still make space between them for the climactic revving-up of breath before that last outstripping rhyme with an already distended "way." For this last and most ordinary word, "day-Ay-ay-Ay-ay," made all but "miraculous" in its own sustained varied shadings, is one more of those moments when, in accurate and gripped close listening, the Streisand sound is found to contain multitudes.

To stress, as I have repeatedly done, the unfailing colloquial note in this opulent sound, its continual *voicing* rather than just singing of a lyric line, is to suggest in turn the tacit dialogic effect this phrasing can have in listening. This is where our hearing the singer's tones as palpable speech opens them to mutable overtones in our own tracing of the sounded sense. Especially so when they are themselves so powerfully opened up in delivery—as in that everlasting long and wavering *a* of "day" (in "Ordinary Miracles") or the utopian but still topographic assonance—and amplitude—of the "some*day*"/ "some*where*" finale from *West Side Story*. Yet such mimetically gauged effects as the extended diurnal hold on that multi-syllabled last word "day" (in the concert's earlier song of perpetual rather than pending miracles) hardly exhaust the premium on wording that Streisand's singing reveals. Her sound, as we know, is equally capable, in its time/space ratios (timed space), of laying open by association a traversed three-dimensional as well as temporal zone within wording. This we have heard yet again, in this same *Concert*, with a latter-day version of her earliest career showstopper. Streisand's first big hit, on call in live performance ever after, gives us a revealing measure of an evolution in the way she hits her biggest notes. After *Funny Girl's* virtual soliloquy version in suspended conversation with Nick on stage and screen—held to a certain normalized talky finish on the three monosyllables of "in the world" ("people who need people" being its luckiest inhabitants)—we audit something new and definitive in later live performances of this song, at least as early as *One Voice*, and then again in both the comeback *Concert* and the later *Timeless*.

What the internal, as well as chronological, shift in question does in rounding out the song is to break the worded "world" first into dual syllables and then upward in pitch on the second. Beyond a surplus press of vocal excitement, this increasingly characteristic Streisand effect offers clear evidence of her pop-rock catalogue's influence on even her more traditional material. Such is the often power-drive variance of pop's inflected high notes that has lent an extra and almost tangibly spatialized "volume" to the now double-thrust last word ("world") spun out in "People." At a newly discovered vocal axis of intonation in the gathering gravity of that soft "uh" vowel, the singer's whole body throws itself into the pulsing one-two punch of a self-unfurled "whir/HURld." Another merely typographic approximation there, alas, of Streisand's phonic topography. But think of this mimetic belling, in its own swoop of global rondure, as a forked tuning of the monosyllable itself. Disclosed in this way is the auto-echo of a rotarized internal rhyme—as taken up in turn by the auditing and enworlded body of response: a "peopled" hearing. What results is a sympathetic vibration within a single lexical unit—and within its capture by the ear's activated magnetic field. The inner liftoff operates on the same spectrum of vocal articulation as any instigated bridgework between separate adjacent words (as with "*BEEE Meee*" earlier in *Funny Girl*). Yes, I know. Indeed, I repeat. Too often in these pages the translucent beauty or verve of Streisand's phrasing has been encumbered by an admittedly clumsy alphabetic transcription meant, however feebly, to index the transferential phonics that I've found no other commentary attempting to celebrate, let alone "spell out." Try as a recast syllabic read-out might, nothing compares, for instance, to actually *hearing* the chiastic dip and rise between those "luckiest" of "PEEEEO/ple"—the *e* so wide in its reach that it almost becomes two syllables in itself, incorporating a trace even of the otherwise silent *o* just before descent—and the electric uptick of "in the wooOOHRLD." So yet again with Streisand's phrasing, any effort to "graph" this supplemental spike of sound at word's end—bursting with its further precipitation of that three-words-in-one cluster (*world/ whirled/ hurled*)—barely begins to register the visceral spin her sound can elicit in lucky us.

But it is the final number of the *Concert*—especially when, just over half a decade later, its last delirious enunciation is actually accentuated by the set design at the end of *Timeless*—that unleashes what is perhaps a wilder syllabic surprise yet. The moment outdoes even the earlier scripted rhyme with "piece of *sky*" from the *Yentl* medley: an achieved elation in that song's closing lyric—elation as elevation—that had further coasted upward not just to, but within, the reverberant afterglow of "watch me flyyy-Hiiigh." Similarly, "halfway there" in ascent of that climactically motivated pyramid in *Timeless*—with the final sounding (probing) of the title word "somewh*ere*"—it is as if we hadn't really heard until now the true aerial reach in Streisand's several definitive performances of this Broadway ballad. With the actress-who-sings turning her voice toward us from a final perch on the set's imposing upward slope, as never before the emphatic laddering-up to and within "suhuhuhmWHERERERAIRRR" is pushed to release exactly the freer "air" of its aspiration and its respiration alike. In a number shared between the *Concert* and *Timeless*, like the first-act knockout with "A Piece of Sky," we hear this particular effect—this induced effusion—in a context that narrates, rather than just deploys, the famous voice in a theatrically staged retrospect of its career. Brought out anew is the way an intrinsic phonic bandwidth in Streisand's enunciation—dramatically phonetic as well as sonic—helps to achieve what she so often seems striving for across the weightless inner contours of her singing. In the terms once more of this book's opening chapter: grain and terrain at once. Time and again we sense her delivery, her timing and its scaled volume, working to map in the act of embodying—here in a microdrama of utopian hope within the last syllable of "Some*where*"—the same rarefied air breathed by her voice. And doing so in this case, with any sense of active wordplay quite aside, as if searching out in the voice's own shimmering vibrato that elusive "place for us" of the song's own yearning.

The result works to transform, by expansion, the final sustained, wavering, richly pitch-bent titular adverb of "Somewhere" into a kind of spacious abstract noun: for a vocal topography or locus, a "place" unto itself, unmistakably staked out across that inimitable clarion peal unprecedented in the history of popular voices. It remains inherent, however, in these two *narrative concerts* mounted by Streisand in the last decade of the century—for all the theatrical calculations of their parallel swooning closures—that when the concert is over we sense the narrative continuing. And continuing (ensuing tours included) in the mode, still, of its own lauded inauguration: a talent having driven the wedge of difference so deeply, on-screen and on record, that performance norms are always getting riven—and refashioned—on the spot.

ENCORES/CURTAIN CALLS

There have been, of course, many curtain calls, including for the sold-out audiences of yet more tours. So, too, besides the scheduled post-finale numbers of those concerts, we have seen the lighthearted encores constituted by the trivial *Focker* films (2004, 2010), *The Guilt Trip* (2012), and those far more entrancing studio promos for recent albums that cross-cut between her home recording den and the Barbra Streisand Sound Stage at Sony, named in her honor after renovations in 1994. And there was the remarkable return to the Greenwich Village club of her youth for a lottery-ticketed *One Night Only* at the Village Vanguard, featuring the jazz standards that Diana Krall had produced with her for the *Love Is the Answer* album in 2009, released in a double CD with a choice between jazz trio or orchestral accompaniment. There are certainly many striking vocal episodes in her later tours as well, often either deftly finessing or lifting above what Broadway historian Ethan Mordden explains not as "fatigue" but as the natural aging of the voice[1]—and doing so in punctuating the throaty warmth of a given number. I'd single out most recently the dazzling after-hours feel of Rogers and Hart's "I Didn't Know What Time It Was," her 2017 concert closer. Piercing through the evening's frequent sunset duskiness of tone, this encore lends a final vocal alchemy to the "Music"/"Mem'ries"/"Magic" promise of that latest tour—in whose video version you can hear her saying to her manager as she comes off stage, half in apology, half in satisfaction: "My voice finally opened up!" Again: amplitude as an inner terrain.

Another moment that bears singling out, from this same most recent tour, came earlier: in the duet with Jamie Foxx on "Climb Every Mountain." What Mordden points out, after a keen-eared tracking of the mostly benign pop-rock influence on Streisand's vocals from mid-career on, is the way she has, as he hears it, reverted to Broadway delivery for this standard from *The Sound of Music*, leaving other musical sounds, so to speak, to Foxx's pop decoration (80). Though Mordden doesn't make the ethnic distinction, on this hearing it's as if—recalling Louis Armstrong's symbolic conjuncture with Streisand in *Hello, Dolly!*—a jazzier Black style has this time separated out distinctly from a sometimes parallel tradition of Jewish stage composition and its vaudeville-evolved divas. Commenting on the recorded rather than the live version, Mordden's intriguing distinction, if one listens closely in either performance, is somewhat overdrawn. The restless glissandos of Foxx's soul-inflected vocal technique (with the little nonsyllabic fillips of his "oh-oh-ohs" punctuating a high note) seem, rather, to have inspired some untraditional slides and inner dips on Streisand's part in this Broadway standard. Hear the bending curve on her noun in "follow every rainboOHoHoh" in its second refrain—or the elevated wiggle room for emotional searching in the descending verb cadences of "fi-i-i-ind your dream," as well that phrase's climactic final noun finding its own scaled conquest in iteration: "dre-e-ea-EA-ea-ea EAmm." Still, in the concert duet, a visceral sense that two different traditions share the stage (in mutual admiration) at this moment—share the impact of musical invention in the harmonics of racial, cultural, and gender rapport—does mark a typical Streisand moment in the iridescent mirroring of difference, within and without, that has defined and varied her "dream" career.

And to this last tour, an addendum, yet another encore: her subsequent Hyde Park concert in 2019, in front of another hundred-some thousand spectators reminiscent of Central Park in 1967, though this time entirely "standing room only." Still holding her sunglasses, darkness not yet wholly fallen by midsummer concert's end, she delivered for the finale an adjusted, gutsy version of the classic last three high notes of "My Man." I subsequently saw and heard this thrilling, newly orchestrated rendition—even cleaner and more confident (judging from the unofficial British cell-phone evidence)—later that summer at Madison Square Garden, from an actual seat in the balcony. Its invested verve certainly eclipsed an occasionally rough or pallid vocal execution in some of her earlier numbers that night, especially marked in the once electrifying "Any Place I Hang My Hat Is Home" from her second album (the opening number cut from the recorded Central Park concert). The last song at the Garden, however, was more than worth waiting for. After this capstone moment of "My Man," and its prolonged ovation, she actually credited the energy of the audience for the success of this tingling, high-wire finish. As if the crowd's support were more than emotional, almost somatic: vocally enhancing in its own right. A month earlier, in Hyde Park, the audience was so packed in that, without chairs, and with no room to lounge on the grass, the crowd was on its feet for the entire concert. But spirits remained high through to the end, if one can again judge from the YouTube sampling. Slotted as the big closing number, this revamped, more ramped-up iteration of "My Man," almost exactly fifty years after its on-screen smash at the end of *Funny Girl*, was more than warmly responded too, in wave after wave of applause—just as later in New York. "Funny," said the star with a laugh, and without the least risk of self-aggrandizement at this moment in the London concert, or at this point in her fabled career, "Since you're already standing, I can't tell if you're giving me a standing ovation or not." Nice touch—but she knew.

NOTES

Overture: Reflection, Refraction, Diffraction

1   All available on YouTube if not otherwise cited.

2   It would be too simple to suggest that the song fame of the actress-who-sings justified the exclusion of any serious attention to Streisand in the academic scholarship on star acting during the very decades when she was widely identified, via lyric keynote, with the celebrity of "I'm the Greatest Star." She gets no mention in James Naremore's compendious *Acting in the Cinema* (Berkeley: University of California Press, 1988) nor, a decade before, in Charles Affron's *Star Acting: Gish, Garbo, Davis* (New York: Dutton, 1979), despite the impressionistic rhapsody of his coda, "The Tunes of Acting," where, regarding the pace and crafted shape of star performances, their very lilt, he proposes that "we submit to their rhythm and their harmony . . . and retain the melody of acting along with countless other memorable tunes" (317). Nor does Streisand appear in Christine Gledhill's anthology *Stardom: Industry of Desire* (New York: Routledge, 1991). A telling exception—though with no allusion to her singing on camera, his brief mentions centering on *The Way We Were*—comes in Richard Dyer's work, where in the second edition of *Heavenly Bodies: Film Stars and Society* (New York: Routledge, 2004), given one of its three chapters on "Judy Garland and Gay Men," the relevance of Streisand would seem inescapable. (Unnoted here is the legendary passing-of-the-baton moment of generational transfer in the two stars' 1963 "Get Happy / Happy Days" contrapuntal sparring match on the Garland TV show, where [a YouTube staple] an anxious tension between a performance norm under siege and its vocal innovation is so intense it almost hurts.) On Dyer's terms, Streisand's underspecified participation in *only some* aspects of his proposed threefold litmus test for gay cathexis in Garland's case—naturalness, androgyny, and camp (156)—goes unexplored. But the contrast with Garland is clear. For Dyer's is an ingenious dialectical argument that sees the inbred *normalcy* of the Garland screen persona as operating, through all her off-screen personal struggles, in alignment with a sense of homosexuality as innate, rather than elective: constituting—however ostracized—its own genetic norm (156). Without Dyer's spelling out Streisand's divergence from Garland within this

naturalizing cultural model (presumably overlapping, as with Katharine Hepburn rather than Diana Ross among his list of gay icons, mostly in regard to the trouser roles of androgyny, rather than anything approaching either naturalness or camp), it would seem that in fact Streisand's appeal right from the start, quite antithetical to Garland's, resides in, or at least derives from, a norm-defying *difference* personified: an embodied cultural anomaly processed by turns through comedy and romantic melodrama in and beyond the musicals. But anomalous, or resistant, only up to a point, Dyer's analysis would be quick to insist. For his political emphasis in *Stars* (London: BFI, 1979)—with its own brief and intermittent treatment of Streisand's work *as work*, down through the "auteurist" voice emerging in *A Star Is Born* (138)—wants to qualify any sense of her system-bucking "interventionist" (38) credentials in seeking better roles for women, noting all this as operating comfortably within the commercial circuit of industrial production. In his grounding Marxist terms, this is a point made even more sharply in *Heavenly Bodies*—with a stress less on Streisand's continually bruited perfectionist investments as actor than on the material "control" at the "shopfloor" level that she exercises in the maintenance of her stardom as part of Hollywood's capitalist production (6).

3   On the matter of Streisand as uniquely self-conscious camera object, I wrote above: "Beyond any narcissistic model, self-scrutiny becomes instead the framed field of disclosure, discovery—and ultimately of performance." So that in the generation of her own screen personae, there is a marked departure from Dyer's constructed-image paradigm for stardom, unremarked by him: something quite beyond that model of image maintenance encapsulated by his opening treatment, in *Heavenly Bodies*, of Eve Arnold's frontispiece photograph of Joan Crawford. Emblematic there is a double mirror image, one looking-glass extending beyond the photo frame while capturing the star studying herself in a smaller, hand-held make-up mirror. The point of the photo, and of Dyer's launching analysis (1–2), is to delve into the constructed image of the star *look*. But, in regard to Streisand's stardom, the present commentary advances another model of reflection from its title page forward. Its touchstone moment: the mirror lineaments of *Funny Girl*'s opening "Hello, gorgeous" line. In this study's titular mirror of self-conscious performance, again and again it is we who, watching Streisand looking into the eyes of her characters, can recognize her not just looking but *watching herself* in the dramatic moment: a matter not of sheer image but of emotional inspection, regularly on the lookout for something in or beyond glass or gaze, something further *enactable*.

1   Here's a case, one among many in the coming pages, where no critic's audio-visual ekphrasis could escape the fact that only seeing is believing: https://www.youtube.com/watch?v=39kpKh3E6aM. But there's another YouTube alert worth posting as well, in the hearing-is-believing spirit. Only late in the refresher course in Streisand performances that constituted the main "research" for this book did online a capella videos begin appearing, just over the last year or so, where new electronic technology allows—in a kind of reverse kara-oke process (AI-powered "vocal remover" software)—the stripping away (un-mixing) of orchestration to reveal the singing in isolation. In every one of these amateur voice-extraction efforts now available, the results are a minor revelation. As, for example, in the atypical valleys of plangent vibrato in "My Coloring Book" from the album rendition: https://www.youtube.com/watch?v=3wYQOF2ltig.

2   Partly disappearing behind the studio applause, and more than in the recorded version, this last note, sung live, would seem to activate very subtly Streisand's gift for the difficult *messa di voce* technique: holding the same pitch through a rise in volume before its graded falling off.

3   See Jack Doyle, "Streisand Rising, 1961–65," 2019, Pop History Dig, https://www.pophistorydig.com/topics/tag/barbra-streisand-leonard-bernstein/.

4   It is a fine mirror symmetry for her to begin rather than end a performance, four decades later, with this number. In *Streisand: Live in Concert* (2006), the last word actually comes in over itself in repetition to extend and amplify the dilation of the time-freed "now"—one of those ingenuities deployed by an aging voice to recharge its native energy.

5   Roland Barthes, *The Pleasure of the Text*, trans. Richard Miller (1973; New York: Hill and Wang, 1975), 67.

6   Roland Barthes, "The Grain of the Voice," in *Image—Music—Text*, trans. Stephen Heath (New York: Hill and Wang, 1977), 181.

7   This book was written during the Covid pandemic, as was another appreciative survey of Streisand's album career in particular—his, done out of professed boredom under lockdown as a do-it-yourself project. See Dylan Hicks (a novelist as well as self-described "obscure 1970s singer-songwriter"), "On Barbra Streisand," *nrmint*, 2020, https://www.nrmint.org/newarrivals/on-barbra-streisand. This witty and colorful guided tour is an extensive, expert, probing, and often critical assessment of material and scoring, as well as of vocals, as

unstinting in lamenting Streisand's missteps as in applauding her home runs. I was particularly interested to find that, after drafting this audit of the Lenny Welch cover, that Hicks, too, singles it out as one of the high points of her pop repertoire—along with a just and subtle appreciation of the *Guilty* album as its triumph.

8   Fil Henry, "Barbra Streisand's Plethora of Technique," *Wings of Pegasus*, 2020, https://www.youtube.com/watch?v=3B5qMKV86Fs. Two years later, by popular demand, Wings of Pegasus has, I find, followed up this microanalysis of breath control in the first bars of "Evergreen" with a fuller tracking of pitch, vibrato frequency, and relaxed anatomical delivery across the whole live number (a capella this time), a fascinating analysis aided by the newly proliferating "voice isolation" technology and a pitch-monitoring video graph. https://www.youtube.com/watch?v=2sDk5nK0FNw.

9   "Down with Love" on *The Judy Garland Show*: https://www.youtube.com/watch?v=wUVd3fy8-pQ.

10 "Bewitched, Bothered, and Bewildered" on *The Judy Garland Show*: https://www.youtube.com/watch?v=t7gjDgSUwqo.

11 Regarding the complexity of sung tones in dramatic performance, it is worth noting another version of aural annotation for the temporal distension of the very word "time," again subordinated to the drive of desire in a song lyric. In his delicate but exacting evocation of vocal nuance across the bridged zone between singing and dramatic vocal acting, Richard Powers's 2003 novel *The Time of Our Singing* (paperback: New York: Picador, 2004), finds its own way of marking the prolongation of notes. He does so not just by repeated alphabetic characters—as I've been doing, most recently with the climactic high note of "t-i-i-I-M-E"—but by a phonetic approximation of the arcs of waver and diphthongization to which any such vibratory enunciation naturally gives way in being so reverberantly "held." In his novel, the closest parallel to the self-transcending "time" of Streisand's inverted (and then normalized) grammar at the peak of "Evergreen" is that same monosyllable's onset in the John Dowland lyric that is part of the tenor-hero's lieder repertoire. Tapping a phonic (deeper than phonetic or phonemic) "thickness before words" (351) reflected upon more than once later in the narrative, the slightly varied refrain from the first two lines of Dowland's art song "Time Stands Still" (3) elicits just this primal resonance. Powers's bravura recitalist Jonah Strom, in a dramatically dilatory and histrionic launch of this opening concert number when later described, "presses on the cylinder of air" behind his hard palate

in the "ravishing sass" (215)—perfect phrase, so it happens, for Streisand's early timing as well—of phonation's delayed-fuse ignition, yielding finally to a "dwarf explosion" after the mimetic suspense of arrested onset. Detonated at last in the pacing-out of the first word is "that fine-point puff of *tuh*" (215)—even the noun "puff" itself being, the dictionaries confirm, of "imitative origin," as well as huffing out in description's own prose its breathy internal echo with "puff." The result is that, from its own emergence in the song's first word, the very sound of "time"—duration and the note itself, hardly monosyllabic after all—"expands, pulling the vowel behind it, spreading like a slowed-film cloud" (215), as if from zero to loud. Any such filmic analogy may well bring to mind the vocal camerawork of Streisand's style, so often hovering in its spun-out luxuriance, elsewhere tightening or widening its lens, homing in or pulling away. Further, the prose phrasing of the Powers text, like its described concert artist's, is heard to be still spreading across its own retards and redirection, even grammatically as well as aurally captured. Incremental prepositions here build to an infinitive ("to transcend") for the full parsing of the single syllable "time" in its broadening vocalic hold: with the opening dental trigger of "tuh" next, with an exaggerated aspirate *h*, "widening to *ta* to *tahee* to *time* to transcend the ear's entire horizon, until the line becomes all it describes" (215). Minimal intervals (one sound bursting, gliding, easing into another) are translated to a layered valence of emotion in the self-designating moment of outplayed time: first with the opening line's "Time stands still," then with its imperative variant (and ambiguous sibilant double) in the second line's "Time stand (s)till." Streisand's "Evergreen," of course, pivots on a similar grammatical surprise—where the ecstatic levitation of a time "we've learned to sail above" (with no sense of "high time" for this hard-won bliss) gives way to its sudden shift into the defiant "explosion" (Powers's term again) of that hard-hit "time" that "can't change the meaning of." And it is there that my graphic stress on escalating volume and pitch in the widening climb of "tiiii-IME" can be heard, in the spirit of Powers's transcription instead—or (better) as well—to be negotiating the phonetic bellows of *tuh/ah/hi/eeme* in pushing, through Barthes's "voluptuousness of vowels," upward toward the iridescent ceiling of Streisand's range.

12   https://www.youtube.com/watch?v=q3dnMKeLgSg.

13   Anthony Tommasini, "Streisand's Fine Instrument and Classic Instinct," https:// www.nytimes.com/2009/09/27/arts/music/27tomm.html. A few gradually declining years later in her vocal instrument, the classical music critic for another major U.S. paper, David Patrick Stearns, writes, in 2016, about the lack of "cosmetic

surgery" for slackened vocal cords but appreciatively about how Streisand has responded not by forcing her former glories but by discovering new and moving routes into her song material, privileged over sheer voice as never before: Stearns, "Barbra Streisand's Year of Singing Dangerously," https://www.inquirer.com/philly/columnists/david_patrick_stearns/20160816_Barbra_Streisand_s_year_of_singing_dangerously.html.

14   Glenn Gould, "Streisand as Schwarzkopf," 1976, http://www.glenngould.tv/2020/05/06/streisand-as-schwarzkopf-the-voice-that-is-one-of-the-natural-wonders-of-the-age-confronts-the-masters-by-glenn-gould/.

15   https://www.bing.com/videos/search?q=He+Touched+Me+Live+streisand.

Chapter 2: Screening the Streisand Sound

1   Pauline Kael, in her review of *Funny Girl* under the title "Bravo!" *New Yorker*, September 28, 1968.

Intermission (1): Genre Triage

1   Bill Manhoff, *The Owl and the Pussycat: A Comedy in 3 Acts* (New York: Samuel French, 1965), 41.

2   This brief episode is located on the DVD at 1.32.20.

Chapter 3: A Star Is Cloned

1   See Matt Howe, *The Barbra Archives*, 2020, https://www.barbra-archives.info/funny_lady_overview, in the entry on *Funny Lady*, which distills print and radio interviews (with *Variety*'s Army Archerd and the BBC) to give a picture of a script Streisand finally warmed to and an appreciation of new songs written not "for me" but for a more ethnic Brice.

2   Pauline Kael, "Talent Isn't Enough," *New Yorker*, March 17, 1975, 112.

3   Camille Paglia, "Sexism and the 'Star Is Born' Films" (guest column), *Hollywood Reporter*, February 20, 2019, https://www.Hollywoodreporter.com/news/camille-paglia-sexism-star-is-born-films-guest-column-1186741.

Chapter 4: *Yentl*'s Lyric Cinema

1   Isaac Bashevis Singer, "Yentl the Yeshiva Boy," trans. Marion Magid and Elizabeth Pollet, in *Collected Stories: "Gimpel the Fool" to "The Letter Writer,"* ed. Ilan Stavans (New York: Library of America, 2004), 457, though in the story Yentl's misfit status is closer to gender dysphoria, registered by her secretly dressing up in her father's clothes long before his death (439)—and by her

being recognized by him otherwise as having "the soul of a man" (439). When asked by Yentl how that could happen: "Even Heaven makes mistakes."

2   Alan Williams, "The Musical Film and Recorded Popular Music," in *Genre: The Musical*, ed. Rick Altman (London: Routledge and Kegan Paul, 1981), 156.

3   Singer, "Yentl the Yeshiva Boy," 456.

Chapter 5: One Voice Twice Over

1   Janet Maslin, "Streisand in 'Nuts,'" *New York Times*, November 20, 1987, https://www.nytimes.com/1987/11/20/movies/film-streisand-in-nuts.html.

2   Tom Topor, *Nuts: A Play in Three Acts* (New York: New American Library, 1980), 32.

3   See Roger Luckhurst, *The Trauma Question* (New York: Routledge, 2008), 150.

Intermission (2): Genre Detours

1   Pat Conroy, *The Prince of Tides* (New York: Houghton Mifflin, 1986), 415.

Chapter 6: Center Stage

1   Later offered as part of a box set DVD as *Barbra Streisand: The Concerts.*

2   Stanley Cavell, *Pursuits of Happiness: The Hollywood Comedy of Remarriage* (Cambridge, MA: Harvard University Press, 1981).

3   Here emerges another link to Cavell's model of the remarriage comedy (*Pursuits of Happiness*)—as a genre of female self-arrival—in his subsequently developed sense of the Hollywood mode's alignment with opera as an earlier genre invented to make space for the often tragic jeopardy of female desire spoken (sung) forth. Not accidentally then, in this light, and internal allusion aside, it isn't the New York Philharmonic itself that our re-bonded couple hears overflowing from the apartment above but the amateur syncing of an opera aria, giving way soon enough to Streisand's favored pop mode. This is hardly an advertisement for the latter against the whole realm of classical singing. Far from it. It operates, rather, in an endorsement of screen passion—even in romantic (as well as musical) comedy—as having some of the force of operatic expansiveness, however much "pitched" (Cavell's term) in a very different key for the "I Finally Found Someone" duet. Paradigms overlap rather than collide. In his chapter in part on diva expressiveness in *A Pitch of Philosophy* (Cambridge, MA: Harvard University Press, 1996), called "Opera and the Lease of Voice," Cavell stresses the stage genre's relation to the kind of assertive self-discovery he has previously traced through screwball screen comedy, so that, in

the opera essay, he sees this yet again as the woman's "demand" to "have a voice in her history" (134). Such is exactly the insistence so fatally chastised in many a death scene aria in the operatic canon—and in this way related to his contrasting sense of screen melodrama as a narrative of the "unknown woman." The sustained emphasis in Cavell, in comic narrative as well as tragic, on the "the creation of the woman" thus runs parallel to the self-instigated female makeover-and-return plot in *The Mirror Has Two Faces*, a re-"creation" story paced, in all its erotic disorientation for the male partner, by the woman's own expressive self-insistence, refused capitulation, and won-back rapport with her estranged husband. A relaxed diva tune of triumph would indeed seem very much in order. In this otherwise non-singing part, the character, via the star's off-screen song, has "finally found" her voice as well as her titular "someone."

4 Barbra Streisand—*Yentl* Medley 2: https://www.dailymotion.com/video/x5n68s.

Encores/Curtain Calls

1 Ethan Mordden, *On Streisand: An Opinionated Guide* (New York: Oxford University Press, 2019), 79. Tart and amusing in his "opining" on the film career, and notable in finding "*Yentl's* direction, I have to say, shockingly good" (103), Broadway historian Mordden, though openly favoring the musical films, sheds more trenchant expertise on a recording career that he deems less uneven. He marks the latter as an epochal break from the smoothly polished 1950s gold standards of Frank Sinatra and Ella Fitzgerald into a newly theatrical style (beyond the Broadway sense): a dynamism of vocal gesture reminiscent of Glenn Gould's emphasis on Streisand as "italicizer." Before a chronology of both films and what Mordden calls album "recitals," however, there is a frontispiece captioned "A Life in Art": Fanny and Nick looking at themselves in that semicircular backstage mirror from *Funny Lady*. In contrast to the double mirror shot of Joan Crawford, found emblematic in Richard Dyer's treatment of stardom's constructed image (see "Overture," n. 3), Mordden's point with Streisand is that the difference caught by reflection in *Funny Lady* is between public and private, professional and personal. For him, this looking-glass (without any reference to its many variants before and after in her film and even concert work) "encapsulates Streisand As Performer"— and not just, in Mordden's fuller caption, through what it incidentally reflects: the well-wishing flowers, theatrical props, make-up, on-stage photo in the background, and the ultimately ironic Victrola (a triggering goad, as we've

heard, in the pending "How Lucky Can You Get" number). In a manner that actually occludes this dressing-room mirror's curved outer edge, and for the star on-camera as much as for the star enacted, Mordden notes how the arched reflection is also suggestively rimmed with congratulatory telegrams that help frame the Streisand image as performing self.

INDEX

pattern, 210; sexual avoidance, 205–7; song-and-dance finale, 210; title scene of reflection, 207–8, *208*; visual allusion to Streisand's lost father, 207

mirror images, 1–2; trivialized in *Emotion* video, 182. *See also individual film titles*

Mitchell, Joni, 156, 179

Montand, Yves, 62

Mordden, Ethan, on directing in *Yentl*, 234n1; pop influence on Streisand's voice, 225

MTV: "Left in the Dark Again," 182; misjudged venue for Streisand, 181–83; "My Heart Belongs to Me," 181. See also *Emotion* (video)

My Fair Lady, 41, 50

My Name Is Barbra (TV), triple exposure on "Happy Days Are Here Again" finish, 22–23, *23*, 218–19

Newman, Paul, 80

Nicholson, Jack, 62

Nielson, Leslie, 173

Nolte, Nick, 187, 189, 209, 210

Nuts: allusion to mirror scene in *Yentl*, 166–67, *167*; apparent turning point in Streisand's dramatic ambition, 177; changes from Off-Broadway source (Tom Topor), 155, 169, 170–72; cinematographic framing and lighting (Andrzej Bartkowiak), 173; debates with director Ritt, 158, 162; eroticism compared to *On a Clear Day You Can See Forever*, 166; flashbacks in, 159, 162–68, *167*; freeze-frame closure in script, 175–76; heroine as snide vocal coach compared to *One Voice*, 174–75, *174*; obverse pairing with *One Voice* concert as further "cloning" of star intensity, 157–58; queering of norms as "creative disruption," 159; return of the repressed compared to recovered memory in *The Prince of Tides*, 169, 170; revised ending, 175–77; Streisand's control as executive producer, 159, 162, 164; Streisand's Method style, 173, 177; unnerving expressivity of close-ups, 172–73; version of play's metatheater, 173; weaponized recall of comic mirror scene from *Funny Lady*, 166

Oklahoma, 50

On a Clear Day You Can See Forever, 8; "Come Back to Me" as parody of dubbing, 67–69; double time frame in superimposition, 65–66, *66*; flashbacks, 63, 64; "He Isn't You," 65; "Hey Buds Below," 69; "Love with All the Trimmings," 64–65; mirror shots, 63, 65; reincarnation plot as allegory of acting's multiple personalities, 61–62; "There's No Melinda," 67; title song closure, 68–72; "What Did I Have That I Don't Have Now?," 66, 70

O'Neal, Ryan, 25, 77

One Hour Photo, 168

One Voice: aerial camerawork ("Over the Rainbow"), 157; "Evergreen," 33–40, *37*; "Somewhere," 157

by Streisand, 11, 34, 106, 120, 121;
John Norman drafting "With One
More Look at You," 110; "Queen
Bee," 103–4; reaction of preview
audience, 188; suicide as *Liebestod*,
111; "The Woman in the Moon" as
feminist ballad, 107–8, *108*, 109–10
Stark, Ray, 55
Stoney End (album), 179
Stradling, Harry, Jr., 3
Streisand, Barbra: actress-who-sings,
9, 10, 22, 69, 79, 197, 198, 227n2;
"ambidextrous" talent, 20; celebrated
technical "genius," 2; change of first
name, 22; early naysaying amid
adulation, 27–28; felt lack of father
figure, 214–18; first Jewish-identified
screen superstar, 2; first three albums,
19, 21; flirtation with MTV, 180–83;
Grammy Legend Award, 14; initial
TV spots, 20; "personality before
a person," 13; self-styled "work in
progress," 197; stage fright, 12, 188,
198; waning of bankable musicals,
73–74; wanting to play Cleopatra on
TV, 74. *See also* close listening; voice;
individual album, concert, and film titles
Streisand—In Concert: as
autobiographical narrative, 198,
200; psychiatry montage, 202–3;
"Somewhere" introduced as rallying
cry in part for gay difference,
204; tour adjustments after Vegas
opening, 201–2; *Yentl* self-duet, 203
Styne, Jule, 191
Sunset Boulevard (Lloyd Webber), 190
Sunset Boulevard (Wilder), 190

Surtees, Robert, 107
synesthesia, 9, 116, 189

Timeless, 11; career genealogy, 198,
200; mirror frame prop, *213*; "Papa,
Can You Hear Me?" / "You'll Never
Know" medley, 213–14; "Something's
Comin'" as career metatext, 212;
staging of "Somewhere," 212–19;
wordplay of script, 213; *Yentl* triptych,
218–19, *219*
Tolins, Jonathan, 206
Tommasini, Anthony, 40
Tonight Show, The, 19
Topor, Tom. See *Nuts*
Tucker, Sophie, 26

Up the Sandbox: aggressive filming-
within-the film, 82; cinematography
for merry-go-round climax,
82–83; fantasy sequences from
discrepant genres, 79–80, 82–83;
feminist wish-fulfilment, 77–80;
First Artists' venture, 80; in-jokes
alluding to Streisand songs, 81;
racial ambiguities, 82; slow-motion
sequence, 83; Statue of Liberty attack
vs. *Funny Girl* identification, 82

vocal motion (reverse-tracking for
breakout numbers): *Funny Lady*, 94,
140; *Hello, Dolly!*, 94; *Yentl*, 140–41,
150
voice (Streisand): analysis by Fil Henry,
33–40; appreciation by Glenn
Gould, 40–42, 43, 234n1; body
language of delivery, 35; echo

voice (Streisand) (*continued*): neurons, 41, 193; effects volumetric and bifocal, 193; "grain" of voice as acoustic "terrain" in the mind's eye, 31–32, 71–72, 192, 194, 222–24; inner cinema of, 9–10, 19, 28, 33, 188, 192; mimetic enunciation, 21, 32, 36, 40, 44, 114, 181, 189, 220, 221, 231; notes on phonetic notation, 22–23, 33; phonetic play, 37, 39, 41, 108–9, 123, 136, 222; pitch bending, 35; semantic overtone of phonetic dilation, 191–92, 193; synesthesia, 9, 116, 189, 192–94, 202; tactile soundscape, 19, 32, 189, 193; vernacular (colloquial, non-operatic) register, 10, 28–29, 34, 41, 71, 220

Walls (album), 21
Watkins, David, 149
Way We Were, The (album), 43
Way We Were, The (film): closing scene compared to *The Prince of Tides*, 187; deleted scene, 84–85, *85*; dramatic departure from early 1970s comedies, 84; film-within-the-film compared to *The Prince of Tides*, 186; home-movie screening, 85–86, *86*
Webber, Robert, 173
Welch, Lenny, 32
What's Up, Doc?: allusions to *Casablanca*, 79; "As Time Goes By," 78–79; difference rebuked, 77–78; and *Hello, Dolly!*, 78; popularity, 77; screwball redux, 76–77; updating of Katharine Hepburn role in *Bringing Up Baby*, 76–77; wordplay in, 77
Wilder, Billy, 190

Williams, Alan, 130
Williams, Robin, 168
Willis, Gordon, 82
Wizard of Oz, The, 157
Wonder, Stevie, 179
Wyler, William, 48

Yentl, 1, 2; camera technique in "The Way He Makes Me Feel," 137–39; deleted scene of Talmudic instruction, 126; direct eyeline launch of last note, *152*; DVD rehearsal tapes, 129, 133, 143; editing as mirror triptych, 151–52; ethnic double talk, 124–26; *Funny Girl* intertext for shipboard climax, 148; gender mis-assigned in original Singer story, 122; gender unmasking, 141–44; genre constraints on the non-dueting star, 153; hero's fear of "pederasty" in Singer story, 141; homoerotic undertones, 142–45; long-take vs. shot–reverse shot, 145–46; metafilmic mirror episodes, 127–28, 131–32, *132*, 133, 134–35, *134*, 136–38, *138*, 139; "No Wonder," 125; revisionary "Film with Music," 121; schematic plot summary, 121–22; sound design of internal monologues, 129–31; Streisand's original opening scene (deleted) as metafilmic model, 124, *124*; tacit vaudeville telos of American voyage, 153–54; "Tomorrow Night," 3–4, *4*, 126, 139; transitional black-outs, 149; widening stream motif, 123, 147

Z, 58

CPSIA information can be obtained
at www.ICGtesting.com
Printed in the USA
JSHW031046081222
34403JS00002B/168